Reflections on Slavery and the Constitution

Reflections on Slavery and the Constitution

George Anastaplo

Lexington Books
Lanham • Boulder • New York • Toronto • Plymouth, UK

Published by Lexington Books
A wholly owned subsidiary of The Rowman & Littlefield Publishing Group, Inc.
4501 Forbes Boulevard, Suite 200, Lanham, Maryland 20706
www.rowman.com

10 Thornbury Road, Plymouth PL6 7PP, United Kingdom

First paperback edition 2013.

British Library Cataloguing in Publication Information Available

Library of Congress Cataloging-in-Publication Data

The hardback edition of this book was previously
catalogued by the Library of Congress as follows:

Anastaplo, George, 1925–
Reflections on slavery and the constitution / George Anastaplo.
p. cm.
Includes index.
ISBN 978-0-7391-7176-9 (cloth : alk. paper) — ISBN 978-0-7391-7177-6 (electronic)
1. Slavery—Law and legislation—United States—History. 2. United States. Constitution. 14th Amendment. 3. Slavery—History. 4. United States—History—Civil War, 1861–1865. I. Title.
KF4545.S5A955 2012
342.7308'7—dc23 2011049524

ISBN : 978-0-7391-7176-9 (cloth : alk. paper)
ISBN : 978-0-7391-8431-8 (pbk. : alk. paper)
ISBN : 978-0-7391-7177-6 (electronic)

To the Memory

of

Richard M. Weaver
(1910–1963)

a North Carolina Patriot

who graced
our Thanksgiving Day Dinners
the Last Years of His Life

Contents

Part Two

Preface

Men! whose boast it is that ye
Come of fathers brave and free,
If there breathe on earth a slave,
Are ye truly free and brave?

—James Russell Lowell,
Stanzas on Freedom

This preface echoes the prefaces prepared for the three predecessor volumes (published by the University Press of Kentucky) in my projected ten-part series of "constitutional sonnets": I. *Reflections on Constitutional Law* (2006), II. *Reflections on Freedom of Speech and the First Amendment* (2007), and III. *Reflections on Life, Death, and the Constitution* (2009). It is hoped that the materials glanced at in this fourth volume (published by Lexington Books) can illuminate, for my fellow citizens, both how the history of race relations in this country should be approached and how seemingly hopeless social and political challenges can be usefully thought about.

The chapters in this volume (as in the other volumes in this series) draw upon my half-century of seminars in the Basic Program of Liberal Education for Adults at the University of Chicago and upon my decades of Constitutional Law and Jurisprudence courses in the School of Law at Loyola University of Chicago. The first five of these *Reflections* form a quintet. (The fifth volume, *Reflections on Religion, the Divine, and the Constitution*, forthcoming) is virtually complete. The second set of five volumes in this series, D.V., has been assigned these titles (forthcoming): *Reflections on War, Peace, and the Constitution*; *Reflections on Race Relations and the Constitution*; *Reflections on Crime, Character, and the Constitution*; *Reflections on Property, Taxes, and the Constitution*; and *Reflections on Habeas Corpus, the Bill of Rights, and the Constitution*.)

This fourth volume (in the first quintet) offers discussions that bear both upon how slavery has come to be regarded worldwide and upon the political struggles that led to the American Civil War. Thereafter, the outbreak of the war, its prosecution, and its aftermath are examined. It is virtually inevitable, when a "sonnet" approach is taken, both that not "everything" can be said in any particular chapter and that some things have to be said again and again if any individual "sonnet" is to be adequately grasped (if only provisionally) on its own. Even so, there have been established in the opening volume of this ten-volume series the vocabulary, format, paragraphing, capitalization and mode of presentation intended for the entire ten-volume series. Thus, there has been developed a discipline which should guide both author and reader throughout.

At the foundation of the series of constitutional sonnets offered in this volume is my first *Abraham Lincoln* collection (1999), for which I much prefer its intended title, *Thoughts on Abraham Lincoln: A Discourse on Prudence*. That Rowman & Littlefield volume bears this dedication:

To
MY CHILDREN'S CHILDREN
and to their Children
with the Reminder that their patriotic Forebears
were among the brave Men
North and South
who both counseled against and fought in
the American Civil War

One cannot reasonably hope to add anything truly original to the voluminous materials long available on slavery, the American Civil War, Abraham Lincoln, and related matters. But perhaps it can be useful to reconsider, however briefly, some of these matters from a somewhat different and hence perhaps fresh angle, particularly if considerations can be brought together which are usually kept separate.

My children and grandchildren (and their fellow citizens of like lineage), who can claim by blood some of the Southern heritage, are provided suggestions about how to begin to think about challenging aspects of their remarkable inheritance. That is, they are encouraged to think about slavery, an institution which *has* become for most of us generally unthinkable. It is well for all of us, upon encountering these melodies, to recall a suggestion made by Abraham Lincoln in his Second Inaugural Address (quoted from at length in the concluding chapter in this volume)—the challenging suggestion that the North shared considerable responsibility historically for slavery in this country. Anticipating this Lincoln suggestion is the following passage taken from the "Concluding Remarks" appended by Harriet Beecher Stowe to her *Uncle Tom's Cabin* (1852):

> Do you say that the people of the free states have nothing to do with [the horrible American slave-trade], and can do nothing? Would to God this were true! But it is not true. The people of the free states have defended, encouraged, and participated; and are more guilty for it, before God, than the South, in that they have *not* the apology of education or custom.
>
> If the mothers of the free states had all felt as they should, in times past, the sons of the free states would not have been the holders, and, proverbially, the hardest masters of slaves; the sons of the free states would not have connived at the extension of slavery, in our national body; the sons of the free states would not, as they do, trade the souls and bodies of men as an equivalent to money, in their mercantile dealings. There are multitudes of slaves temporarily owned, and sold again, by merchants in northern cities; and shall the whole guilt or obloquy of slavery fall only on the South?
>
> Northern men, northern mothers, northern Christians, have something more to do than denounce their brethren at the South; they have to look to the evil among themselves.
>
> But what can any individual do? Of that, every individual can judge. There is one thing that every individual can do,—they can see to it that *they feel right*. . . .

One prerequisite, I presume to add, to "feel[ing] right" about momentous matters in a sustained and useful way is that of *thinking right*—that is, recognizing the critical issues of one's day and trying to understand the enduring questions and answers illuminating such issues.

This volume of chapters is offered as a contribution to the hardheaded and yet compassionate investigation required here. Such an investigation can usefully begin with reminders of observations about slavery made by two of our most revered presidents. President Lincoln observed, in an 1864 letter, "If slavery is not wrong, nothing is wrong." The following year he confessed in a speech, "Whenever I hear anyone arguing for slavery, I feel a strong impulse to see it tried on him personally." In 1786 George Washington (who ordered the emancipation of his own slaves at his death) announced, in a letter, "I never mean, unless some particular circumstances should compel me to do it, to possess another slave by purchase, it being among my first wishes to see some plan adopted by which slavery in this country may be abolished by law." Such a plan for eventual abolition, Abraham Lincoln was to argue, was in effect initiated (even before Washington became president) by the enactment in 1787 (by the Articles of Confederation Congress) of the Northwest Ordinance with its remarkable prohibition of slavery in what was then the principal undeveloped Territory of the United States.

Even earlier, Thomas Jefferson (himself a longtime owner of slaves) had proposed, as a grievance (about both slavery and the slave trade) to be included in the Declaration of Independence of 1776, the following complaints about the King (that is, about the British government):

> he has waged cruel war against human nature itself, violating it's most sacred rights of life and liberty in the persons of a distant people who never offended him, captivating and carrying them into slavery in another hemisphere, or to incur miserable death in their transportation thither. this piratical warfare, the opprobrium of *infidel* powers, is the warfare of the CHRISTIAN king of Great Britain. determined to keep open a market where MEN should be bought and sold, he has prostituted his negative for suppressing every legislative attempt to prohibit or to restrain this execrable commerce: and that this assemblage of horrors might want no fact of distinguished die, he is now exciting those very people to rise in arms among us, and to purchase that liberty of which *he* has deprived them, by murdering the people upon whom *he* also obtruded them; thus paying off former crimes committed against the *liberties* of one people, with crimes which he urges them to commit against the *lives* of another.

The only element of this proposed grievance that was included in the Declaration of Independence was the complaint that the King "ha[d] excited domestic Insurrections amongst [them]." And, a decade later, delegates from South Carolina and Georgia in the Constitutional Convention managed to have had suspended until 1808 any power the prospective Congress of the United States would have had to forbid the importation of slaves into the United States.

The intermittent Jefferson anguish with respect to the slavery that the South had somehow to deal with came to be repudiated by Southern leaders who could even learn to celebrate the controversial institution they had inherited. Alexander Hamilton Stephens of Georgia, as vice president of the newly established Confederate States of America, embraced chattel slavery as a Positive Good for everyone fortunate enough to be involved. Thus, he can be described in this way in the *Dictionary of American Biography*:

> His most notable expression in this period was the "Corner-stone Speech" at Savannah, Georgia, March 21, 1861. In this he surveyed the conditions of the Confederacy, praised its Constitution [adopted in Montgomery, Alabama, March 11, 1861], and appealed for wise and patriotic support of the cause. As to Negro slavery, he said that the architects of American independence, as exemplified in Thomas Jefferson, had contemplated a theoretical equality of races; but, he continued: "Our new government is founded upon exactly the opposite idea: Its foundations are laid, its corner-stone rests upon the great truth that the Negro is not equal to the White man; that slavery—subordination to the superior race—is his natural and normal condition." . . . In the same speech he said: "We are now the nucleus of a growing power, which if we are true to ourselves, our destiny, and high mission, will become the controlling power on this continent."

Thoughtful Southerners, ever since, have had to come to terms with what their secessionist forebears were "really" dedicated to. This challenge may be seen in the concluding ("Lost Cause") chapter in this *Reflections* volume. It may be seen as well in the following remarks (a half-century ago) by Richard M. Weaver, a University of Chicago English professor from North Carolina (*The Southern Tradition at Bay*, p. 148):

> The issue of Southern separatism inevitably raised the question of differences between Southern and Northern people, and it was natural that champions of the lost cause would make the most of comparisons advantageous to them. If two people are so unlike that they can be happy only in separate political courses, the yoking of them together is an act of violence which can be justified only by casuistry or in terms of some mystical belief in a joint mission. Southern spokesmen realized that in the right of self-determination of people they had a powerful argument—*somewhat vitiated, it is true, by the awkward presence of the Negro*—and they were not slow to quote the Declaration of Independence on the necessity of dissevering political bonds [emphasis added].

The Weaver sensibleness is reflected in his recognition that the Southern insistence upon "self-determination" *was* "somewhat vitiated . . . by the awkward presence of the Negro"—that is, by the plight of millions of people whose self-determination had been rigorously suppressed for generations (however much better off their descendants may seem to be today in this country than are the descendants of those *not* kidnapped into slavery in the African territories from which the slaves had been taken). (Thus, Americans of African descent may be, with respect to their relatives in "the old country," much as Americans of European or of Asian descent are likely to be with respect to *their* relatives elsewhere.) It is a fair-minded sensibleness that is reflected as well in the way Mr. Weaver (of *Ideas Have Consequences* fame) responded (in November 1957) to an Illinois bar admission committee's "Cold War" question put to him about whether he had "ever heard any question raised as to [a particularly controversial bar] applicant's adherence to and support of the principles of the Constitution of the United States":

> I have heard that this question was raised some years ago in connection with [this applicant's] application for admission to the bar. It has surprised me, however, that this should have happened. I have never seen any sign that [this applicant] harbors ideas of an unpatriotic tendency, and I am thinking of patriotism here in the old-fashioned sense. He has always seemed to me too keen and too independent a thinker ever to allow himself to be committed to a radical program. My own publications have often been attacked for their conservatism, but I must say that [this applicant] has shown a better and a more sympathetic understanding of the point of view expressed in them than the vast majority of students I meet. Everything I know about the applicant leaves me feeling that he is an unusually intelligent, balanced, and helpful American citizen. [See 18 Ill. 2d 182, 207–209 (1959). Compare, for the quite different "reaction" to this controversy by another distinguished scholar, "An Instructive Encounter with Professor Sidney Hook of New York City," www.anastaplo.wordpress.com.]

The distinctiveness of the South continues to be recognized, however much the long-standing racial discrimination in that region has been ameliorated. Thus, for example, it has recently been reported (by the Death Penalty Information Center) that the South still has by far the highest murder rate in this country and that the South accounts for over 80 percent of executions in the United States. To what extent, and in what way, is this (at least in part) a legacy of centuries of dubious race relations? Certainly all this may be, the official abolition of slavery in 1865 could not immediately endow the ex-slaves and their descendants with the attributes of effective citizenship in a republic. This was recognized, a generation after Emancipation, in an 1881 oration by Robert Charles Winthrop (a prominent Massachusetts politician [born in 1809] associated with Daniel Webster) (*Bartlett's Quotations*):

> Slavery is but half abolished, emancipation is but half completed, while millions of freemen with votes in their hands are left without education. Justice to them, the welfare of the States in which they live, the safety of the whole Republic, the dignity of the elective franchise, all alike demand the still remaining bonds of ignorance shall be unloosed and broken, and the minds as well as the bodies of the emancipated go free.

The challenge here may be even more formidable now if the most gifted among the country's citizens (of whatever color) can no longer be expected to be as thoughtful as the more competent of their forebears could *at times* be. In any event, there may be seen, in Appendix F of this volume, the demoralizing consequences for the enslaved (even when they are talented and well-educated) of the desperate accommodations that they must make to powerful masters who regard them as "nothings" to be exploited at will.

The tension perhaps intrinsic to the American regime founded in 1776 may be seen at its most intense in the Civil War of 1861–1865. That desperate conflict may also be seen even to have deepened the American soul, perhaps making it more interesting as well as more vulnerable. Indeed, the juxtaposition in this country between the founding era and the Civil War may be usefully linked to the juxtaposition, among the Ancient Greeks (so critical to the Western heritage), between the cosmology-providing Hesiod and the crises-minded Homer (with Abraham Lincoln somehow serving as our Odysseus [about which I hope to say much more later]). It should also be remembered here what Socrates does with Odysseus in the closing pages of Plato's *Republic*.

Publication of this book was financially supported by a Loyola University of Chicago School of Law subvention.

Hyde Park
Chicago, Illinois
September 3, 2011

PART ONE

1. Slavery in Ancient Greece

I

Slavery, we are told by the *Encyclopedia Britannica*, is a "condition in which one human being is owned by another." A slave, we are further told, "was considered in law as property, or chattel, and was deprived of most of the rights ordinarily held by free persons." Slavery is said to have "existed in various forms throughout almost the whole of recorded history."

Indeed, it seems, slavery may have been widespread, rather than the exception, in the ancient world. The *Britannica* provides this account of how enslavements came about:

> Slaves were obtained in a number of ways. Most often enslavement was involuntary, being achieved by such procedures as capture in war, kidnapping, or slave raiding; punishment for criminal acts; payment for debts; direct sale by one's parent, guardian, or chieftain; or the transfer of ownership from one master to another. The children of slaves themselves usually, but not invariably, became slaves.

"Freedom from slavery," it is said, "could usually be gained only by the granting of manumission by the master, although in the nineteenth century there were several proclamations of mass emancipation by the governments of various Western nations."

"Throughout most of Greek and Roman civilization," it is further said, "slavery was an accepted way of life, and slaves often assumed managerial and secretarial posts as well as their usual domestic and agricultural duties." That is, the more advanced the culture of a community, the more likely that the humanity of the slave would be recognized and made use of. Our concern in this chapter, in providing some background for discussions in this volume on slavery in the United States, is primarily with slavery in Ancient Greece (with additional background provided in the next two chapters, where slavery in ancient Israel and in ancient Rome are glanced at).

II

A convenient place to begin is with the slavery associated with the Trojan War, which has been usefully summed up in this way in the *Chronology of World Slavery*:

> C. 2000 B.C. Probable date of the Trojan War, which was memorialized in Homer's epic, the *Iliad* (probably composed in the eighth century B.C.), but accounts of it are highly fictionalized with mythological references. In the thirteenth century B.C., there was economic rivalry in the Aegean world between the Achaean Greeks and the residents of Troy, a city in Asia Minor. Homer's work suggests that Greeks of the archaic period believed that conquest in battle entitled the victors to the spoils of war, including the right to take enemy captives and make slaves of them.

This account, stressing as it does the economic factors in the Trojan War, neglects the erotic element in the conflict. After all, much *is* made by the poets of the elopement of Helen, someone who is presented (in the *Iliad* and especially in the *Odyssey* of Homer, as well as in several Greek plays) as a woman with a will of her own, not as the mere object of male acquisitiveness.

Critical to the causes leading to the quarrel between Achilles and Agamemnon, around which the *Iliad* turns, is the affection Achilles has for a captive woman who had been awarded to him as a prize of war. Other slavery-connected men and women are treated with respect, including Ajax's half-brother Teucer, whose mother had been a slave. And, in sequels to the Trojan War, the Greek playwrights report, the Andromache carried off into slavery (after the death of Hector, her Trojan husband) becomes the progenitor of an illustrious royal lineage among the Greeks.

Other slaves in the Greek plays are presented as men and women of character and ability. After all, the Greek audience would know that important cities were conquered from time to time, leading to the enslavement of quite respectable people. Even Heracles, a son of Zeus, could find himself condemned to a series of remarkably onerous labors.

III

Enslavement of cultivated cities (not just of primitive or barbaric peoples) was known among the Greeks of the fifth and fourth centuries. Thucydides, in his *History of the Peloponnesian War*, tells the story of the subjugation by the Athenians of the entire population of Melos, a people with some admirable traits (along with occasional bad judgment, perhaps). And then there were the thousands of Athenians cruelly enslaved after their city's ill-conceived Sicilian Expedition collapsed.

Plato, in his dialogues, has Socrates suggest, here and there, how slaves should be treated. For one thing, it is urged, Greeks should not enslave Greeks. It might even seem to be suggested at times that barbarians who are enslaved may be benefitted by the experience.

Still, it is recognized that slaves do not have to be treated as well as citizens are. Thus, in Plato's *Euthyphro*, Socrates presents himself as astonished that a zealous young man is prosecuting his own father because he had conducted himself so negligently that he had caused the death of a runaway slave. That the victim had been a recaptured homicidal slave seemed to make the son's apparent impiety even harder to justify.

IV

Perhaps the most telling Platonic commentary on the institution of slavery may be found in the *Meno*. It is in this dialogue that a slave boy is recruited by Socrates to demonstrate that "learning" is really a kind of "recollection." This is done by having the boy work through, and evidently discover, a variation of what we know as the Pythagorean Theorem.

The boy is taken from the entourage of a wealthy aristocrat who had himself proved woefully incapable of following the arguments offered by Socrates. It does not matter that the boy *is* a slave. The only question Socrates has about him is, "He is Greek, then, and speaks Greek?"

Socrates is assured by the slave boy's owner, "By all means, very much so; he was born in the house." The boy so conducts himself, with opportune prompting by Socrates, that Socrates can say to his master at the conclusion of this exercise:

> And now those very opinions [the boy has expressed] have just been stirred up in him, like a dream. But if someone were to ask him these questions many times and in different ways, you know that he will finally understand them no less precisely than anyone else.

We can wonder what the Greek reader thought of slavery when an enslaved boy can be presented as apparently distinguishing himself in this fashion.

V

Just as Socrates' best student can be understood by us to have been Plato, so Plato's best student can be understood to have been Aristotle. I draw here, for some suggestions about the Aristotelian approach to slavery, upon the epilogue to my *Abraham Lincoln* book. These suggestions were originally developed for a 1986 conference organized by Mortimer J. Adler, who was intrigued by (even as he differed from) what is indicated here about the natural slave.

Critical to what Aristotle says about various topics in his *Politics* (as well as in his *Nicomachean Ethics*) is his understanding of the *polis*. Central to his account of these matters is this series of suggestions from the *Politics* (in the not-yet-published Laurence Berns translation):

> Since we see that every *polis* is some kind of association [*koinonia*] and every association is constituted for the sake of some good (for all men do everything they do for the sake of what seems to be good), it is clear that while all associations aim at some good, there is one which is most authoritative of all and comprehends all the others and does so in the highest degree and aims at the good which is most authoritative of all. This is the one called *polis*, the political association.

The proposition that all associations aim at some good is, for the modern reader, put to a severe test upon studying such barbarities as the eighteenth-century international slave trade.

We can be challenged further upon encountering what Aristotle had to say about *the natural slave*, a subject which I have introduced in this way in my *Abraham Lincoln* book:

> It seems that the critical practical issue with slavery is not so much who will rule but rather who will be ruled. Can those who are to be ruled as slaves, and especially those who are to be permanently ruled, be reliably identified? It is clear to Aristotle that permanent rule over others in the capacity of slaves can be justified only in the case of natural slaves. Who are they? What, if anything, are they good for?

I have attempted to answer these questions thus:

> Vital to reliable identification of the natural slave is the expectation that he and perhaps his master will be better off because of their association than ei-

> ther of them is likely to be on his own. It would seem, therefore, that there is something inherently defective about the natural slave. But he is not so defective as to be utterly helpless, and hence useless, just as he is not constituted to be as useful as free, self-reliant human beings are apt to be. If we should report to Aristotle that we know of no human beings who would be better off under the rule of a master, he might suggest that our circumstances may be such that no natural slaves can be reliably identified or justly managed among us. He might well add the caution that we should not neglect something presupposed not only by natural slavishness but also, and even more important, by sound politics—that the intellect should be primary, that reason should rule over bodily elements and over most if not all of the passions. That is, he would caution us against repudiating nature along with belief in natural slavery.

How unreliable an ally Aristotle is for conventional slavery is further suggested by these remarks in my first *Abraham Lincoln* book:

> Natural differences among men, Aristotle says, begin to become evident at birth. Even so, he does not suggest that slaves are naturally bred from slaves. Rather, he can be taken as recognizing that the son of a slave may be equipped to be a master—and that the son of a master may be fit only to be a slave. This is hardly a doctrine that the typical slaveholder is likely to cherish.

VI

One suspects that the apologists for slavery in modern times (including some in the Old South) who make use of Aristotle as an ally have not read him with the care that he invites and requires. We turn now, with Aristotle, from the relatively few who are naturally slavish to most of the slaves found in the typical slaveholding community. Such slaves, along with the institution of slavery, should be called into question for the thoughtful reader by Aristotle's analysis of the natural slave.

I continue this discussion by drawing further, for the history of slavery, on my *Abraham Lincoln* book:

> Most enslaved people, Aristotle recognizes, come from war, especially when victors enslave prisoners whom they might otherwise kill. Included among these wars are hunting expeditions for slaves. These expeditions, he hints at the very end of his discussion of slavery, are simply unjust. Ordinary wars may also be unjust, of course—and when they are, a question may be raised about the propriety of permanently enslaving the resulting prisoners. The slave, it should not be forgotten, can always purchase his freedom by death—by refusing to surrender when defeated in battle or by committing suicide (or by starving himself to death) if he should happen to be captured. The slave,

therefore, is usually someone who prefers life at the cost of servitude. He may be quite sensible in making this choice, however degraded his life may be in some respects, at least for a while.

And then we can notice:

Such a trade-off may be a form of ransom or a form of reparations, designations with which we are much more likely to be comfortable. What the victors are truly entitled to depends in part upon their merits. The victors even in an unjust war usually exhibit some virtue (or excellence), the trait at least of superior power (which can depend upon discipline, strategy, . . . etc.). Thus, even here, Aristotle suggests, there is likely to be some natural basis for enslavement. He thereby recognizes the unsentimental truth ratified by nature that, generally speaking, it is usually better to be strong than weak, . . . it is usually better to win than to lose.

To this extent, then, I recall, Aristotle acknowledges the justice that there may be in the large-scale conventional slavery of his day.

The conventional slavery of Aristotle's day, like that in nineteenth-century America, required this continuation of my *Abraham Lincoln* discussion:

It must at once be added that this justice is most limited. Certainly, any recourse to war in order to secure an ample supply of slaves cannot help but expose the dubious foundations of conventional slavery. Besides, as Aristotle notices, the fortunes of war are such that good men are all too often enslaved. That good men were enslaved in Aristotle's time was most likely to be noticed when Greeks enslaved Greeks. And so the Greeks came to believe, as Aristotle indicates, that barbarians were far preferable to Greeks as slaves. This seems to have been a tacit deference by them to the promptings of nature: the strangeness of barbarians, especially with respect to language, must have made it easier to avoid facing up to the fact that human beings were all too often enslaved who were no more destined by nature for slavery than were their masters.

That discussion is brought to a close with these observations:

Aristotle leaves it to us to make explicit one argument against even natural slavery which can be said to be implicit in his recognition that most conventional slavery was, at best, dubious. The distinction between the relatively rare natural slave and the multitude of conventional slaves is likely to be lost sight of because of the selfish interests of any ruling class. This can lead to the thoughtless or even cynical defense of unjust enslavements, or at least to the permanent political subjugation of a large part of the population (as had happened in Sparta). This kind of selfishness, when it is noticed, can lead to the

> prudent conclusion that any sustained recognition in public of natural slavery is politically irrelevant if not pernicious, whatever its intrinsic validity. Aristotle in his tough-mindedness would have us notice, if only in passing, that conventional slavery has itself permitted enduring salutary developments in communities that might not have been possible otherwise.

Aristotle would also have brought to our attention how carefully an "intellectual" in Athens (or in the antebellum South) might have been obliged to talk about so critical an institution as chattel slavery.

VII

Natural slaves are few and far between. Nor are they likely to be as useful as many conventional slaves that a community has chanced to acquire (by "the fortunes of war" or otherwise). Advertisements for the sale of slaves in nineteenth-century America often emphasized the talents and reliability of the slaves put on the market.

Slaves in the Old South probably appeared most eligible for enslavement when first "broken to harness" after their importation from Africa. It was then that they must have seemed virtually of a species apart. The longer they were in this country, we notice again and again in this volume, the more like their masters they would appear.

A further complication can be noticed here, if only in passing. Nineteenth-century American slaves might even come to share some of their ancestors, as well as most of their language and religion, with their masters of the day. May not this have been the case as well in Plato's *Meno*?

VIII

Socrates makes it clear in various dialogues who the real (or most obvious) slaves are in any particular time and place. They are the ignorant and the impassioned. That is, there are always far more slaves around than the community either "officially" recognizes or provides for.

The Socratics (and these, of course, include Aristotle) would have endorsed the sentiment recorded in Henry Thoreau's journal on the eve of the American Civil War:

> Talk about slavery! It is not the peculiar institution of the South. It exists wherever men are bought and sold, wherever a man allows himself to be made a mere thing or a tool, and surrenders his inalienable rights of reason and conscience. Indeed, this slavery is more complete than that which enslaves the

> body alone. It exists in the Northern States, and I am reminded by what I find in the newspapers that it exists in Canada. I never yet met with, or heard of, a judge who was not a slave of this kind, and so the finest and most unfailing weapon of injustice. He fetches a slightly higher price than the black man only because he is a more valuable slave.

Perhaps Thoreau (here as elsewhere) went too far with the sweep of his brush. That is, one can be enslaved by a sophisticated cynicism as well as by ambition, ignorance, and passion.

Useful here are the plays of William Shakespeare, for they can remind us (they can help us "recollect"?) what ambition and passion can do to a man (as well as to an occasional woman?). Consider the varieties of slavishness seen even in some of the Shakespearean heroes we tend to admire. Perhaps the most Socratic and hence the most liberated of them all (at the other extreme from, say, Plato's *Euthyphro*) is the prudently pious Edgar of *King Lear*, someone who appears at times the most self-deprecating of heroes, but one who learns from his suffering.

IX

A system of slavery in a law-abiding regime may tend to develop humanizing features. Even so, harsh necessities may "have" to be resorted to from time to time in order to make the system "work." One form that these can take is indicated in a story used in the chapter on Grotius in this volume, the story drawn from Plutarch's *Life of Titus Flamininus*.

That is, there are, in any system of conventional slavery, ugly features that can manifest themselves in unexpected ways. One consequence can be the promotion of fearfulness among the masters, "masters" who can come to dread what their slaves might be incited to do "someday." That is, "masters" are sometimes moved to imagine what *they* would do to anyone who had treated them as they "have" to treat their slaves.

The sense of vulnerability among masters (even when they are truly superior) can sometimes take awful forms, as may be seen in the story Thucydides tells of how the Spartans once "had" to protect themselves against their Helots. This was at a time when the going was particularly rough for the Spartans in their war with Athens:

> The Spartans were glad to have an excuse for sending some of the Helots out of the country, for fear that the present [difficult state of affairs for Sparta] might encourage the Helots to move against them. Indeed fear of the Helots' numbers and obstinacy even persuaded the Spartans to the action which I

> shall now relate, the Spartan policy at all times having been governed by the necessity of taking precautions against the Helots. The Helots were invited by a proclamation to pick out those of their number who claimed to have most distinguished themselves against the enemy, in order that they might receive their freedom; the object being to test them, as it was thought that the first to claim their freedom would be the most high-spirited and the most apt to rebel. As many as two thousand were selected accordingly, who crowned themselves and went round the temples, rejoicing in their new freedom. The Spartans, however, soon afterwards did away with them, and no one ever knew how each of them perished.

It can be saddening to recognize that the men who planned and executed this strategy, in the interest of protecting Sparta from the feared consequences of her centuries-long subjugation of the Helots, could themselves have been grandsons of the very Spartans who had conducted themselves so gloriously at Thermopylae in the noble campaign to save Greece from Persian subjugation.

2. Slavery and the Bible

I

Alexander Hamilton Stephens (1812–1883) is introduced in this fashion by the *Encyclopedia of the American Constitution*:

> A successful self-taught Georgia lawyer, [he] was a Congressman (1843–1859, 1873–1882), Vice President of the Confederacy (1861–1865), and a life-long defender of States' Rights. As a Southern Whig, [he] sought [both] to protect State sovereignty and [to] preserve the Union.

Stephens was a slaveowner who declared that he was "no defender of slavery in the abstract." He seems to have regarded himself as an independent thinker.

The *Encyclopedia* suggests that Stephens "opposed the Mexican War because of his unrelenting hatred of President James K. Polk, his honest belief that the war was unjust, and his fear that it would reopen the divisive issue of Slavery in the Territories." "But," the entry continues, "once the war was over he advocated opening the Mexican Cession to slavery." Similarly, he did serve as vice president of the Confederacy after vigorously opposing the secession of his native Georgia.

"On slavery," we are told, Stephens was by 1861 quite "sound." "As early as 1855," the *Encyclopedia* recalls, "he had defended slavery on biological and

Biblical grounds, as well as its role in creating Southern society, which [he] believed was the greatest in history." It is further recalled,

> By 1861 [Stephens] owned more than thirty slaves. In March 1861 he told the South and the world, in his most famous speech, that slavery was the "cornerstone of the Confederacy."

II

In short, Stephens can be remembered as a Southern patriot. He can even be considered to have been deliberately pious in the political stance he took. That is, he was determined to identify himself with the Southern cause that he had (somewhat reluctantly?) inherited.

Five years after the Civil War Stephens published a massive treatise, *A Constitutional View of the Late War Between the States; Its Causes, Character, Conduct and Results*. This treatise denied "the rightful powers of the Federal Government over [the Institution of Slavery], to interfere with it in any way, except as is expressly provided in the Compact." Our *Encyclopedia of the American Constitution* entry calls the Stephens treatise "a ponderous and tedious book."

However that may be, the treatise does reflect long-held Southern convictions about American constitutionalism. We can even notice the uses by Stephens of "expressly" and "Compact." He continued to speak of the Constitution in the way common in the 1860–1861 Ordinances of Secession promulgated by various States—that is, as a "Compact" for which the "expressly" of Article II of the Articles of Confederation could be used in the effort to emphasize the limited, if not even the provisional, character of the 1787–1789 constitutional enterprise.

III

Stephens, in his post–Civil War treatise, "stated in the outset that the right or wrong of [the] institution [of slavery] did not legitimately come within the purview" of this exposition. It can be wondered, however, whether grand political events, including the development of a cataclysmic crisis, can be understood without an assessment of the moral issues posed by institutions vital to the controversy. However that may be, Stephens was moved to defend pre–Civil War slavery against a then-recently-expressed judgment that it had been a "sin in the sight of men and in the sight of God."

These remarks, he says, "demand notice," which should be as "briefly as possible." "I know," Stephens says, "of but one sure standard in determining what is, and what is not sin or sinful." "That standard," he argues, "is the written law of God as prescribed in the Old and New Testaments."

This means, in effect, a reliance upon whether slavery is regarded in the Bible as sinful. It means, that is, that practice is relied on, not principle, albeit a practice believed to be somehow sanctioned by divine authority. No effort is made to identify the principles or standards implicit in the divinely sanctioned practice.

IV

Reassurance is found by the Southern slaveholder in the institution of slavery as it was divinely sanctioned among the Israelites. Therefore, it is recalled by Stephens,

> Abram, afterwards called Abraham, the father of the faithful, with whom the Divine Covenant was made for man's salvation and the redemption of the world from the dominion of sin, was a slave-holder.

The Southern champion of slavery could thereby hold up the long-exalted Abraham as a model.

Biblical precedents of slaveholding by righteous men must have reassured many Southerners. Typical of the reassurances available was a sermon, preached in the First Presbyterian Church of Augusta, Georgia, by Joseph R. Wilson (the father of Woodrow Wilson) on January 6, 1861 (that is, as Georgia was preparing to secede from the United States). The sermon was entitled, "Mutual Relations of Masters and Slaves as Taught in the Bible."

The Wilson sermon does not, however, rely only on the precedent of Biblical institutions. It is several times suggested (by this Presbyterian minister who had been brought up in Ohio) that the servile race, as in the South, can be improved by a properly administered system of slavery. In this way, "a lower race [can be saved] from the destruction of heathenism," even as the "superior race" can be "refine[d], exalt[ed], and enrich[ed]."

V

The Stephens Biblical precedents included the career of Job. He was, the reader is reminded, "certainly one of the best men we read of in the Bible." We are also reminded,

> [Job] was a large slave-holder. So, too, were Isaac and Jacob and all the Patriarchs.

It is then noticed, "The chosen people of God, by the Levitical Law, proclaimed under divine sanction, were authorized to hold slaves—not of their own race . . . but of the Heathen around them." Not noticed here by Stephens is that the Biblical slaves could be white men and women and, perhaps even more important, that the slavery sanctioned in the Bible (or, for that matter, in Classical Greece and Rome) was never evidently dependent on anything comparable to the horrific international slave trade of modernity. Were not virtually all the slaves that Stephens was personally familiar with either brutally kidnapped from Africa or the descendants of such victims?

Thus, Biblical slavery, insofar as it appeared to have Divine sanction, did not depend on the kind of enterprise that had been generally condemned as piracy by the time Stephens was born. The persistent Southern fear of servile uprisings testified (we have noticed) to the awareness that masters had of how *they* would feel about anyone who had captured and enslaved them as their slaves had been. Biblical precedents would have done little to moderate their own resentment in such circumstances.

VI

Stephens finds support for slavery in the New Testament as well. It does not seem that either Jesus or his Apostles owned slaves. They certainly did not have the material resources of Abraham, Job, and the like.

But, Stephens recalls, "Slavery existed when the gospel was preached by Christ and his Apostles, and where they preached it was all around them." He then argues,

> And though the Scribes and Pharisees were denounced by Christ for their hypocrisy and robbing widows' houses and diverse other sins, yet not a word did he utter, as far as we are informed, against slaveholding. On the contrary, he said he had not found so great *faith* in all Israel, as in the slave-holding Centurion. Was he truckling to a Slavery Oligarchy when he made this declaration?

How *is* silence about a questionable institution to be regarded, including, say, the modes of capital punishment employed (whether stoning, by the Jews, or crucifixion, by the Romans)?

Stephens continues thus in his assessment of how the Bible regarded the established institutions of slavery in Jesus's time:

> In no place in the New Testament is the relation of master and slave spoken of as sinful. Several of the Apostles alluded to it, but none of them, not one of them, condemned it as sinful in itself, or as violative of the laws of God, or

> even of Christian duty. They enjoin the relative duties of both masters and slaves. Paul sent a fugitive slave, Onesimus, back to Philemon his master. He did not consider it any violence to his conscience to do this, even when he was under no stipulated obligation to do it. He frequently alludes to Slavery in his letters to the Churches, but in no case speaks of it as sinful. . . . Can we suppose that Paul would have so written, if he had considered that there was anything morally wrong in the relation of master and slave, much less if he had looked upon it as the "summation of all iniquity," and if our Ministers of the Gospel did continue to teach the same doctrine, to enjoin the same duties upon master and slave, can it be justly said that they thereby "desecrated the Temples of the Living God"?

Thus, the arguments of the abolitionists, insofar as they relied upon Christian sensibilities, are questioned by Stephens as un-Biblical, if not even as anti-Biblical. Indeed, he seems to suggest that such abolitionists had in effect "blasphemed" "the name of God and *his* doctrine."

VII

Stephens returns to this assessment shortly thereafter as he brings to a close this "digression" about the alleged sinfulness of slavery:

> To maintain that Slavery is *in itself sinful*, in the face of all that is said and written in the Bible upon the subject, with so many sanctions of the relation by the Deity himself, does seem to me little short of blasphemous. It is a direct imputation upon the wisdom and justice, as well as the declared ordinances of God, as they are written in the inspired oracles, to say nothing of their manifestation in the universe around us.

One can suspect that Stephens was trapped here by the allegiances he had chanced to inherit. Indeed, the modern critic might even wonder whether the Stephens argument elevated slavery or lowered the Apostles (if not even Jesus himself) in the eyes of thoughtful observers.

The role of chance here is further indicated in the constitutional observation Stephens relies upon in this "essay" on sin and slavery:

> It is not, as I have said, within the purview of this discussion, to speak of the right or wrong of Slavery morally, or the evils of the Institution politically, arising from an abuse of power under it, any more than it is to speak of the institution of marriage, or the relation of parent and child, as it is regulated in any State. These are matters which under the Federal system belong exclusively to the several States.

It seems to be suggested here that it had not been a proper concern either of the General Government or of the citizens of the free states how slaves had been treated in the slave states. Of course, might not free state citizens have been morally obliged to wonder what kind of life awaited those fugitive slaves that they were obliged to return to their "lawful" masters?

Even more critical—and it is this issue around which the presidential election of 1860 obviously seemed to turn—was whether slavery should be permitted in the remaining Territories of the United States. It must have always been difficult to see, no matter what the 1857 *Dred Scott* case ruled, that this determination "under the Federal system belong[ed] exclusively to the several States." Could any conscientious citizen anywhere in the country, upon considering whether slavery should be extended, deliberately ignore questions about "the right or wrong of Slavery morally?"

VIII

Alexander Stephens's post-war discourse on the issue of the sinfulness of slavery reminds us of the challenges that conscientious Southerners had had to confront for decades. These may be seen, for example, in a note Stephens adds (in his 1870 treatise) to the discourse on sin that we have been examining, a note about the controversy a quarter-century before:

> James H. Hammond of South Carolina, one of the most intellectual men this country ever produced, when Governor of his State, in 1844, in reply to a communication he received from the Free Church of Glasgow, Scotland, upon this subject of Slavery, amongst other things, said: "Your memorial, like all that have been sent to me, denounces Slavery in the severest terms; as 'traversing every law of nature, and violating the most sacred domestic relations, and the primary rights of man.' You and your Presbytery are Christians. You profess to believe, and no doubt do believe, that the laws laid down in the Old and New Testaments for the government of man, in his moral, social and political relations, were all the direct revelation of God himself. Does it never occur to you, that in anathematizing Slavery, you deny this divine sanction of those laws, and repudiate both Christ and Moses; or charge God with downright crime, in regulating and perpetuating Slavery in the Old Testament, and the most criminal neglect in not only not abolishing, but not even reprehending it, in the New? If these Testaments came from God, it is impossible that Slavery can 'traverse the laws of nature, or violate the primary rights of man.' What those laws and rights really are, mankind have not agreed. But they are clear to God; and it is blasphemous for any of His creatures to set up their notions of them in opposition to His immediate and acknowledged Revelation. Nor does our

> system of Slavery outrage the most sacred domestic relations. Husbands and wives, parents and children, among our Slaves, are seldom separated, except from necessity or crime. The same reasons induce much more frequent separations among the white population in this, and, I imagine, in almost every other country." (See *Speeches and Letters* of Hon. J. H. Hammond, p. 107.)

We notice here that recourse was had by Governor Hammond to the Bible in an effort to counter a denunciation of slavery as "traversing every law of nature, and violating . . . the primary rights of man."

It is evident, therefore, that the arguments that Stephens drew on had long been relied upon by defenders of slavery. It is also evident that decent Southerners had had to come to terms with such features of their established system of slavery as that which permitted the separation of parents and children. It is this "phenomenon," we can recall, that is critical to the appeal in the North, and indeed worldwide, of *Uncle Tom's Cabin*.

Whatever reservations we are obliged to have about the case for slavery, it must be conceded to the likes of Alexander Stephens that they recognized, both before and after the Civil War, how important the slavery issue was for the secessionists. This is in marked contrast to how determined some champions of the Lost Cause in our time seem to be to discount slavery as critical to the secessionist efforts during the Civil War. Do not such champions concede, in effect, that the cause, as originally understood by the secessionists, no longer makes sense?

IX

We need not question the sincerity of the pre–Civil War apologists for slavery. Their sensibleness, however, is another matter. Not least among the distortions fostered by slavery were the constitutional doctrines developed by Southerners and their Northern allies (such as Stephen A. Douglas), especially with respect to the power of the General Government to shape and regulate the Territories of the United States.

The intellectual, as well as the moral, distortions promoted, perhaps even required, by slavery are illustrated by the kind of rationalizations that Alexander Stephens is reduced to in presenting his two-volume treatise *A Constitutional View of the Late War Between the States*. Distortion may be seen at the outset in the substitution of "War Between the States" for "Civil War," if not even for "Rebellion." Particularly sobering can be the recollection that the most impressive speech heard by Abraham Lincoln during his one term in Congress was evidently from Alexander Stephens, a representative from Georgia.

Benjamin Franklin is reported to have observed, "Sin is not hurtful because it is forbidden, but it is forbidden because it is hurtful." One of the most grievous sins engendered by slavery seems to have been what it did to the souls of decent Southerners who considered themselves duty-bound to defend (if not even to praise) it as an institution. In Alexander Stephens's case the standards he believed he was invoking in defense not so much of slavery as of the right to have slaves—these standards may have been constantly recalled by the name of his estate, *Liberty Hall.*

3. Hugo Grotius on Slavery and the Law of Nations (1625)

I

Hugo Grotius (1583–1645) was a citizen of Holland. He has been identified in this way for us by Richard H. Cox:

> A veritable prodigy of learning as well as a man of action, Grotius was a diplomat, lawyer, magistrate, scholar, and teacher; but essentially he was a jurist. He regarded his greatest work, the *De Jure Belli ac Pacis* (1625) or *The Law of War and Peace*, as a legal treatise rather than as a treatise in political theory; and he explicitly distinguished his intention as that of a jurist from Aristotle's intention in the *Politics* as that of a political scientist.

It is then suggested,

> Grotius' work is not, however, simply a treatise on positive law. Nor is it—in spite of its title—limited to the treatment of the law of war and peace, which is to say to international law as we know it today. On the contrary, it is, as its subtitle indicates, a general treatise on "the law of nature and of nations" (*jus naturae et gentium*), and on the main points of "public law" (*jus publicum*). And although it is true that Grotius focuses upon the law of war and peace, he constantly places that particular branch of jurisprudence within the framework of a general juristic analysis of law and government.

Grotius proclaims in his grand treatise, "An unjust cause of war is the desire for freedom among a subject people." He then argues:

> Liberty, whether of individuals or of states, that is "autonomy," cannot give the right to war, just as if by nature and at all times liberty was adapted to all persons. For when liberty is said to be an attribute by nature of men and of peoples this must be understood of the law of nature which precedes all human conditions, and of liberty "by exemption," not of that which is "by opposition"; that is to say, that by nature no one is a slave, but not that man has the right never to enter slavery, for in that sense no one is free.

It is no surprise then that Jean-Jacques Rousseau, who opened his *Social Contract* with the challenging observation, "Man is born free, and yet we see him everywhere in chains," should pronounce (not altogether fairly) this judgment on the Dutch jurist:

> Grotius denies that all human power is established for the benefit of those who are governed; and he instances slavery in proof of his assertion. But his constant manner of reasoning is to establish right by fact. A more satisfactory mode might be employed, but none more favourable to tyrants. It is therefore doubtful, according to Grotius, whether the whole human race belongs to about one hundred men, or this hundred men to the human race; and he appears throughout his book to incline to the former opinion, which is also the idea of [Thomas] Hobbes: so that, according to them, mankind is divided into herds of cattle, each herd having its master who protects it in order to devour it.

It follows from all this that there was not for Grotius any provision, in his theory, for the sovereignty of the people. A further consequence of his approach is (as we shall see) that there is not that right of revolution recognized in the Declaration of Independence. We should not be surprised, therefore, to find Grotius much more tolerant of slavery than we have become.

II

Another scholar, Martin Wight, provides us a useful introduction to Grotius on slavery:

> [N]atural law is [for Grotius] not necessarily *Christian* theory at all. On the other hand, consider the principles of slavery: liberty is attributed to men by nature; by nature no one is a slave, slavery is contrary to nature. (By contrast, elsewhere Grotius quotes Aristotle's *Politics*: "Aristotle said that some men are

> by nature slaves, that is, are suited to slavery, so there are some people so constituted that they understand better how to be ruled than to rule.")

This scholar then reports on one way, according to Grotius, that slavery can be properly established (however base Grotius himself regards this kind of self-enslavement):

> [I]t is not a right of man never to be enslaved; it is not in conflict with natural justice that slavery should have its origin in a human act. There is a form of voluntary subjection; complete slavery in exchange for certainty of lifelong support.

Furthermore, we are told, Grotius recognized, "According to the law of nations all persons captured in a war that is public become slaves."

This way of properly establishing slavery is, also, a kind of exchange. That is, the captive in war has his life spared by becoming a slave. Otherwise, his captors might be reluctant to go the trouble of preserving someone who is of no use to them, someone who they cannot afford either to release or to maintain.

Thus, Grotius justifies, and builds upon, the sovereignty of nations as they have long conducted themselves. His considerable use of poets, as well as of historians, reflects his desire to report and build upon the way that peoples do conduct themselves. A "fact of life," so to speak, is a system of relations among states which has provided for and accepted slavery.

III

Properly enslaved captives are those prisoners taken by a nation engaged in a just war. The principal forms of a just war have to do either with self-defense or with the suppression of great evils. There seem to be for such campaigns both Biblical and Classical precedents.

"The rights [to enslave captives]," Grotius argues, "have not been introduced by the nations in vain." He continues:

> This we may perceive from what happens in civil wars, in which we find that on many occasions captives have been killed because they could not be reduced to slavery.

Grotius thereby exhibits again and again respect for the way that states have long conducted themselves (which means, in practice, that slavery may have to be recognized whether or not generated by a just war?).

To take account of practice in this way does not ignore moral standards. Rather, Grotius might have argued, it is irresponsible not to take account of, and to try to make sense of, how people are likely to act. We return to Martin Wight for an appraisal of these matters that should at least be noticed:

> To simplify crudely: if you are apt to think the moral problems of international politics are simple, you are a natural, instinctive Kantian; if you think they are non-existent, bogus, or delusory, you are a natural Machiavellian; and if you are apt to think them infinitely complex, bewildering, and perplexing, you are probably a natural Grotian.

IV

Even so, one can venture the opinion that even "a natural Grotian" would have found it difficult to justify the system of slavery that the American South found itself stuck with by 1800. Perhaps enslavement of some of the native population of North America could have been justified on Grotian terms. Some of *them*, that is, did become captives in the course of wars with the European settlers.

Whether those settlers had ever been entitled to the territory they occupied *has* been debated, as has been the justice of the wars carried on against indigenous tribes, in "self-defense" or in programs of expansion. However that may have been, the captives gathered during such wars were not, it seems, readily converted into slaves. Grotius might even find support for his overall analysis in the observation that the victors in those wars, finding the native tribesmen unwilling to submit to slavery in order to save themselves, did not have the incentive to spare any captives' lives in order to make use of them.

However uncertain the justice of the treatment of the native population of North America by European settlers was, the campaigns in which African slaves were acquired were never wars in which Europeans had any rights or duties. Indeed, they were not truly wars but rather (it seems) programs of systematic pillaging that destroyed villages (if not even regions) and murdered uncooperative villagers. Still, Grotius, even though he could not have justified the slave-gathering campaigns in Africa, might have wondered how many generations it would take thereafter for Southerners to begin to be justified in the measures they "had" to rely on to retain the slaves originally acquired in this lamentable fashion.

V

The most startling passages for the modern reader in Grotius's great treatise are those in which it is questioned "whether it is permissible for those who have been captured [in a war] to flee." If captives make their escape to their own people *while the war is still in progress*, Grotius explains, they properly attain their freedom. But "if they flee to others, or [even] to their own people, after peace has been made, they must be given up to the master who claims them."

Such "worldwide" respect for the sanctity of property in slaves is dramatized for us in an account of a remarkable constraint placed upon a victorious Roman general, Titus Flamininus (230?–174 BC). This is (according to Plutarch) what happened in Achaea while Titus Flamininus and his victorious army were there after having protected the Achaeans from the Spartans:

> [Some] Romans, who in the [earlier] war with Hannibal had been taken captives, were sold about here and there [throughout the Mediterranean world], and dispersed into slavery; twelve hundred in number were at that time in Greece. The reverse of their fortune always rendered them objects of compassion; but more particularly, as well might be, when they now met [in Achaea], some with their sons, some with their brothers, others with their acquaintances; slaves with their free, and captives with their victorious countrymen. Titus Flamininus, though deeply concerned on their behalf, yet took none of them from their masters by force.

What can seem astonishing to us is a reported state of affairs which had the Romans who then controlled Greece "unable" to liberate twelve hundred former Roman soldiers held in slavery in Greece.

Such glimpses of everyday life can alert us to the difficulties we may have in understanding the ways of another people distant in time or space. In Achaea itself, however, things turned out well for its enslaved Romans:

> The Achaeans, redeeming [these slaves] at five pounds a man, brought them altogether into one place, and made a present of them to [Titus Flamininus], as he was just going on shipboard [for Rome], so that he now sailed away with the fullest satisfaction; his generous actions [as a victorious but restrained general?] having procured him as generous returns, worthy of a brave man and a lover of his country.

We can wonder, of course, whether someone of a Machiavellian turn of mind in Titus Flamininus's entourage (if not the general himself) had let it be known to the Achaean authorities that, one way or another, the enslaved Roman soldiers thereabouts would have to be emancipated—and that was done here without explicitly undermining the system of slavery upon which so many relied throughout the Mediterranean world.

VI

It seems, in any event, that Grotius was receptive to the Roman way of dealing with slavery, a way that Southerners, in the first half of the nineteenth century, probably "appreciated." It is a way that is celebrated in the opening stanza of the Southern Civil War song, "The Bonnie Blue Flag":

> We are a band of brothers
> And native to the soil,
> Fighting for the property
> We gained by honest toil . . .

The Kantian might wonder, of course, about the justification for the two claims, "native to the soil" and "property . . . gained by honest toil."

Canadians, too, must have wondered about the basis of Southerners' claims to that quite mobile "property . . . gained by honest toil." Were there ever any serious doubts, among thoughtful nineteenth-century Canadians, about the propriety of receiving (and hence effectively emancipating) slaves who managed to enter their country? Indeed, was this the only species of property smuggled into Canada at that time which was exempt from reclamation by its "owners"?

Thus, in still another way, a Grotian might have been inclined to question the legitimacy of Southern slavery. That is, he could well have considered to be revealing the asylum given to runaway slaves by so respectable a part of the British Empire. After all, the Canadians were drawing, in effect, on the lesson taught by John Locke and then by Lord Mansfield in *Somerset v. Stewart* (1772) (a case discussed in the next chapter in this volume).

VII

The status of slavery does seem to depend considerably on chance circumstances. Thus, for example, relations and inhibitions that were considered routine among, say, the Romans can strike us as peculiar, if not even as unbelievable. But, then, the slavery-enthralled secessionists of 1860–1861 could sincerely see themselves as dedicated to liberty and justice.

How much one can be shaped by one's circumstances may be seen in the career of Grotius himself. Martin Wight informs us:

> [Hugo] Grotius and [Johan van] Oldenbarnevelt were arrested and tried for treason [during Dutch civil strife in 1618]; the latter was beheaded, Grotius was imprisoned for life. He was kept in Loevestein Castle from 1619 to 1621 with his wife, children, and books. He wrote several books there . . . and, aided by his wife, escaped in 1621 in a chest of books, [even] while questioning "whether it is permissible to use ruse or deceit in war"!

Would Grotius have been equally as flexible, as to whether one can properly escape from slavery, if he had found himself personally enslaved for life after being taken captive in a battle?

One might find support for the announced Grotian anti-flight rule by recalling Socrates' refusal to take advantage of the plan, financed by Crito, to get him out of Athens before his death sentence could be carried out. Still, one can usefully wonder what a *much younger* Socrates might have done, especially if he recognized that he still had much to contribute to the proper development of both his city and philosophy. After all, it is said that Aristotle once fled that city when threatened with death, explaining that he would not permit Athens to sin against philosophy twice.

VIII

The Grotian defense of slavery *can* be seen as a humanitarian measure, intended to reduce the cruelty of war by offering victors a motive for clemency toward captives. Thus he points out,

> [T]he opportunity of claiming a slave and restraining him, and further, of putting him in bonds and retaining his property, was enough to induce captors to spare captives. If the captors were so ferocious as not to be influenced by these advantages, certainly they would not have been affected by the imposition of any moral restraint.

A system of slavery, he insists, is really humanitarian, curbing as it does all but the most ferocious of captors.

Elsewhere in his treatise Grotius offers an alternative to slavery as a restraint upon the ferocity of captors. Such restraint, of course, is for him to be found in (and encouraged by) the influence of Christianity:

> Christians . . . have as a whole agreed that those who are captured in a war which has arisen among themselves do not become slaves so as to be liable to be sold, constrained to labour, and suffer the fate of slaves in other respects. In this they are surely right, because they have been, or should have been, better

> instructed in the teachings of Him who has sanctioned all charity than to be unable to be restrained from the slaughter of unfortunate men in any other way than by the concession of a lesser cruelty.

This, it seems, is an influence that Grotius wants to encourage, even as he remains "realistic" about how to appeal to those not yet (or not still) moved by Christian sentiment.

Perverse support of the Grotian approach may be found in how the Nazis conducted themselves in their determination to slaughter all the Jews they could get their hands on. In the closing years of the Second World War (it is noticed in Appendix F of this volume) the Nazis, hard pressed for labor, did spare able-bodied Jews who could be put to work for them. Should this be considered somewhat equivalent to the enslavement inducement offered by Grotius to otherwise ferocious military captors?

IX

We have noticed that there was not, for Grotius, any provision in his theory for the sovereignty of the people. He seems to have regarded such a doctrine as too unsettling. Nor, we have also noticed, does he seem to have had a place for the right of revolution.

That the doctrine of the right of revolution, too, can be unsettling is acknowledged in the Declaration of Independence, where it is recognized, "Prudence . . . will dictate that Governments long established should not be changed for light and transient Causes." But it is also recognized in the Declaration, by way of reassurance, "[A]ll Experience hath shewn, that Mankind are more disposed to suffer, while evils are sufferable, than to right themselves by abolishing the Forms to which they are accustomed." This seems to be a caution in the Grotian spirit.

Also in the Grotian spirit, it would seem, is the development in recent centuries of international law with respect to the proper treatment of prisoners of war. Respect for that law makes dependence upon enslaving military captives obsolete as a humanitarian measure. Slavery in general may also be made less attractive if not even obsolete, at least in the Western world, by the remarkable development of technology.

4. *Somerset v. Stewart* (1771–1772) and Its Consequences

I

We are told by Lord Mansfield, in May 1772, about a slave who had had recourse to a writ of *habeas corpus* to prevent being returned against his will to Jamaica from England. The Mansfield account begins thus:

> [T]he negro [*James Somerset*] had been a slave to Mr. [*Charles*] *Stewart*, in Virginia, had been purchased from the *African* coast, in the course of the slave-trade, as tolerated in the [*North American*] plantations [of *Great Britain*]; that he had been brought over to *England* by his master, who intending to return, by force sent him on board of Captain [*John*] *Knowles's* vessel, lying in the river [*Thames*]; and was there by the order of his master, in the custody of Captain *Knowles*, detained against his consent, until returned in obedience to [a] writ [of *habeas corpus*, in December 1771].

The case is sometimes said to have done little, but it still had a profound effect on how slavery was to be understood ever after among the English-speaking peoples.

A leading American student of this case, William M. Wiecek, has provided us a quite useful account of the case, its background, and its uncertain consequences. This account may be found in his 1974 article, "*Somerset*: Lord Mansfield and the Legitimacy of Slavery in the Anglo-American World." Professor Wiecek summed up Somerset's case and its influence in a one-paragraph-long entry in the *Encyclopedia of the American Constitution* (reprinted here in its entirety, except for its cross-references to other articles):

> The case of *Somerset* v. *Stewart* decided by King's Bench (the highest common law court in England) in 1772, profoundly affected the constitutional status of slavery in England and in the United States after independence (because the precedent had become part of American common law). In a brief opinion, Lord Mansfield, Chief Justice, held that slavery "must be recognized by the law of the country where it is used." He further declared that "the state of slavery is of such a nature, that it is incapable of being introduced on any reasons, moral or political; but only [by] positive law." *Somerset's Case* did not abolish slavery in England or America, but until the 1850s it was interpreted to mean that slavery did not exist where it was not established by positive law (which, according to Chief Justice John Marshall in *The Antelope* [1825], might include custom as well as statutory law). Abolitionists construed Mansfield's words to mean either that slavery was universally illegitimate or that it had a legal existence only where affirmatively established by a slave code. They denied that the federal government had power to establish slavery in any territory or district, or to protect it anywhere. This argument became the basis of the Republican "Freedom national, slavery local" slogan of the 1850s and was reflected in Stephen A. Douglas's *Freeport Doctrine* of 1858. *Somerset's Case* also complicated interstate relations in the matter of fugitive and sojourning slaves; some free states in the 1850s refused to recognize the continuation of an individual's slave status in a free jurisdiction. Southern jurists responded by repudiating the liberating potential of the *Somerset* doctrine after 1851, dismissing Mansfield's words as *obiter dicta* or error.

The uncertain consequences of *Somerset* are anticipated by what William Blackstone had said about the law of slavery (as recalled in the 1974 Wiecek article already referred to in this essay):

> In the first edition of his *Commentaries on the Law of England*, published in 1765, Blackstone had emphatically declared that slavery in its pure form "does not, nay cannot, subsist in England" and had laboriously repudiated three origins of slavery that Continental writers had recognized as legitimating it (captivity in war, self-sale, inherited status). . . . Blackstone had ventured the opinion that as soon as a slave comes into England, he becomes free. . . . [He] had gone on, though, to suggest that slavery might have a contractual basis, and that whatever rights an English master derived on this basis continued in force and were unaffected by [a slave's conversion to Christianity].

The 1974 Wiecek article continues thus:

> Troubled by the uses to which [some English abolitionists] were putting the more libertarian parts of his writings, and not wishing [he said] "to pronounce decisively on a matter which is *adhuc sub judice*," Blackstone cautiously modified the relevant passages in his third edition to remove the implications that slavery rested on a contractual basis and that a slave enjoyed "liberty" under English laws. He stated that "whatever service the heathen negro owed to his American master, the same is he bound to render when brought to England and made a christian;" he also revised an earlier statement that a slave becomes free upon coming to England to read that he merely comes under the "protection of the laws, and so far becomes a free man: through the master's right to his service may possibly still continue." These were disastrous shifts of emphasis from [the abolitionist's point of view].

However all this may be, the concluding passage (set forth here) from the Mansfield Opinion in *Somerset* has had profound implications ever since for the discussion of slavery in the English-speaking world:

> The power of a master over his slave has been extremely different in different countries. The state of slavery is of such a nature, that it is incapable of being introduced on any reasons, moral or political; but only [by] positive law, which preserves its force long after the reasons, occasion, and time itself from whence it was created, is erased from memory: It's so odious, that nothing can be suffered to support it, but positive law. Whatever inconveniences, therefore, may follow from a decision, I cannot say this case is allowed by the law of *England*; and therefore the black must be discharged.

II

One important feature of the *Somerset* case is rarely noticed. The writ of *habeas corpus* was used on that occasion to call a non-governmental party to account, the captain of a ship. Even though the significance of this might be explained away by noticing that a ship captain may be licensed by some government, it is still suggestive about how the writ may be used to rein in those who act with seeming authority, including perhaps those who act in accordance with what public opinion seems to require.

Certainly, the master of this slave was thwarted in what he attempted to do. He was not permitted to take with him, when he left England, the slave he had brought with him from the Americas. We can be reminded here of how much slavery does depend on a system grounded in public opinion, whatever the state of the law may be.

The respect with which the writ of *habeas corpus* is treated in common law jurisdictions testifies to the importance of liberty in Anglo-American constitutionalism. The *Encyclopedia of the American Constitution* begins in this way its entry on the subject:

> *Habeas Corpus.* (Latin: "You shall have the body.") Habeas corpus is the most celebrated of Anglo-American judicial procedures. It has been called the "Great Writ of Liberty" and hailed as a crucial bulwark of a free society. It is a symbol of freedom, as well as an instrument. . . . Habeas corpus is accorded a special place in the Constitution. Article I, section 9, of [that] basic document, included even before the Bill of Rights was appended, contains the following provision: "The Privilege of the Writ of Habeas Corpus shall not be suspended, unless when in Cases of Rebellion or Invasion the public Safety may require it."

All this is in dramatic contrast to the kind of lawlessness we have come to associate with the Bastille and Guantánamo.

III

Lord Mansfield, at the outset of his two-part Opinion, noticed that James Somerset "had been purchased from the African coast." Further on, he identifies Somerset as "a negro of Africa." One was reminded thereby of the slave trade—that is, the systematic kidnappings—which continued at that time to supply the slaves "needed" for English plantations in the Americas.

Whatever the status of slavery in England, in Lord Mansfield's time, English ships were very much involved in the African slave trade. However "odious" slavery may have been, no suggestion is made by Lord Mansfield about how the masters of slaves should be regarded. Nor is anything said about the character of those ship captains who deliberately seek (or at least knowingly accept) cargoes of kidnapped human beings to carry across the Atlantic.

This source of slaves in the eighteenth century stands in dismal contrast to the principal source in antiquity of slaves (that is, prisoners of war). Africa, it is obvious, was there to be exploited, no matter what the immense human cost of the original captures and of the subsequent transportation of such captives to the Western Hemisphere. Those origins and their inevitable consequences have darkened American race relations down to our day.

IV

Whatever the "theory" of English liberty in Lord Mansfield's time, there *were* the dubious "practices" of everyday life in that country. This ambiguity is evident in the jurist's professed reluctance to decide this case. The discussion of this case in my *Abraham Lincoln* volume includes these observations:

> *Somerset*, it can be said, was not "really" about slavery but rather about conflict-of-laws issues and about the problem of the relation of municipal law to the general principles of the common law. These matters can be put, as Mansfield put them, in rather prosaic terms.

"Mansfield's purported desire to go no further than he had to," I suggest, "is reflected in the efforts he made to avoid having to decide the case at all." I then add,

> In effect, he issued several warnings to the would-be owners of slaves in England. Everyone was put on notice as to what the court was likely to do if it was pressed to decide the case.

Mansfield even made a point of noting that several such controversies had been settled out of court in recent years, evidently by simply emancipating or otherwise satisfying in each instance the slave in question.

I wonder, at this point in my *Abraham Lincoln* account of *Somerset*, whether the pressured owners of emancipated slaves had been compensated theretofore by other slave owners in England who wanted to avoid a definitive ruling. My speculations continue along these lines:

> It is obvious that Mansfield gave the owners of other slaves being held in England time both to have this particular controversy settled and to get out of the country with their slaves at once if they planned to leave, especially since they had evidently come to rely on the security of their property in England. One wonders, considering Stewart's failure to respond to the threat implicit in Mansfield's remarks, whether this was a contrived case, with abolitionists really behind Stewart, the ostensible owner of Somerset. Although I have seen no evidence of this, the situation does look odd. However that may have been, Mansfield recognized that there were thirteen to fourteen thousand slaves being held at that time in the country, with a total value of some £700,000. This, in short, was serious business. It was clear that Mansfield wanted everyone to understand that the law could not be cavalier about the property and expectations of so many people, especially in the light of "official" remarks (however ill-conceived)

> that had been made some decades before about the status of property in slaves in England. Assurances had once been given to owners of slaves, it seems, and now some warning was needed before a critical change in the effective rules could be announced, even if that announcement merely recognized a change of opinion that had already taken place.

We can see here how the common law judges instinctively worked, something drawn upon in my final quotation here from my first *Abraham Lincoln* volume:

> If liberty is to mean anything, Mansfield seems to say, property and not-unreasonable expectations must be respected. This must have seemed only fair. The very liberty sought by slaves depends upon moderation, including respect for recognized property rights. This approach is to be expected from a great commercial-law judge such as Mansfield: the significance of what he holds is enhanced by his obvious insistence upon the rule of law.

V

The informed caution of the commercial-law judge may be seen in how various facets of this kind of issue are distinguished in *Somerset*. Thus, Lord Mansfield points out,

> Contract for sale of a slave [elsewhere?] is good here; the sale is a matter to which the law properly and readily attaches, and will maintain the price according to the agreement.

He at once adds, "But here the person of the slave himself is immediately the object of enquiry; which makes a very material difference."

And thus the liberty of a human being, right there in England—not on an African slave-trade ship or in a colony across the Atlantic—has to be dealt with. At the heart of all this, it should be remembered, is that the court *is* dealing with an institution that it recognizes to be simply "odious." It is such an assessment that decent Southerners in the United States, trapped for generations in the system they inherited, had to reckon with.

Indeed, so odious is modern slavery that Lord Mansfield considers himself obliged to put at risk considerable property that up to then had been confidently and comfortably held in England. In short, Lord Mansfield indicates, no one will be entitled to protest that he was surprised by what the court ruled on this occasion, especially since the judge had evidently held five separate hearings before he ruled. This is not to suggest, however, that it was certain what the immediate consequences of that ruling would be, aside from what happened to James Somerset personally.

VI

The limitations of the *Somerset* ruling should have been evident to students of the law. The Wiecek article provides this summary:

> Technically considered, the judgment in *Somerset* settled only two narrow points of English law: a master could not seize a slave and remove him from the realm against the slave's will, and a slave could secure a writ of *habeas corpus* to prevent that removal.

"Yet," it is recognized,

> many contemporaries, as well as historians, thought *Somerset* abolished slavery in England; a few thought it challenged slavery in the colonies as well.

Certainly, the reputation of *Somerset* was exploited by those opposed to slavery. That opposition bore fruit, early in the nineteenth century, in the substantial suppression of the African slave trade, that commerce in which British ships had been notorious. The Congress of the United States itself made illegal, as of January 1, 1808, any importation of slaves from Africa into this country.

Once the battle in Parliament over the slave trade was more or less won, the campaign against slavery in the remaining British colonies in North America followed. I have summed up this development thus in my first *Abraham Lincoln* book:

> The appeal of the antislavery movement in Great Britain is dramatized by the career of William Wilberforce [after whom a college in Ohio is named]. When Wilberforce [born in 1759] died in 1833 he was, by the unanimous wish of Parliament, buried in Westminster Abbey. His coffin was followed through the streets of London by immense crowds. His principal claim to fame was his decades-long campaign against the international slave trade, a cause in which he could bring together in Parliament such political rivals as William Pitt, Charles Fox, and Edmund Burke. Even so, it is obvious from a study of Wilberforce's career that he was (like Lincoln, a generation later) more the instrument than the shaper of a great development.

That development culminated, in Great Britain, in the 1833 Act of Parliament which abolished slavery in that country's colonies in the Western Hemisphere.

VII

Is it known today what happened after *Somerset* to the tens of thousands of slaves that Lord Mansfield said were then being held in Britain? It may have been partly a matter of chance who among them learned about the *Somerset* ruling and its implications for them personally. James Somerset, it can be assumed, was not the only one immediately benefited by that ruling.

We are told, in the Wiecek article, that "an unknown number of free blacks lived in the realm, numerous enough to create a special group of London beggars known derisively as 'St. Giles' blackbirds.'" The prospect of destitution in Britain may have moved some, perhaps most, slaves held there (who did happen to hear of the *Somerset* ruling) to decide to remain in their masters' service, wherever it might take them. Besides, many of them may have had families in the colonies to whom they would want to return.

These are the kinds of problems and considerations attendant upon any announcement of a change in official policy on a momentous issue. Lord Mansfield's awareness of the problems in such circumstances is reflected in his insistence that an "application to parliament" is "the best, and perhaps the only method of settling" points of "great commercial concern." This is counsel that the United States Supreme Court in the *Dred Scott* case (1857) might well have taken seriously.

VIII

"The decision and the arguments in *Somerset*," we are told in the Wiecek article, "became known almost immediately in the mainland colonies" in North America. Extracts from English discussions of this controversy were soon reprinted in Philadelphia and Boston. We are also told,

> Of course, [these *Somerset* discussions] did not fall on an American mind that was *tabula rasa* where antislavery ideas were concerned. Rather, they were just one added element in a ferment of antislavery activity in the northern colonies.

We are further told that respectable opinion had attacked slavery in the Massachusetts Bay Colony as early as 1700; Quakers in the Middle Colonies, including the remarkable John Woolman, had long agitated against slavery. The Wiecek article recalls how this agitation came to be connected with the Independence movement:

> James Otis denounced slavery twice shortly before the beginning of the Revolution, first in his argument in the *Writs of Assistance Cases* (1761) and then at greater length in *The Rights of the British Colonies Asserted and Proved*, where he insisted that all Americans, "white or black", "are by the law of nature freeborn." Otis's efforts were followed by an outpouring of antislavery agitation from Boston that scorned white Americans for their efforts to overthrow the comparatively mild form of "slavery" imposed on them by Britain, while forcing the real thing on their black fellow-countrymen.

"These activists," we are then told,

> were supported by the New England clergy, who preached Biblical antislavery messages to congregations in Boston, Newburyport, and Hartford. So widespread was antislavery sentiment in the Boston area that the topic assigned for the formal debate at the Harvard College commencement exercises in 1773 was whether slavery was "agreable [*sic*] to the law of nature" even though sanctioned by positive law. The same subject had been canvassed earlier (1768) in a commencement debate at the College of Philadelphia (the predecessor of the University of Pennsylvania). The impact of *Somerset* in the colonies, and particularly in Massachusetts, took various forms. Some of the most revealing reactions came from blacks. Whether enslaved or free, blacks were not indifferent to the rhetoric of liberty they heard about them daily. As a group of black slaves in Massachusetts wrote, possibly through a white amanuensis, in a petition to the General Court, "the efforts made by the Legislature of the province in their last sessions to free themselves from Slavery, gave us, who are in that deplorable state, a high degree of satisfaction." Thus attentive to the whites' notions of liberty, blacks hearing of *Somerset* brought suit in the Massachusetts courts against their masters, seeking not only freedom but also recovery on *quantum meruit*. In these freedom suits, the blacks contended that they could not be enslaved because there was no positive law permitting anyone to hold a human in slavery, and that slavery was contrary to the common law. These suits, according to a contemporary account, were uniformly successful.

We can see here the seeds of that abolitionist movement that became so controversial in the United States during the opening decades of the nineteenth century. It can even be wondered whether American Independence delayed the abolition of slavery in all of North America, insulating as it did the former mainland colonies from the actions taken by the British Parliament to suppress, first, the international slave trade and, then, slavery itself. On the other hand, if the colonies had not rebelled when they did, might there not have been, considering the passions and resources of the Southern colonies on the mainland, an American Declaration of Independence issued in 1833, not in 1776, and in a cause and with language that would be painful to contemplate today?

IX

Such language, on behalf of slavery, may be seen of course in the 1860–1861 Ordinances of Secession and Declarations of Causes discussed in chapters 7 and 8 of Part Two of this volume. There had been by that time three-quarters of a century during which to develop authoritative responses to Lord Mansfield's challenging evaluation of modern slavery (an evaluation which recognizes the ultimate subordination of any judiciary to its legislature): "[Slavery is] so odious, that nothing can be suffered to support it, but positive law." Thus, it is suggested, slavery is not only without any grounding in nature; it is simply *un*natural.

This meant, among other things, that modern chattel slavery had to be recognized as based on *might*, not on *right*. The more high-minded Southerners, trapped by their circumstances, had to work out a rationale for slavery that permitted them to retain both their self-respect and their troubling privileges. It can be said to have been "natural," therefore, that leaders such as John C. Calhoun even found themselves obliged to argue for the positive good of slavery—good for the benighted Africans as well as for their enlightened masters.

Lord Mansfield observed, upon hearing the remarkable oral arguments in *Somerset*, "I cannot omit to express particular happiness in seeing young men, just called to the bar, have been able so much to profit by their reading." He expresses thereby his confidence in the tradition and discipline upon which the proper practice of law depends. It can be wondered whether any of these young men, upon hearing the ruling that "the black must be discharged," recognized that this was a critical step in a development that would eventually discharge not only many other slaves but also such slaves' spiritually oppressed masters, at least in the English-speaking world.

5. John Wesley and the Sins of Slavery (1774)

I

We are told by the *Encyclopedia Britannica* that John Wesley (1703–1791) was an Anglican clergyman, evangelist, and founder (with his brother Charles) of the Methodist movement in the Church of England. We are also told:

> In London John [Wesley, already an ordained clergyman] met a Moravian . . . who convinced him that what he needed was simply faith, and he also discovered Martin Luther's commentary on the *Letter of Paul to the Galatians*, which emphasized the scriptural doctrine of justification by grace through faith alone. On May 24, 1738, in Aldersgate Street, London, during a meeting composed largely of Moravians under the auspices of the Church of England, Wesley's intellectual conviction was transformed into a personal experience while Luther's preface to the commentary to the *Letter of Paul to the Romans* was being read. From this point onward, at the age of 35, Wesley viewed his mission in life as one of proclaiming the good news of salvation by faith, which he did whenever a pulpit was offered him. The congregations of the Church of England, however, soon closed their doors to him because of his enthusiasm. He then went to religious societies, trying to inject new spiritual vigour into them.

This *Britannica* entry closes with the report, "Toward the end of his life, Wesley became an honoured figure in the British Isles."

Among Wesley's causes was the abolitionist movement. He contributed to it, in 1774, a tract, *Thoughts Upon Slavery*. An American edition of this tract was published in 1848, upon which I draw in this chapter.

Wesley's enthusiastic turn of mind is reflected in how he can speak of slaveholding as "utterly inconsistent with mercy." "A man," he says in judging those who trade in slaves, "can be under no necessity of degrading himself into a wolf." I am reminded, by the passion exhibited in Wesley's 1774 tract, of the revivalists I heard from time to time in the southern Illinois town where I grew up.

II

"Slavery," Wesley observes, "imports an obligation of perpetual service, an obligation which only the consent of the master can dissolve." Such a system "allows the master to alienate the slave, in the same manner as his cows and horses." And it extends in perpetuity, "descend[ing], in its full extent from parent to child, even to the last generation."

The beginning of slavery, we are told, "may be dated from the remotest period of which we have an account in history." He continues, "[Slavery] commenced in the barbarous state of society, and in process of time spread into all nations." The "all nations" and "history" referred to, it soon becomes evident, are those of the West.

Slavery, we are then told by Wesley, "prevailed particularly among the Jews, the Greeks, the Romans, and the ancient Germans; and was transmitted by them to the various kingdoms and states which arose out of the Roman empire." It is then suggested,

> But after Christianity prevailed, [slavery] gradually fell into decline in almost all parts of Europe. This great change began in Spain about the end of the eighth century; and was become general in most other kingdoms of Europe, before the middle of the fourteenth [century].

Thus, Wesley would not have been surprised to learn that the slaves in *Uncle Tom's Cabin* (1852) could find solace and hope in Methodist hymns.

III

Little is said by Wesley about the slavery of antiquity. The reemergence of slavery, in the Western World, after the Christian discouragement of it, is described: "[S]lavery was nearly extinct till the commencement of the sixteenth century, when the discovery of America, and of the western and eastern coasts of Africa, gave occasion to the revival of it." Critical here were "the Portuguese, who, to supply the Spaniards with men to cultivate their new possessions in America, procured negroes from Africa, whom they sold for slaves to the American Spaniards."

Thereafter, it seems, it became difficult, if not simply impossible, for European rulers to rein in the slave trade. Further on in this tract, Wesley describes the "manner [in which slaves] are generally procured [in Africa], carried to, and treated, in America." Both fraud and force are used by Europeans seeking slaves in Africa.

It soon became evident to European slave-traders that it was dangerous for them to attempt to capture Africans on their own. The most efficient way for them to proceed was to prevail "upon [Africans] to make war upon each other, and to sell [to the Europeans] their prisoners." Before this practice was developed, we are told by Wesley, African peoples

> seldom had any wars; but were in general quiet and peaceable. But the white men first taught them drunkenness and avarice, and then hired them to sell one another. Nay, by this means, even their kings are induced to sell their own subjects.

IV

Descriptions are provided by Wesley of the wars and bloodshed promoted, in effect, by the European slave-traders in order to collect their human cargoes. He then comments,

> Such is the manner wherein the negroes are procured! Thus the Christians preach the Gospel to the Heathens!

"Thus they are procured" in Africa, he observes before asking, "[I]n what manner are they carried to America?"

The conditions in which these human cargoes were carried have always appalled authors who have undertaken to describe them. Grim indications of those conditions are provided by the mortality rates that have been reported. It is suggested by Wesley that almost one-third of the Africans picked up by the slave-traders perished before they were delivered to the slave markets on the other side of the Atlantic.

We need not concern ourselves about the accuracy of the statistics relied upon. It seems to have been generally understood, by all who have investigated these matters, that the entire operation was simply horrible. Wesley can sum up his own account with the observation, "So that it is no wonder, so many should die in the passage; but rather, that any survive it."

V

Readers today of these slave-trade accounts can be reminded of the horror elicited by accounts (such as the one drawn upon in Appendix F of this volume) of the Nazi camps during the Second World War. It was inevitable, therefore, that the transatlantic slave-trade came to be condemned even by those in North America who intended to retain the slaves they did have. Wesley undertakes to challenge those who argued that the Africans who did manage to settle in North America were better off than their counterparts in Africa.

That is, he undertakes to instruct those who "may desire to know what kind of country [in Africa] it is from which the negroes are brought, what sort of men, of what temper and behavior are they in their own country." At the heart of our Wesley "sermon" is this passage:

> [W]hat kind of country is that from whence they are brought? Is it so remarkably horrid, dreary and barren, that it is a kindness to deliver them out of it? I believe many have apprehended so; but it is an entire mistake, if we may give credit to those who have lived many years therein [that is, in Africa], and could have no motive to misrepresent it.

The accounts that follow argue that the lands from which slaves were brought were generally peaceful and productive, at least when not manipulated by ruthless Europeans.

One of Wesley's sources could be reminded, by the people of Guinea, "of our first parents"—that is, of Adam and Eve in the Garden. Even so, it remains a mystery, at least for the casual Western observer today, what the conditions were in sub-Saharan Africa that made its peoples so susceptible, for so long, to the depredations of ruthless slave-traders. Political insufficiencies may have made them particularly vulnerable, but also (curiously enough) their habituation to an agricultural life (unlike most of the native tribes of North America).

VI

Wesley, as he prepares to conclude his condemnation not only of the slave trade but also of that slavery which had become settled and far less bloody, "add[s] a few words, to those who are more immediately concerned, whether captains, merchants, or planters." As he does so, beginning with the captains, he recapitulates (in the fashion of the determined revivalist preacher) critical points that he has made:

> Most of you [captains] know the country of Guinea . . . and the kingdom of Angola. Perhaps, now, by your means part of it is become a dreary, uncultivated wilderness. . . . But you well know how populous, how fruitful, how pleasant it was a few years ago. You know, the people were not stupid, not wanting in sense. . . . Neither did you find them savage, fierce, cruel, treacherous, or unkind to strangers. On the contrary, they were, in most parts, a sensible and ingenious people. They were kind and friendly, courteous and obliging, and remarkably fair and just in their dealings. Such are the men whom you hire their own countrymen to tear away from this lovely country; part by stealth, part by force, part made captives in those wars which you raise or foment on purpose.

Then the revivalist can proclaim, "You [captains] have forced them into your ships like a herd of swine—them who had souls immortal as your own."

Wesley addresses thereafter "every merchant who is engaged in the slave trade." He reminds these men,

> It is your money that is the spring of all, that empowers [the English villain] to go on; so that whatever he or the African [villain] does in this matter is all your act and deed. And is your conscience quite reconciled to this? Does it never reproach you at all?

He can even exhort the merchant,

> Have no more any part in this detestable business. Instantly leave it to those unfeeling wretches who "laugh at human nature and compassion!" Be you a man, not a wolf, a devourer of the human species! Be merciful, that you may obtain mercy!

Addressed next are the planters, that class of owners and users of slaves in the English colonies of North America. The challenge issued by Wesley to them should be of particular interest to us, for it can help us assess the thoughts and deeds of the nineteenth-century champions of slaveholding in the country both of the Declaration of Independence and of the Constitution of 1787 (with its Bill of Rights):

> And this equally concerns every gentleman that has an estate in our American plantations; yea, all slaveholders, of whatever rank and degree: *seeing men-buyers are exactly on a level with men-stealers*. Indeed you say, "I pay honestly

> for my goods; and I am not concerned to know how they are come by." Nay, but you are; you are deeply concerned to know they are honestly come by. Otherwise you are a partaker with a thief, and not a jot honester than him! But you know they are not honestly come by; you know they are procured by means nothing near so innocent as picking of pockets, house breaking, or robbery upon the highway. You know they are procured by a deliberate series of more complicated villainy (of fraud, robbery, and murder) than was ever practised either by Mohammedans or Pagans; in particular, by murders, of all kinds: by the blood of the innocent poured upon the ground like water. Now, it is your money that pays the merchant, and through him the captain and the African butchers. You therefore are guilty, yea, principally guilty, of all these frauds, robberies, and murders. You are the spring that puts all the rest in motion; they would not stir a step without you; therefore the blood of all these wretches who die before their time, whether in their country or elsewhere, lies upon your head. "The blood of thy brother" (for, whether thou wilt believe it or no, such he is in the sight of Him that made him) "crieth against thee from the earth," from the ship, and from the waters. O, whatever it costs, put a stop to its cry before it be too late. Instantly, at any price, were it the half of your goods, deliver thyself from bloodguiltiness! Thy hands, thy bed, thy furniture, thy house, thy lands, are at present stained with blood. Surely it is enough, accumulate no more guilt; spill no more the blood of the innocent! Do not hire another to shed blood; do not pay him for doing it! Whether you are a Christian or no, show yourself a man! Be not more savage than a lion or a bear! Perhaps you will say, "I do not buy any negroes; I only use those left me by my father." So far is well; but is it enough to satisfy your own conscience? *Had your father, have you, has any man living, a right to use another as a slave? It cannot be, even setting Revelation aside.* It cannot be, that either war, or contract, can give any man such a property in another as he has in his sheep and oxen. Much less is it possible that any child of man should ever be born a slave. Liberty is the right of every human creature; as soon as he breathes the vital air; *and no human law can deprive him of that right which he derives from the law of nature* (Wesley's emphases).

Wesley can then add, anticipating in effect those nineteenth-century Southerners who became so desperate as to resort to the positive good rationale:

> If, therefore, you have any regard to justice, (to say nothing of mercy, nor the revealed law of God,) render unto all their due. Give liberty to whom liberty is due, that is, to every child of man, to every partaker of human nature. Let none serve you but by his own act and deed, by his own voluntary choice. Away with all whips, all chains, all compulsion! Be gentle toward all men; and see that you invariably do unto every one as you would he should do unto you.

VII

The principal influences on Wesley seem to have been Christian doctrine and English constitutionalism. The latter is drawn on (as we have seen) in what he says about "the law of nature" and a natural right to liberty. Bolstering his arguments here is what he has chanced to learn from the *Somerset* case (decided only two years before) and from Blackstone's *Commentaries* (published the preceding decade).

Thus, Wesley provides, early on, a citation to "Mr. Hargrave's Plea for Somerset, the Negro." The passage cited is found at the beginning of the Wesley tract:

> The variety of forms in which slavery appears, makes it almost impossible to convey a just notion of it, by way of definition. There are, however, certain properties which have accompanied slavery in most places, whereby it is easily distinguished from that mild domestic service which obtains in our country.

That is, whatever reservations one may have about the exploitation of the working class in Britain, the evils of slavery are far worse.

Further on, Wesley can strike "at the root of [the] complicated villainy [of slavery]" by "absolutely deny[ing] all slaveholding to be consistent with any degree of natural justice." He then says that he "cannot place this in a clearer light than that great ornament of his profession, Judge Blackstone, has already done":

> The three origins of the right of slavery assigned by Justinian, are all built upon false foundations: (1.) Slavery is said to arise from captivity in war. The conqueror having a right to the life of his captive, if he spares that, has then a right to deal with him as he pleases. But this is untrue, if taken generally,—that, by the laws of nations, a man has a right to kill his enemy. He has only a right to kill him in particular cases, in cases of absolute necessity for self-defence. And it is plain, this absolute necessity did not subsist, since he did not kill him, but made him prisoner. War itself is justifiable only on principles of self-preservation: therefore it gives us no right over prisoners, but to hinder their hurting us by confining them. Much less can it give a right to torture, or kill, or even to enslave an enemy when the war is over. Since therefore the right of making our prisoners slaves, depends on a supposed right of slaughter, that foundation failing, the consequence which is drawn from it, must fail likewise. It is said, secondly, slavery may begin by one man's selling himself to another. And it is true, a man may sell himself to work for another; but he cannot sell himself to be a slave, as above defined. Every sale implies an equivalent given

> to the seller, in lieu of what he transfers to the buyer. But what equivalent can be given for life or liberty? His property likewise, with the very price which he seems to receive, devolves ipso facto to his master, the instant he becomes his slave: in this case, therefore, the buyer gives nothing, and the seller receives nothing. Of what validity, then, can a sale be, which destroys the very principles upon which all sales are founded? We are told, thirdly, that men may be born slaves, by being the children of slaves. But this, being built upon the two former rights, must fall together with them. If neither captivity nor contract can, by the plain law of nature and reason, reduce the parent to a state of slavery, much less can they reduce the offspring.

Wesley sums up all this with the observation, "It clearly follows, that all slavery is as irreconcilable to justice as to mercy."

VIII

We can see, in Wesley's 1774 tract, the kinds of arguments, grounded in both religious and political doctrines, that were featured in the campaigns of nineteenth-century abolitionists in the United States. Anticipating these developments was the career of John Woolman (1720–1772). He is described thus in the *Encyclopedia Britannica*:

> British-American Quaker leader and Abolitionist whose *Journal* is recognized as one of the classic records of the spiritual inner life. Until he was 21 Woolman worked for his father, a Quaker farmer. He then moved to Mount Holly, N.J., to enter trade. At that time he made his first appearance as a preacher of Quaker doctrine, exercising his ministry without financial remuneration, in keeping with his religion's practice. In 1743 he took up tailoring, which afforded a modest income, supplemented at times by other work. From 1743 he made frequent and often arduous preaching journeys, visiting, among other places, Maryland's east shore, where he carried his message against slaveholding, and the Rhode Island coast, where he brought his antislavery doctrine to the attention of shipowners. In Indian villages of the Pennsylvania frontier, he supported Moravian missionary attempts, sought to curtail the sale of rum to the Indians, and worked for a more just Indian land policy. Woolman maintained a strict manner of life, making his trips on foot whenever possible, wearing undyed garments, and abstaining from the use of any product connected with the slave trade. He was successful in getting Quaker communities to go on record against slavery and in persuading many individuals to free their slaves.

Woolman describes, in his remarkable *Journal*, the spiritual experiences that he considered to have practical applications in eighteenth-century

America. Wesley, too, draws on his own experience in America when he assesses the then-common insistence that only Africans could work the land in what we know as the Deep South. Such an insistence may be seen, for example, in documents issued by secessionist states in 1861 (discussed in chapters 7 and 8 in Part Two of this volume).

The climate justification for slavery (of which much *is* made later) is addressed in this fashion by Wesley:

> For white men, even Englishmen, are well able to labor in hot climates; provided they are temperate both in meat and drink, and that they inure themselves to it by degrees. I speak no more than I know by experience. It appears from the thermometer, that the summer heat in Georgia is frequently equal to that in Barbadoes, yea, to that under the line. And yet I and my family (eight in number) did employ all our spare time there, in felling of trees and clearing of ground, as hard labor as any negro need be employed in. The German family likewise, forty in number, were employed in all manner of labor. And this was so far from impairing our health, that we all continued perfectly well, while the idle ones round about us were swept away as with a pestilence. It is not true, therefore, that white men are not able to labor, even in hot climates, full as well as black.

Wesley does not leave the argument at this, however, for he goes on to insist, "[But even if white men are not able to labor in hot climates, full as well as black], it would be better that none should labor there, that the work should be left undone, than that myriads of innocent men should be murdered, and myriads more dragged into the basest slavery." We can see here the kind of passion that moved men such as John Brown to resort to the desperate deeds they did, without regard to immediate material costs and political consequences.

IX

A letter, of February 26, 1791, was evidently written in London by John Wesley, four days before his death, to the English abolitionist William Wilberforce. The opening paragraph of this short letter reads:

> Unless the Divine power has raised you up to be as *Athanasius contra mundum* [Athanasius against the world], I see not how you can go through your glorious enterprise, in opposing that execrable villainy, which is the scandal of religion, of England, and of human nature. Unless God has raised you up for this very thing, you will be worn out by the opposition of men and devils. But, "if God

> be for you, who can be against you?" Are all of them together stronger than God? O "be not weary in well doing!" Go on, in the name of God, and in the power of his might, till even American slavery (the vilest that ever saw the sun) shall vanish away before it.

The difficulties to be encountered by the champions of slavery on this continent in the nineteenth century are anticipated by this judgment (whether or not fair) by a distinguished clergyman, that American slavery was "the vilest that ever saw the sun."

Wesley's letter to Wilberforce continues with this observation about the slave codes in North America:

> Reading this morning a tract, wrote by a poor African, I was particularly struck by that circumstance,—that a man who has black skin, being wronged or outraged by a white man, can have no redress; it being a law, in all our colonies, that the oath of a black against a white goes for nothing. What villainy is this?

At the core of whatever "villainy" there may be here are elementary questions about what it means to be human. What use *did* sensible slaveowners in the South make, we may well wonder, of what their slaves knew and felt—and how did that affect how "owners" treated those fellow human beings known as "slaves"?

These and like questions can help us investigate the grounding there may be in nature, as well as in theology, for the system of slavery that developed in the United States. Two years after the Wesley tract, *Thoughts Upon Slavery*, was published, the Declaration of Independence was proclaimed. The grounding of that Declaration in theology, as well as in nature, was much more profound than might have been recognized by most (if not all) of the Declarers of 1776.

6. The Declaration of Independence and the Issue of Slavery (1776)

I

It was natural that the insistence in the Declaration of Independence that "all Men are created equal" would be invoked more and more in the following decades by those who questioned the institution of chattel slavery. A variety of responses, in support of the use of African slaves, was developed during the four score years after this "created equal" insistence in 1776. These responses ranged, among apologists for slavery, from the limitation of this language to "all Europeans" to its dismissal as being simply not true.

It is not only in the "all Men" language that all of humanity is seen as decisively similar. That similarity extends even to the necessity of dividing up humanity into various peoples. At times, "it becomes necessary for one People" to separate itself from another with whom they had been "connected."

Even so, the case for separation had to be put in terms that could be assessed by "a candid World," which once again seems to recognize affinities among "all Men." The United States can be proclaimed in this Declaration, completing a separation which had evidently been developing for some time. Was a different kind of separateness relied upon, by defenders of slavery, with regard to "people" routinely held as slaves in North America?

II

To speak of "all Men" may be to recognize a common humanity worldwide. But (we have noticed) it is also recognized in the same instrument that the human race does have to be divided if it is to be ministered to effectively by governments and the social order. Thus, even the ties of kinship ("the Voice of . . . Consanguinity") may have to be disregarded if an effective political order is to be recovered or to be developed and maintained.

The decisiveness of the experience of immigration for the people of the United States is recognized in the Declaration. The political order relied upon by them very much depends on the law. Law is critical not only if a people is to be governed effectively, but also if (as *Somerset* v. *Stewart* [1772] had noticed) any people is to be permanently subjugated anywhere.

Effective governance includes considerations of who rules where. For two centuries it had seemed "natural" enough that thousands, and then millions, of people along the Atlantic coast in North America should continue to be ruled by a government three thousand miles away. But it was argued in 1776 that that government (like any other?) should be constantly subject to review and authoritative assessments by those it purported to rule.

III

Particularly to be guarded against is *tyranny*. The authors of the Declaration could see, in the way that the British had been conducting themselves, "a design to reduce them under absolute Despotism." It is obvious, they argue, that the "repeated Injuries and Usurpations" that they had encountered had "in direct Object the Establishment of an absolute Tyranny" over them.

Tyranny may be seen in the insistence by the British government that it was "invested with Power to legislate for [its Colonies] in all Cases whatsoever." At this very time, it is alleged, "large Armies of foreign Mercenaries [were being transported] to compleat the Works of Death, Desolation, and Tyranny." Further on it can be noticed, "A Prince, whose Character is thus marked by every act which may define a Tyrant, is unfit to be the Ruler of a free People."

There seems to be throughout the Declaration an emphasis upon liberty and self-government as distinctively English. It should not be surprising that such an emphasis could eventually come to threaten the case made for chattel slavery in the United States. It seemed obvious enough to more and more citizens in this country, once independence could be generally regarded as secure, that such slavery was an extreme form of that tyranny decried in the Declaration of Independence.

IV

At the heart of the grievances systematically cataloged in the Declaration is the imposition of taxes "without our Consent." It did not matter, it seems, that some of those taxes were justified as necessary to pay for vital services that the colonies had wanted and gotten from the British government during the French and Indian War. What mattered was the sense of vulnerability, if not even of humiliation, that taxation imposed in this fashion promoted.

The objection here can be said to go back to Magna Carta, which itself invoked standards and practices from well before 1215. The accustomed liberty of the English-speaking peoples is thus drawn upon and developed. We can be reminded of William Wordsworth's engaging lines:

> We must be free or die, who speak the tongue
> That Shakespeare spake, the faith and morals hold
> Which Milton held.

It did not require much effort to see, in a system of chattel slavery, presuppositions and practices that seemed very much in opposition to the principles of English liberty. In due time, the slaves themselves could also be "infected" by English notions about these matters, for they could well come to see the grievances they naturally had as the most extreme form of "taxation" without consent. That is, such slaves had steadily acquired a vocabulary which taught them arguments they might add to those that they naturally had as permanently exploited human beings.

V

The "self-evident" truth, "that all Men are created equal," is questioned after 1776, and not only by Southern slaveholders. It seems to be questioned, in some respects, even in the Declaration itself. Particularly challenging here is its final grievance:

> [The present King of Great-Britain] . . . has excited domestic Insurrections amongst us and has endeavoured to bring on the Inhabitants of our Frontiers, the merciless Indian Savages, whose known Rule of Warfare, is an undistinguished Destruction of all Ages, Sexes and Conditions.

The "domestic Insurrections" condemned here seem to have been the slave uprisings that the British were believed to be inciting. Such incitements anticipated what John Brown could be reviled for having tried to do in 1859 at Harpers Ferry and what President Lincoln was condemned by Southerners as having done in his Emancipation Proclamation of 1862–1863. Thus, it seemed to be argued in the Declaration of Independence that the right of revolution extolled therein was not something that slaves should be encouraged to rely upon, at least at that time and place.

To speak as the Declaration does of "the merciless Indian Savages" suggests that even though "all Men are created equal," some can be considered so corrupted by their circumstances that they are in need of restraint. This grievance recognizes also that other critical distinctions should be made among "all Men," distinctions that recognize differences in "Ages, Sexes and Conditions." Even so, a decade later, in the Northwest Ordinance of 1787, residents in the Northwest Territory were instructed by the Continental Congress,

> The utmost good faith shall always be observed towards the Indians; their lands and property shall never be taken from them without their consent; and in their property, rights and liberty, they never shall be invaded or disturbed, unless in just and lawful wars authorized by Congress; but laws founded in justice and humanity shall from time to time be made, for preventing wrongs being done to them; and for preserving peace and friendship with them.

VI

We have noticed that the imposition of taxes "without our Consent" lies at the heart of the Declaration's grievances. We have also noticed that slavery can be regarded, at least by some, as an extreme form of such usurpation. It was this recognition that prompted Samuel Johnson to ask about the American revolutionaries, "How is it that we hear the loudest yelps for liberty among the drivers of negroes?"

American abolitionists, in the first half of the nineteenth century, challenged slavery as in principle incompatible with the principles of their regime. We have seen that troubling accommodations had had to be made to slavery interests in the 1780s, but once the Republic was firmly established it was time to take its principles seriously enough to see slavery for what it was, a tyranny far worse than that which had justified a people's rebellion in 1776. Such a dire assessment of slavery was evident in the passage about the slave trade (reproduced in the preface of this volume) that Thomas Jefferson had proposed for the Declaration of Independence.

Of course, Southerners could come to resent Northern challenges to slavery as, in effect, "imposing Taxes on [them] without [their] Consent." This resentment had been anticipated by that which had been aroused by the Northern exploitation of tariffs to encourage Northern manufactures, tariffs which in effect imposed an economic burden on Southern exporters of raw materials. Indeed, some Southern whites even came to regard themselves as enslaved by a Northern money-grubbing plutocracy.

VII

Some, among Southerners, were troubled in 1776 by any explicit public questioning of slavery, whatever may have been implied by the expression of pieties about "all Men." Among the challenges encountered by Southerners, we have noticed, had been the proposal made by Thomas Jefferson that the king should be condemned in the Declaration of Independence for having prevented the colonies from forbidding the importation of slaves. A decade later South Carolina and Georgia chanced to be in such "need" of slaves, because of the ravages of the Revolutionary War, that they kept the Constitutional Convention from empowering the new Congress to act immediately against the international slave trade.

Would not a condemnation of that trade be a condemnation, in effect, of slavery? This would have been more troubling for some slaveholders than a public recognition that "all Men are created equal." What *that* meant could be indefinite in its applications and consequences, but not an explicit condemnation of the international slave trade.

Of course, the international slave trade would come to be substantially suppressed by European nations early in the nineteenth century. By that time, however, the slavery interests in the United States were capable of providing themselves all the slaves they "needed" (if not even more than they needed in the existing slave states) without having to rely on continued importations from Africa. Besides, there evidently was still the expectation, or at least the hope, among some of the more sophisticated citizens in the United States (in the South as well as in the North) that slavery was indeed in the course of ultimate extinction.

VIII

Economic and social conditions changed enough by, say, 1820, however, to make it ever harder for the slave states to contemplate giving up their slaves. And it came to be obvious to some of them that they could not maintain slavery if they could not share in the economic and political exploitation of the Territories acquired by the United States because of the Louisiana Purchase of 1803 and the Mexican War of 1846. This is in marked contrast to the insistence in the Northwest Ordinance of 1787 that there should never be any slavery in the Northwest Territory, which was then the major Territory of the United States.

Two principal causes have been suggested for the enhanced determination of Southerners to retain, perhaps even to expand, slavery. One had to do with the economic rewards that developed with respect to products such as cotton. The other had to do with the horrific race war that followed in 1791 upon the abolition of slavery by the French in Santo Domingo.

One of the grievances collected by the Framers of the Declaration of Independence had been that the British had "transport[ed] [Americans] beyond Seas to be tried for pretended offences." Another grievance had been that "[the King] ha[d] constrained [their] fellow Citizens taken Captive on the high Seas to bear Arms against their Country." It can be wondered whether slaves being held in the United States and moved into the Territories ever saw themselves as entitled to express grievances of this kind, especially after they had become familiar with the spirit as well as with the language of the Declaration of Independence.

IX

Of course, it can also be wondered, here and elsewhere, whether the typical master of slaves ever recognized himself as indulging in the tyranny challenged in the Declaration of Independence. The obligation to address a "candid World" suggests that it matters what people elsewhere do think. It also suggests that there are relevant standards to be invoked here that transcend national boundaries.

To speak of "all Men" as being entitled to various rights is to recognize that there are standards that draw on informed opinions about humanity and rationality. To speak of "the most barbarous Ages" is to recognize that there *are* better and worse ways of organizing human communities. Thus, standards were invoked by which the institution of modern chattel slavery would be judged more and more, beginning (as we have seen) with a nigh-universal condemnation of the African slave trade.

Even so, the apologists for slavery in the slave states and the apologists for a "hands-off" policy in the free states were able, during the first half of the nineteenth century, to make a substantial case for at least the toleration of slavery where it was. So effective were these apologists that it may have become less obvious than it had seemed to be in 1776 that it was a "self-evident Truth" that "all Men are created equal." This shift was tacitly recognized by Abraham Lincoln at Gettysburg, by which time a critical "self-evident Truth" of 1776 had become (for too many of his countrymen) no more than a "proposition" that had to be tested by "a great civil war."

7. Human Nature and the Constitution

I

The understanding of human nature in the Constitution of 1787 is both high-minded and shrewd. Aspirations are recognized and affirmed. Cautions are provided, sometimes in considerable detail.

The uses of forms of *nature* in the Constitution are limited to rather prosaic provisions with respect to natural-born citizens and naturalization. This is in marked contrast to the Declaration of Independence, where "the Laws of Nature and of Nature's God" are dramatically invoked. The reliance upon nature in the Constitution is less obvious, but it *is* there in various manifestations.

Thus, an awareness of *nature*, in the more or less physical sense, may be seen in the provisions for the immaturity of some citizens considered for public office and for the incapacity or death of others. It is natural as well to identify some people as like-minded and thereafter to provide for them and to rely upon them. And it is expected that other peoples have comparable allegiances and duties, both immediately and for the foreseeable future.

II

Among the cautions provided for in the Constitution are those with respect to the compensation of various officers of government. It is recognized, that is, that officers might be either intimidated or led astray by what is threatened or offered with respect to compensation. So it is provided, "The President shall, at stated Times, receive for his Services, a Compensation, which shall neither be encreased nor diminished during the Period for which he shall have been elected, and he shall not receive within that Period any other Emolument from the United States, or any of them."

A different arrangement had to be made, however, for judges who would have indefinite appointments. Inflation must be taken into account—and this is done by the provision that judges would not have *their* compensation "diminished during their Continuance in Office." It is also provided, "The President, Vice President and all civil Officers" are subject to removal from office "on Impeachment for, and Conviction of, Treason, Bribery, or other high Crimes and Misdemeanors."

The financial misconduct of members of Congress is anticipated in another way, as may be seen in the Twenty-seventh Amendment, which was originally proposed in 1789: "No law, varying the compensation for the services of the Senators and Representatives shall take effect, until the election of Representatives shall have intervened." In the same spirit, it can be said, is the provision (reflecting British experience) in Article I, Section 8 of the Constitution: "Congress shall have Power . . . To raise and support Armies, but no Appropriation of Money to that Use shall be for a longer Term than two Years." In these ways, therefore, the "natural" misuse of money is anticipated, as it is in provisions (among others) with respect to the punishment of counterfeiting, and to an insistence upon uniformity in duties and other taxes.

III

Assurances are given that the official acts in one state are duly respected in other states of the Union. Thus, "Full Faith and Credit shall be given in each State to the public Acts, Records, and judicial Proceedings of every other State." Cautions that take the form of criminal laws may be seen in the provisions with respect to the treason, bribery, and counterfeiting already referred to.

All this is reinforced by the provision in Article IV of the Constitution, "A Person charged in any State with Treason, Felony, or other Crime, who shall flee from Justice, and be found in another State, shall . . . be removed to the State having Jurisdiction of the Crime." It is also recognized in Article IV that persons who are held as slaves in one state may "escape" into another state. It seems to be recognized as well that the states receiving such escapees might prefer to accept the self-emancipation of these slaves.

The "created equal" language in the Declaration of Independence must have called into question, for some, the legitimacy of slavery anywhere in the country. That antipathy is reflected in the care that has to be taken to permit states to import slaves until 1808, that care which extends to the assurance that this permission cannot be amended out of the Constitution. Within a generation, however, substantial questioning began to be heard (naturally enough, we might say) not only about the propriety of returning fugitive slaves but also about the justice of any system of slavery anywhere in the Union.

IV

The cautions grounded in an awareness of how human nature can work may also be seen in provisions with respect to the impeachment of officers of government. No persons shall be convicted in an impeachment proceeding "without the Concurrence of two thirds of the Members [of the Senate] present." When the president of the United States is tried, the Chief Justice presides.

That is, the vice president, who usually presides over the Senate, is excused from service there when the president is tried. Is this because he might covet the office of the president? Or is it that he may be (or may seem to some to be) too much of an ally of the president?

The appearance or prospect of partisanship is reined in elsewhere as well, as in the provision that it takes "the Concurrence of two thirds" of the members of a House of Congress to expel a member. Not unrelated to this is the assurance in Article V that "no State, without its Consent, shall be deprived of its equal Suffrage in the Senate." Not unrelated, also, may be the provision in Article II, that electors for president must "vote by Ballot for two persons, of whom one at least shall not be an inhabitant of the same State with themselves."

V

Aspirations, grounded somewhat in nature, may be seen in the Preamble to the Constitution, with its invocation of justice, the general welfare, and the blessings of liberty. This may be seen elsewhere as well, of course, as in the Necessary and *Proper* Clause. The expectations of an enlightened age, inspired somewhat by such influences as Francis Bacon's project of "the conquest of nature," may be seen in the promotion of "the Progress of Science and useful Arts."

The workings of nature can be expected in that "Law of Nations" deferred to in the Constitution. Precisely what nature ordains is not spelled out, with the explicit references to the natural (with respect to "natural born" and "Naturalization") dependent not truly upon natural features but rather upon artificial boundaries and the like. Still, it can be said, a people naturally attempts to identify itself as somehow natural, especially when sacrifices seem to be needed.

The influence of nature can also be expected in the workings of that common law which the Constitution takes for granted throughout. It is further evident throughout that a substantial political heritage and a reliable ethical system are relied upon. This is a people with considerable experience in self-government, experience that was drawn upon in the Constitutional Convention and shortly thereafter in the ratification of the Constitution and then in its competent implementation.

VI

It is not generally noticed that there are no qualifications, with respect to age, residence, or even citizenship, for the judges empowered by the Constitution. What does that say about the duties judges should perform, how they should think, what standards they should apply? Reason and a respect for justice seem to be looked for in judges, wherever these traits may be found.

Of course, political considerations may very much affect who are selected for judges. But does not the lack of formal judicial qualifications in the Constitution itself reflect an opinion as to the standards to be drawn upon by judges? Does it not presuppose as well that judges should not involve themselves directly in political controversies?

Questions can be raised here, therefore, about the propriety of the involvement by the United States Supreme Court in the year 2000 presidential election controversy. Questions can be raised as well about that Court's sustained supervision of legislative reapportionment measures. Do judicial interventions in political matters tend to be too mechanical for sound political determinations, something illustrated most dramatically perhaps by what was done in the *Dred Scott* case in 1857?

VII

Political determinations, in any event, have to be sensitive to chance developments, more so perhaps than judges need be in applying enduring principles in particular cases. It can be in part a matter of chance what territories make up a country and who its people are. Yet, it can seem natural for a people to consider as "destined" whatever borders it happens to have—or, at least, whatever borders it happens to have had for some time.

The workings of chance may even be seen perhaps in where chattel slavery "thrived" in North America. Neither Canada nor Mexico developed and maintained the system of slavery found in the United States. Developments prior to 1800 could have differed enough in some respects from what *did* happen as to forestall the deep divisions that led to the Civil War in 1861.

A recognition of the workings of chance may remind us of how difficult it can be to implement continually in a community the aspirations that nature prescribes. Still, standards can be perceived that do provide guidance for all officers, of both the national and the state governments, who are obliged (by Article VI) to support the Constitution of the United States. Such support, it is assumed, is both possible and meaningful.

VIII

The obligation to support the Constitution is secured, in Article VI, "by Oath or Affirmation." The language there, permitting something other than *an oath*, reflects long-standing religious sensitivities. Still, the solemnity of one's recognition of a fundamental political allegiance is to be displayed for all to witness.

It is at once added, however, "[N]o religious Test shall ever be required as a Qualification to any Office or public Trust under the United States." It was known by the Framers of the Constitution that religious allegiances varied from state to state in the Union. Even so, there *was* enough that was similar nationwide to exempt Sundays from the ten days that the president has to consider bills passed by Congress.

Does nature suggest standards as to how religion should be used by the political order? Is religion, we might venture to ask, kept in its proper place for the political order when it is protected by provisions such as the First Amendment? Thus, a variety of religious expressions is protected even as only one form of government—a republican form of government (whatever that may mean)—is permitted in the United States, suggesting thereby an authoritative *political* creed.

IX

Republicanism is the sovereign form of government relied upon by the Constitution. But, it should be remembered, the Constitution does provide means for its amendment. "To amend," it can be remembered, means "to improve"—and this is what has been officially attempted some two dozen times since 1787.

The Constitution itself provides detailed guidance to *how* it should be amended, with virtually no explicit guidance as to *what* its amendments might be, aside from what its Preamble may suggest. It seems to have been presupposed by the Framers that standards outside (and above) the Constitution would have to be looked to in ratifying the proposed Constitution and thereafter in developing and ratifying Amendments. Here, once again, we can see how nature, and particularly human nature, might be looked to for guidance.

The tension in these matters between *liberty* and *equality* (as well as between fears and aspirations?) seems to be evident in the amendments developed over two centuries. A dedication to *liberty* is evident in the first ten amendments, but with the Civil War amendments, a dedication to *equality* seems to have become more influential. We can well wonder what nature teaches us about the balance to be struck, in a variety of circumstances, between liberty and equality as fitting and proper for both the effective governance and the enduring happiness of human beings.

8. The Compromises with Respect to Equality in the Constitution (1787)

I

Americans, however dedicated they may be to the principle of liberty, seem to have an instinct for equality. This may be partly because of the way that they (or their forebears) settled on this continent. The privileged did not tend to move to the New World from Europe.

The sanctity of equality is proclaimed in the Declaration of Independence with its insistence that "all Men are created equal." This understanding is reinforced by constitutional prohibitions against granting titles of nobility. It is reinforced as well by the restriction of elected officeholders to short terms (of two, four, or six years).

It should be instructive to notice how else the respect for equality is manifested in the Constitution of 1787. This may be found in provisions that take equality for granted. But it may be found as well in provisions deemed necessary to permit departures from an overall insistence upon equality.

II

The provisions that take equality for granted are many. At the outset of the Constitution, for example, it is understood that the distribution of seats in the House of Representatives would be allocated among the several states according to population. This allocation would be adjusted every ten years based on the periodic census provided for.

Membership in the House of Representatives is open to a wide range of citizens. One need only be twenty-five years old and an inhabitant of the state in which one is chosen. The electorates for such Representatives are broadly based, reflecting the electorates for state legislative posts.

All this is reinforced by the invocation, at the outset of the Preamble of the Constitution, of "We the People." It is that People which is depended on to ratify the proposed Constitution. That People retains the power not only to select various officers of government but also to change the Constitution itself when that is deemed necessary.

III

Other provisions that take equality for granted deal with financial matters. Thus, taxes are to be collected uniformly, an approach that seems to be challenged for some by a progressive income tax. Uniformity is seen also in how the various ports of the Union are to be treated by the regulations of Congress.

The devotion to equality can further be seen in how the various states are to be treated. Particularly telling here is the understanding that the new states in the Union are to be on the same footing as the original states. That is, there are not to be states with inherited titles of nobility.

An aspect of equality may perhaps be seen as well in the reliance upon the militia of the several states for military service on behalf of the Union. This kind of sharing of burdens may be seen thereafter in the broad basis of participation by "everyone" in the Civil War and the Second World War. Things do appear quite different today when not all classes are called upon to share the risks and burdens of military services, a tendency anticipated by the ability of the privileged (including two future presidents of the United States of the right age) to avoid combat service during the Vietnam War, a war during which conscription was relied upon by the United States.

IV

Significant departures from reliance upon the principle of equality may be seen here and there in the Constitution. These departures were usually due to circumstances that required compromises if the Union was to be maintained. Such compromises could be troubling for those obliged to make them.

Particularly pervasive in its workings was the agreement to treat the states as equals for some purposes. Thus, we have seen, the states were to have equal votes in the Senate. Changes in the relative populations of the states never affect this distribution, unlike what is provided for the House of Representatives.

It is not only in the Senate, however, that the states are treated as equals. They are also treated as equals in the amendment process. They are treated thus as well whenever the election of the president is to be decided by the House of Representatives.

V

The most glaring departure from the principle of equality proclaimed in the Declaration of Independence is, of course, the recognition in the Constitution of slavery. This may be seen, for example, in the provision that prevents, until the year 1808, any prohibition by Congress of the importation of slaves into the United States. It is said that this "had" to be agreed to, in the Constitutional Convention, if Georgia and the Carolinas, who had lost many slaves during the Revolution, were to ratify the Constitution.

Another provision that is often disparaged as exhibiting a refusal to recognize slaves as truly human, and hence as equals, is the "three-fifths" measure in counting slaves for purposes of allocating seats in the House of Representatives. But here, as elsewhere, it is easy to misread the implications of what is (and is not) said in the Constitution. For, it should be noticed, the slaveholding interests in the Constitutional Convention themselves must have preferred a "five-fifths" to a "three-fifths" measure in counting slaves for purposes of representation.

After all, such Southerners could argue, slaves *are* human beings. The fact that they, as slaves, could not vote was irrelevant. Children and most free women could not vote either, and yet they were obviously to be counted in determining the allocation of seats in the House of Representatives.

VI

The "1808" assurance and the "three-fifths" measure are reinforced by the fugitive slave provision in Article IV of the Constitution. Slaveholding states are thereby assured:

> No Person held to Service or Labour in one State, under the Laws thereof, escaping into another, shall in Consequence of any Law or Regulation therein, be discharged from such Service or Labour . . .

Rather, such persons are to be "delivered up on the Claim of the Party to whom such Service or Labour may be due."

Is it not tacitly recognized by this provision that the slaves were the equals of whites, at least to the extent that they would prefer to do what their masters would do if given an opportunity—that is, flee from lifelong servitude? After all, the eloquent slaveholder Patrick Henry had proclaimed in 1775, "Give me liberty, or give me death." It was also recognized that many citizens elsewhere, and perhaps entire states in the Union, would welcome and protect fugitive slaves if they were not in effect forbidden to do so by the Constitution—and such protection might make slavery itself vulnerable as an institution.

Even so, the fugitive slave clause is distinguished in its wording from the clause that immediately proceeded it which provides for the return of any person "flee[ing] from Justice." The Framers of the Constitution evidently refused to accept any suggestion that fleeing slaves be regarded as fugitives "from Justice." Again and again one sees in the Constitution reluctant accommodations to the institution of slavery as it existed in 1787.

VII

This reluctance may even be seen in how Southern slaveholders could speak of their "peculiar institution." Slavery was widely regarded by the more thoughtful of them, at least at the time of the establishment of the Constitution, as a "necessary evil." Slavery, they insisted, was an institution that they had inherited, an institution that they had to continue and to deal with as best they could before it could be safely eliminated.

Chance, it could be said, was critical both in determining which states still had slavery in 1787 and in determining who became slaves and how they were treated. We have noticed that historical events, such as the invention of the cotton gin and the Santo Domingo racial strife, discouraged nineteenth-century Southerners from contemplating the eventual emancipation of all their slaves, something that their more thoughtful predecessors could hope for. Rather, we have noticed, slavery could even come to be recognized by some determined Southerners (well before the Civil War) as a "positive good" for everyone involved.

When we return to consideration of the equality sought for in the status of the states in the Senate and elsewhere, we can again notice the workings of chance. Such workings can be seen in precisely where state borders were drawn and in how populated various states would be from time to time. Thus, the way states happened to be arranged at one time or another could be all-important (even affecting matters of life and death) for the parties involved, sometimes even negating (in effect) the equality among states that had been provided for.

VIII

That the two provisions just noticed here—the 1808 slaves-importation provision and the Senatorial equality of the states—were troubling was apparent to the Framers of the Constitution. This is evident in the Article V provisions for amending the Constitution, where assurances had to be given both that the slave-trade protection would not be amended prior to 1808 and that "no State, without its Consent, would be deprived of its equal suffrage in the Senate." Of course, even these two Article V assurances could have been gotten around by first amending *them* out of the Constitution and *then* by reallocating seats in the Senate and by permitting Congress to forbid the importation of slaves before 1808.

But such maneuvers would have been repudiated as acts of bad faith. We can be reminded thereby of the implicit understandings upon which a healthy constitutionalism depends. Thus there is likely to be a tacit constitutionalism upon which an explicit constitutionalism depends.

The troubling aspects that some resent in the allocation of seats in the Senate—troubling as a compromise with the vital equality-principle—have been largely taken care of by the emergence of political parties in the United States. This means, among other things, that Senators *tend* to be defined more by their political allegiances than by the sizes of the states they represent. The emergence of political parties has substantially affected as well other arrangements in the Constitution, such as those for the election of the president.

IX

The slaves-importation assurance became obsolete, of course, after 1808. It can still be pointed to, however, as a reminder of the unseemly compromises that the Framers of the Constitution had made with slavery. But its very presence (and the way it had to be protected in the amendment article) should also serve to remind us of how fragile the guarantees on behalf of slavery could be.

This was apparent, well after 1808, in the difficulties often encountered by slave owners in recovering "their" fugitive slaves. Particularly troubling for them was the steadily growing disapproval of slavery, especially in the North, once the institutions provided for by the Constitution had been firmly established. The concern slave owners had about recovering fleeing slaves was eventually superseded by the concern that they had about whether they could safely take their slaves into the Territories of the United States.

The volatility of the slavery issue, particularly for an equality-minded regime, is evident in the repeated concerns about the *movements* of slaves. First, there was the concern about importing slaves from abroad; then there was the concern about recovering slaves who would not stay put; and then there was concern about being able to take and retain slaves in the Territories of the United States. Thus, the issue of slavery and its aftermath should be taken as supporting the proposition that no issue is truly settled among any sensible people until it is settled right, with rightness *here* very much respectful of the deeply rooted American instinct for equality.

9. The States in the Constitution (1787)

I

We hear considerable talk, more at some times than at others, about Federalism, states' rights, and state sovereignty. This kind of talk is reinforced by the uses made of *The Federalist*, that series of newspaper articles written in 1787–1788 during the contest in New York state over the ratification of the proposed Constitution. These eighty-five articles, written by Alexander Hamilton, James Madison, and John Jay, were published over the name of Publius, a name hearkening back to the Roman Republic.

United States Supreme Court Justices, in citing these *Federalist* articles, often follow the lead of scholars in attributing the articles to Hamilton or Madison (with Jay rarely drawn on). It is not generally appreciated, that is, that these politicians (two of them New Yorkers, the third a Virginian) would probably have spoken otherwise on some of the issues discussed if they had written in their own names. What is said in *The Federalist* is what "Publius" is presented as saying about matters of particular concern from time to time for the New York electorate.

"Publius" was more "federalist" in his sympathies than was Hamilton, and was less "federalist" than Madison was to become. A critical step in the campaign to secure ratification of the Constitution in 1787–1788 was the politic appropriation of the label "Federalists" by advocates of the proposed Constitution. Critics of that Constitution could, with justice, insist that that instrument was far more nationalist or consolidationalist than its advocates conceded.

II

The status of "federalism" in the system provided by the Constitution of 1787 can be gathered by the uses made of the states in that Constitution. Critical to those uses is the considerable reliance upon the states for the electoral processes that determine who the president and members of Congress should be. Also critical is the reliance upon the states in the processes provided both for the initial ratification and for any subsequent amendments of the Constitution.

The Constitution was to be considered to be in effect when nine (of the original thirteen) states ratified it, binding thereby all those who had ratified. By the time that the First Congress was assembled, in the spring of 1789, eleven of the thirteen states had ratified. The other two, North Carolina and Rhode Island, were to come along later.

The amendment procedures require that three-fourths of the states agree to any proposed amendment before it can be considered part of the Constitution. These procedures (laid down in Article V) even permit the states to take over not only the ratifying but also the proposing phase of this process. But the process also assumes that a state will be bound by duly-ratified amendments even if it had rejected them, which is quite different in spirit from the original arrangement that a state was bound by the Constitution itself only if it ratified it.

III

There is relatively little said explicitly in the Constitution about what the states are to do once the system provided for is established. The Declaration of Independence had claimed for the United States that they as "Free and Independent States," would have "full Power to levy War, conclude Peace, contract Alliances, establish Commerce, and to do all others Acts and Things which Independent States may of right do." All of these powers (except as to the complete control of commerce) are pretty much assigned by the Constitution to the General Government, not to the state governments.

The states do have some power of self-defense, but even this power is, or can be, subordinated to supervision and control by the General Government. Thus, the state militias can be taken over, when need be, by that government. In the meantime, the way a state militia is to be trained makes it suitable for use when needed as part of the consolidated armed forces of the United States.

It is recognized in the Constitution that the states are to have, and are to be able to retain, territories of their own, just as they are to retain equal votes in the Senate. It is also recognized that the states will be able to raise revenues for their use. It is recognized as well, such as by the provision about fugitives from justice, that the states will continue to have judicial systems of their own.

IV

It can be inferred from the Constitution that the states are expected to engage in those proper activities of government that the General Government is not authorized to handle. The states may do as well some of the things that the General Government does. Both the General Government and the state governments, for example, can exercise authority over the "needful Buildings" that they erect.

Restrictions are placed upon what the states may do. Some of these restrictions are the same as those placed upon the General Government, such as prohibitions upon "pass[ing] any Bill of Attainder [or] ex post facto Law." Other restrictions are evidently designed to keep the states from interfering with the effective operations of the General Government, such as the prohibitions upon "grant[ing] Letters of Marque and Reprisal [and] coin[ing] Money."

It was argued by some advocates for the Constitution that the General Government was bound to respect the kind of rights that had long been recognized by the English-speaking peoples. This was said in order to reassure those citizens troubled by the failure of the Constitutional Convention to provide a Bill of Rights when it drafted the Constitution. To the extent that such rights were considered long-established, they would also seem to govern as well the state governments, something that is now said to have been recognized by the 1868 Fourteenth Amendment's extension of the 1791 Bill of Rights to govern the states as well.

V

The Ninth Amendment to the Constitution provides, "The enumeration in the Constitution of certain rights shall not be construed to deny or disparage others retained by the people." Such rights, it would seem, should be retained by the people against the state governments as well, with or without the Fourteenth Amendment. The people's rights, that is, should trump states' rights.

Perhaps the most critical directive in the Constitution as to how the states should conduct themselves may be seen in the provision, "The United States shall guarantee to every state in the Union a Republican Form of Government." No such directive is provided with respect to the General Government, presumably because a republican form of government is implicit in the institutions and operations spelled out in the Constitution for *that* government. The republicanism of the General Government, it seems to be assumed, requires for its perpetuation and effectiveness that the people in the several states be routinely shaped by and practiced in the workings of republican governments on the local level.

The Territories of the United States, out of which have been carved almost all the states subsequent to the original thirteen, were governed by the General Government. It is left to Congress to determine when any part of those Territories is ready to be admitted to the Union of states. And, of course, those Territories were apt to be settled by citizens from existing states, which made it highly likely that they would "naturally" be republican in their inclinations.

VI

The states, created for the most part by the United States (that is, after the original thirteen), are obliged to recognize the supremacy in various respects of the General Government. This may be seen in restrictions placed in the Constitution upon the military, revenue, and commercial policies of the states. It may be seen as well in the restrictions upon the states that follow from the legislation that Congress is authorized to enact.

The preeminence of the Union, even before 1789, is assumed in the Article VI provision, "All Debts contracted and Engagements entered into, before the Adoption of this Constitution, shall be as valid against the United States under this Constitution, as under the Confederation." Thereafter it is provided,

> This Constitution, and the Laws of the United States, which shall be made in Pursuance thereof, and all Treaties made, or which shall be made, under the Authority of the United States, shall be the supreme Law of the Land . . .

Among the provisions in this Constitution are those which, indirectly as well as directly, require that the states recognize and respect various acts of other states in the Union.

Thus, it is ordered in Article IV, "Full Faith and Credit shall be given in each State to the public Acts, Records, and judicial Proceedings of every other State." In the same spirit is a provision (previously referred to), also in Article IV,

> A Person charged in any state with Treason, Felony, or other Crime, who shall flee from Justice, and be found in another State, shall on demand of the executive Authority of the State from which he fled, be delivered up, or be removed to the State having Jurisdiction of the Crime.

Here, as elsewhere, it is assumed (and sometimes explicitly indicated) that the territory of each state is to be recognized and respected both by the United States and by the other states.

VII

A sensitive aspect of the question of the place of the states in the constitutional system is evident in how slavery is dealt with. It has been said that the slavery issue was fundamental to the divisions in the 1787 Constitutional Convention, even though slavery was not made much of explicitly in that assembly. The sensitivity of this matter is reflected in the need to add a special provision for the return of fugitive slaves, human beings that the Convention (we have noticed) would *not* permit to be designated (with others in Article IV) as "flee[ing] from Justice."

Slavery may have been a fundamental issue, but (we have also noticed) it was in part a matter of chance which states had slaves from time to time. Climate may have been of some effect here, but political decisions were often critical as to which Territories would permit slavery. Where borders would be drawn with a view to slavery could eventually engage Congress in debates that shook the entire country.

The intense struggle, in the decades preceding the Civil War, depended ultimately on how slavery was to be regarded, especially in the light of the insistence in the Declaration of Independence that "all Men are created equal." Republicanism was evidently considered in some quarters to be consistent with slavery. In other quarters slavery was believed to undermine that respect for labor which would permit the development and maintenance of a population, made up largely of working people, who would be suitable for the proper use and perpetuation of republican institutions.

VIII

The slavery issue became more and more divisive as the population of the North grew significantly more than did that of the South. The North's superiority in rate of growth was probably due in large part to the effect of slavery on immigrants who were not inclined to go where their labor would tend to be depreciated because of its identification with what slaves did. Indeed, it is said that the North was even able during the Civil War to replace by immigration the men it lost on the battlefields of that war.

Pre–Civil War Southern leaders, as they saw their region steadily falling behind in the population ratios that determined political power with respect to the presidency and the House of Representatives, insisted more and more on the federalist character of the Union. States' rights were made much of, with "Compact" (or "Confederation") coming to mean more in their political vocabulary than "Nation" (or even "Union"). The election of a "Free Soil" Republican to the presidency in 1860 seemed to them an ominous sign of what the future would be like if the South remained in the Union.

The Confederate Constitution of 1861, it is evident in Appendix E of this volume, was obviously patterned on the Constitution of 1787. The 1861 changes made, in large part with a view to protecting slavery, placed those states in a much stronger position than they had been vis-à-vis their General Government. One indication of this is that constitutional amendments were to be thereafter completely under the control of the states, with Congress having no power even to propose amendments.

IX

The steady subordination of the states that led to the Civil War was anticipated by the recognition in the Constitution of the law of nations. This was a reminder of principles and ends that went beyond the interests and inclinations of particular countries. Such looking beyond local interests and practices may be seen elsewhere as well in the Constitution, as in the indication that there are pre-existing "Privileges and Immunities" that states are obliged to respect, rights that were to be recognized thereafter in the Ninth Amendment and in the Fourteenth Amendment.

The effects of the national growth in commerce and military power were bound to reduce the influence of local governments relative to the General Government. This development has been intensified by the "globalization" that we have witnessed in our own time. Thus, the states have tended to be subordinated nationally, although they obviously continue to do a lot for and to us.

In the course of these developments domestic slavery has been largely eliminated in the developed nations of the world. If it exists for us, it is principally (some would argue) in the indirect form of our exploitation of distressingly cheap labor abroad. It remains to be seen whether the long-term interests of those thus employed (especially when no other employment seems available for them) can be adequately developed by the countries to which *they* owe political allegiance.

10. *The Federalist* on Slavery and the Constitution (1787–1788)

I

The Federalist, a series of eighty-five newspaper articles published between October 1787 and May 1788, was prepared (we have noticed) by a Virginian (James Madison) and two New Yorkers (Alexander Hamilton and John Jay). These articles (we have also noticed) were offered by an author designated as "Publius." By the time New York delegates met in a convention (in July 1788) to consider the proposed Constitution, more than enough states had ratified it to "establish" it "between the States so ratifying it."

It must have been obvious, however, that the agreement of New York was critical, perhaps essential, for the new constitutional arrangement to be successful. The proponents of the Constitution (we have noticed as well) managed, early on in the 1787–1788 contest, to appropriate to themselves the name of "Federalists," leaving the opponents of the Constitution (the true federalists?) with the name of "Anti-Federalists." That is, some of the critics of the proposed Constitution regarded its proponents as "Consolidationists."

Be that as it may, the arguments developed in *The Federalist* were addressed to the people of the state of New York. The arguments made in that state were not always those made in other states on behalf of the Constitution. Indeed, such arguments made at one point in the 1787–1788 campaign could be quite different from those made even in the same state at another point as circumstances changed.

II

Among the topics tailored for the New York electorate, as distinguished from a Southern state electorate, was that of slavery. The principal *Federalist* articles in which that topic is discussed are No. 42 and No. 54. Scholars assign both of these articles to Madison, but even if so (we should note) it is a Madison speaking as this Publius would.

Federalist No. 42 opens with a consideration of that "class of powers, lodged in the general government, [which] consist of those [powers] which regulate the intercourse with foreign nations." These powers include, New Yorkers were told, "a power to prohibit, after the year 1808, the importation of slaves, and to lay an intermediate duty of ten dollars per head, as a discouragement to such importations." To describe this power thus makes it appear that the provision referred to (in Article I, Section 9, Clause 1) is more an *empowerment* of the General Government to restrict the international slave trade than it is a restriction upon that government (a restriction that Madison himself had lamented in the Constitutional Convention).

Further on, in *Federalist* No. 42, Publius must say more about the 1808 provision. He begins with this observation:

> It were doubtless to be wished that the power of prohibiting the importation of slaves had not been postponed until the year 1808, or rather that it had been suffered to have immediate operation. But it is not difficult to account either for this restriction on the general government, or for the manner in which the whole clause is expressed.

It may not have been "difficult to account" for this provision, which had had to do with the insistence of South Carolina and Georgia delegates in the Constitutional Convention that their states would not ratify the Constitution if they could not continue to import slaves from Africa for twenty more years.

III

It seems to have been recognized that nothing would be gained by singling out states for criticism. Rather, the best face was to be put on this unfortunate slave-trade concession. And so the passage just quoted continues:

> It ought to be considered as a great point gained in favor of humanity that a period of twenty years may terminate forever, within these States, a traffic

> which has so long and so loudly upbraided the barbarism of modern policy; that within that period it will receive a considerable discouragement from the federal government, and may be totally abolished, by a concurrence of the few States which continue the unnatural traffic in the prohibiting example which has been given by so great a majority of the Union.

Although it may not have been "difficult to account" for this provision in the proposal Constitution, no account is provided. It seems that it would not have been prudent to say more than this about the practices and motives of some of the states in the Union. Instead, the passage continues:

> Happy would it be for the unfortunate Africans if an equal prospect lay before them of being redeemed from the oppressions of their European brethren!

This is probably not a fair representation of the steadily growing revulsion in the Western World against the international slave trade. This diversionary tactic by Publius continues with the observation, "Attempts have been made to pervert this [1808] clause into an objection against the Constitution by representing it . . . as a criminal toleration of an illicit practice." Carefully read, Publius's observation here concedes in effect that the slave trade is indeed "an illegal practice" that it was necessary (but *not* criminal) to put up with in order to preserve and consolidate the Union.

IV

The other principal *Federalist* article dealing with the handling of slavery in the Constitution is found in No. 54, which opens thus:

> The next view which I shall take of the House of Representatives relates to the apportionment of its members to the several States, which is to be determined by the same rule with that of direct taxes.

The critical provision here, that people in New York were evidently troubled by, was that found in Article I, Section 2, of the proposed Constitution:

> Representatives and direct Taxes shall be apportioned among the several States which may be included within this Union, according to their respective Numbers, which shall be determined by adding to the whole Number of free Persons, including those bound to Service for a Term of Years, and excluding Indians not taxed, three fifths of all other Persons.

Everyone knew that the partial counting of slaves for allocating seats in the projected House of Representatives was provided for here—that is, the counting of "property" as "people."

Publius's response to this challenge begins with an emphasis upon what this provision means for the tax liability of the slave states:

> It is not contended that the number of people in each State ought not to be the standard of regulating the proportion of those who are to represent the people of each State. The establishment of the same rule for the apportionment of taxes will probably be as little contested; though the rule itself, in this case, is by no means founded on the same principle. In the former case, the rule is understood to refer to the personal rights of the people, with which it has a natural and universal connection. In the latter, it has reference to the proportion of wealth of which it is in no case a precise measure, and in ordinary cases a very unfit one. But notwithstanding the imperfection of the rule as applied to the relative wealth and contributions of the States, it is evidently the least exceptionable among the practicable rules, and had too recently obtained the general sanction of America [in the Articles of Confederation?] not to have found a ready preference with the convention.

It is sensed, however, that this argument may not suffice—and so Publius continues:

> All this is admitted, it will perhaps be said; but does it follow, from an admission of numbers for the measure of representation, or of slaves combined with free citizens as a ratio of taxation, that slaves ought to be included in the numerical rule of representation? Slaves are considered as property, not as persons. They ought therefore to be comprehended in estimates of taxation which are founded on property, and to be excluded from representation which is regulated by a census of persons. This is the objection, as I understand it, stated in its full force. I shall be equally candid in stating the reasoning which may be offered on the opposite side.

In short, it can be troubling to have slaves counted for representation, albeit at a reduced rate.

It is evident that something extraordinary has to be done. This is done by having Publius speak *not* as he has been speaking for more than fifty issues of *The Federalist*, but rather as "one of our Southern brothers [might] observe." The collaborators producing these articles (long reduced, by this time, to Hamilton and Madison) must have enjoyed having a Southerner (either as author or as co-author of *Federalist* No. 54) speaking as a New Yorker pretending to be a Southerner for some four pages of print.

V

The argument made by "one of our Southern brethren" begins with observations that seem to question the kind of argument that Chief Justice Roger B. Taney relied upon in the *Dred Scott* case (1857) in order to conclude that people of African descent (at least the descendants of those imported as slaves) could never become citizens of the United States. My readers can assess for themselves the arguments made by Publius's "Southerner" in *Federalist* No. 54. This assessment could well begin with the concession made by Publius in this number immediately after "one of [the] Southern brethren" finishes his extended argument:

> Such is the reasoning which an advocate for the Southern interests might employ on this subject; and although it may appear to be a little strained in some points, yet on the whole, I must confess that it fully reconciles me to the scale of representation which the convention have established.

Thus, the perceptive reader in New York is put on notice that much of what has just been said is in need of qualification. On the other hand, the Southern reader is reminded that the slave is, after all, a human being, a moral agent, however "debased [he may be] by servitude." The fundamental problem with slavery is suggested by the fact that such questionable arguments as are found in *Federalist* No. 42 and No. 54 "have" to be made.

The most critical American provision with respect to slavery in 1787–1788 is not mentioned in *The Federalist*. This is what was done, in the summer of 1787, by the Articles of Confederation Congress: the enactment of the Northwest Ordinance with its prohibition of slavery in what was then the principal Territory of the United States. This strict exclusion of slavery from the Northwest Territory turned out to be much more than a counterpoint to the leniency toward slavery displayed in the Constitution's 1808 provision.

VI

The high-minded sophistry resorted to by Publius in dealing with the accommodations to slavery in the proposed Constitution may be seen as well in how the absence of a bill of rights is justified. This is referred to, in the next-to-last article (No. 84), as "[t]he most considerable of [the] remaining objections" to the proposed Constitution. One wonders, of course, whether the Framers would have included a bill of rights in their 1787 document if they had anticipated the opportunity given to opponents of the proposed Constitution by the absence of a bill of rights.

The extended justification for the lack of a bill of rights culminates with this argument in *Federalist* No 84:

> On the subject of the liberty of the press, as much has been said, I cannot forbear adding a remark or two: In the first place, I observe that there is not a syllable concerning it in the constitution of this state [New York], and in the next, I contend that whatever has been said about it in that of any other state, amounts to nothing. What signifies a declaration that "the liberty of the press shall be inviolably preserved?" What is the liberty of the press? Who can give it any definition which would not leave the utmost latitude for evasion? I hold it to be impracticable; and from this, I infer, that its security, whatever fine declarations may be inserted in any constitution respecting it, must altogether depend on public opinion, and on the general spirit of the people and of the government. And here, after all, as intimated upon another occasion, must we seek for the only solid basis of all our rights.

Of course, once the Constitution was ratified, James Madison undertook, early in the First Congress, to develop in the House of Representative a bill of rights to be proposed to the states for ratification. A decade later he was to draw on the First Amendment in developing the Virginia Resolutions in opposition to the Sedition Act of 1798.

All this can remind us that we should be cautious in treating *The Federalist* as an authoritative interpretation of the Constitution. It is more like the closing argument in a trial, an argument which draws upon (and is limited by) the record that has been made during the trial. As such, it can be instructive, and particularly so when one recognizes the limitations that a talented advocate had had to take into account.

VII

It was, then, partly a matter of chance what Publius had to say in *The Federalist*, with his argument depending, in part, on what had come out of the Constitutional Convention. It also depended on what was happening in New York during the seven months that this series of articles ran in that state. This could even mean (we have noticed) that Publius's positions on various issues would have to shift in response either to what the opposition was saying or even to what was happening elsewhere in the United States.

The reader can be challenged to determine, for example, what Publius really said about judicial review of Acts of Congress for their constitutionality. To determine what Publius "meant" may be impossible, inasmuch as he *is* a contrived character designed to deal with a series of challenges. Perhaps it can be said that "he" did "mean" to say whatever was needed to get the proposed Constitution ratified exactly as it was drafted.

Our inquiry, then, about Publius and the slavery issue should perhaps be directed not at what Publius "meant" but rather at what it seems that the New York electorate probably thought about slavery. We have seen, for example, that the virtual licensing of the African slave trade until 1808 was evidently troubling. The attempt to deal with that in *Federalist* No. 42 was anticipated by an observation in *Federalist* No. 38:

> Is the importation of slaves permitted by the new Constitution for twenty years? By the [already ratified Articles of Confederation], it is permitted forever.

VIII

What, it can be wondered, must Madison have learned about the slavery problem from his efforts to minister to New York public opinion? Did New Yorkers appear to him to be impractical with respect to this problem? Or was he sobered, and perhaps instructed, upon learning how difficult it was to justify slavery when dealing with Northerners who otherwise seemed sober and reliable?

Madison, back in Virginia, could be expected to recall the lessons promulgated in *Federalist* No. 10 about the need to curb the contests of destructive factions. "[T]he most common and durable source of factions," it is argued there, "has been the various and unequal distribution of property." Perhaps Madison's New York experience might have suggested to him thereafter that the most unequal, and hence a particularly dangerous, "distribution of property" is that which finds some so reduced in property that they are considered the possessions of others.

He could have been expected to recall as well sentiments found in the opening paragraph of *Federalist* No. 1. It is there that this inspiring challenge is recorded:

> It has been frequently remarked, that it seems to have been reserved to the people of this country, by their conduct and example, to decide the important question, whether societies of men are really capable or not, of establishing good government from reflection and choice, or whether they are forever destined to depend, for their political constitutions, on accident and force. If there be any truth in the remark, the crisis, at which we are arrived, may with propriety be regarded as the aera in which that decision is to be made; and a wrong election of the part we shall act, may, in this view, deserve to be considered as the general misfortune of mankind.

Madison could well have wondered what course of action with respect to slavery would be dictated thereafter by a proper reliance upon "reflection and choice."

IX

The course of action to be pursued here was not one that could be left only to Southerners to determine. After all, there were in the South two classes of slaves. There were, of course, the multitude of Africans in bondage, but there were also their supposed masters.

The Africans recognized, by and large, the plight they were in, a condition perhaps contributed to somewhat by endemic misgovernment back in Africa. But their supposed masters faced the indefinite prospect of sophisticated self-delusion. The most gifted among them may have been at the greatest risk during the opening decades of the nineteenth century.

The Southerners who could endorse, in 1776 and thereafter, the insistence that "all Men are created equal" could, understandably, recognize their system of slavery as "a necessary evil," something to be eventually eliminated in a manner beneficial to all parties. But, we have been obliged to notice, their most gifted successors came to insist instead upon slavery as "a positive good," something to be cherished indefinitely not only by the enslavers but even by the enslaved. And when they talked thus, they never conceded (as Publius did in *Federalist* No. 54), that their "reasoning . . . may appear to be a little strained in some points."

11. Hannah More and Other Poets on Slavery (1798–1847)

I

It has been said of Hannah More (1745–1833) that she was the most influential female member of the Society for Effecting the Abolition of the African Slave Trade. Her poem on slavery has been acclaimed as one of the more important poems of the abolition period in Great Britain. It was published originally in London in 1788, in 294 lines, and in an expanded version in 1801 (with three dozen lines modified and with more than five dozen lines added).

It is very much an Englishwoman speaking in this poem, someone quite aware of English letters and especially respectful of William Shakespeare. She is quite aware as well of the importance of liberty in what Britain stands for. Liberty and freedom are referred to a dozen times (more or less interchangeably) in her "Slavery" poem.

The anti-slavery movement, of which Hannah More was a conspicuous part, came to be dominated (we have seen) by William Wilberforce. Distinguished poets who also had occasion to speak about the slavery of More's time included Robert Burns, William Cowper, John Greenleaf Whittier, and William Wordsworth. Hannah More's most spectacular successor, as a literary polemicist against slavery, was another woman, Harriet Beecher Stowe.

II

Hannah More, like Harriet Beecher Stowe, was very much influenced by Christian sensibilities. The 1801 version of the More poem tended to made its argument even more Christian than it originally was. This may be seen in the eight lines added to the very end of the expanded poem:

And Thou! great source of Nature and of Grace,
Who of one blood didst form the human race;
Look down in mercy in thy chosen time,
With equal eye on Afric's suff'ring clime:
Disperse her shades of intellectual night,
Repeat thy high behest—Let there be Light!
Bring each benighted, great God, to Thee,
And with thy wide Salvation make them free!

Christian sensibilities were very much in evidence in the abolitionist movement that was to develop in the United States early in the nineteenth century. One manifestation of this was the growing emphasis in some quarters upon the sinfulness of slavery, a characterization (as we have seen) that many Southerners were to find offensive. Insofar as slavery could be regarded by some as deeply sinful, prudential considerations could themselves be condemned as unacceptable compromises with evil, a response epitomized perhaps by the career of John Brown in Kansas and Virginia.

We notice that Hannah More, in the lines appended in 1801 to her "Slavery" poem, regarded the Divine as the "great source of Nature and of Grace." The half-dozen other uses of "Nature" (or "Unnatural") in her poem also seem to presuppose that Nature is an instrument of the Divine, not that guide upon which philosophy depends for any independent authority manifested in the sovereignty of Prudence. A subordination of the rational to the spiritual seems implicit in the central lines of the More poem:

Plead not, in reason's palpable abuse,
Their [the Africans'] sense of feeling callous and obtuse:
From heads to hearts lies Nature's plain appeal,
Tho' few can reason, all mankind can feel.

III

Freedom (or liberty) is so critical to the English-speaking peoples that Hannah More can speak of Britain as the place "where the soul of freedom reigns." Much is made of the need, even the duty, to liberate those deprived of their freedom by slavery. Still, the reservations expressed about an unfettered, or undisciplined, liberty are very much in the traditional English spirit.

Britain does bask in freedom's "full blaze of light," but it is a "sober goddess" to whom the English defer. Hannah More, early in her 1788 poem, has lines that can be understood to have anticipated Edmund Burke's reservations (during the following decade) about the excesses of the French Revolution. Thus she distinguishes the influence of the "sober goddess" from

> . . . that unlicens'd monster of the crowd,
> Whose roar terrific burst in peals so loud,
> Deaf'ning the ear of Peace: fierce Faction's tool,
> Of rash Sedition born, and mad Misrule;
> Whose stubborn mouth, rejecting Reason's reign,
> No strength can govern, and no skill restrain;
> Whose magic cries the frantic vulgar draw
> To spurn at Order, and to outrage Law . . .

One can hear echoes throughout her poem of the sobriety of such champions of a regulated liberty as John Milton, William Blackstone, and Lord Mansfield. Slavery is condemned, of course, as a cruel deprivation of liberty for many at the hands of privileged men who misuse their own liberty. Such men are condemned as "WHITE SAVAGE[S]," who are moved either by "lust of gold [o]r lust of conquest."

IV

Much of Hannah More's effort in this poem is to assign the correct names to things. Thus, the "WHITE SAVAGE" lays claim to the name of "hero," when he should be known instead as "robber." What is critical here is to recognize that such a man pleads an "impious claim to wealth or fame."

The foreign policy of European nations needs to be called by its right name. "Conquest," we are told, "is pillage with a nobler name." Implicit in the More poem may be deep reservations about the empire that her country is ruling.

At times she makes explicit how she understands and judges what Europeans are doing to the Africans:

> Does thirst of empire, does desire of fame,
> (For these are specious crimes) our rage inflame?

And closer to home is what the British say and do, beginning with a line on which we have already drawn:

> Shall Britain, where the soul of freedom reigns,
> Forge chains for others she herself disdains?
> Forbid it, Heaven! O let the nations know
> The liberty she loves she will bestow;
> Not to herself the glorious gift confin'd,
> She spreads the blessing wide as human kind,
> And, scorning narrow views of time and place,
> Bids all be free in earth's extended space.

In short, Hannah More can be understood especially to have counseled her fellow citizens against hypocrisy.

V

Sensitivity with respect to the naming of things, which is evident throughout this poem, may be seen in what happens to the title of her poem. It was, in 1788, simply "Slavery," but in 1801 it was "The Slave Trade." This seems to recognize what the primary focus of British abolitionists was in the closing decades of the eighteenth century.

The emphasis in the 1788 version of the poem does seem to be on "th' opprobrious commerce." It is that commerce—the systematic kidnapping of men and women from the coasts of Africa—which was at the heart of the atrocities of modern slavery. And it was that commerce, known as the slave trade, which was under severe attack by the shapers of the international law of the day.

The potency of the attack is recognized in Article I of the Constitution of 1787, where assurances had to be given to Carolinians and Georgians that Congress would not shut off before 1808 their access to slaves newly stolen from Africa. Congress did provide that such importations could not continue past January 1, 1808. By that time such a slave trade had come to be recognized as piracy under international law.

VI

Much of the More poem is, in effect, an argument for regarding Africans as fully, or truly, human beings. Americans making the same argument would insist upon the universality of the "created equal" language of the Declaration of Independence. Hannah More emphasizes this identification by observing, in a note to her poem, "Nothing is more frequent than this cruel and stupid argument, that [Africans] do not feel the miseries inflicted on them as Europeans would do."

However this may be, it can be wondered whether the shift to "The Slave Trade" tacitly recognized that the problem of how slavery itself should be dealt with, wherever it was established, was much more complicated than the problem of how the international slave trade should be dealt with. Although Great Britain did not recognize slavery as a domestic institution, it still permitted it in its North American colonies. The abolition of it in those colonies by Parliament in 1833 proved to be memorable, and was celebrated in such poems as John Harris's "The Fall of Slavery."

It was difficult enough for Parliament to abolish slavery in distant colonies. It proved dangerous for Congress to attempt to limit slavery in the United States. An overriding issue, of course, was how former masters and former slaves would live together, especially in a free country (even if that country did not include the economies of some states devastated by emancipation).

VII

The modern reader of Hannah More's poem is apt to question her anthropology. It is assumed again and again that Africa is a benighted place, and this independent of the devastation wrought there by European slave-traders. Thus it can be asked, in the opening stanza of the poem,

> While Britain basks in [Heaven's] full blaze of light,
> Why lies sad Afric quench'd in total night?

We have seen, in the lines added in 1801 to the end of the poem, that Africa was regarded as in need of light, that she chances to suffer from "intellectual night." Such assessments may be seen throughout the poem, even though it is said, early on,

> Perish th' illiberal thought which would debase
> The native genius of the sable race!

It is indicated that the inferior condition of Africa had made its peoples vulnerable to the depredations of slave-traders.

The modern reader might even be troubled by what the poet evidently regarded as an exhibition of nobility on the part of a slave, that exhibition recorded in an episode described in a Hannah More footnote (citing "Ramsay's Essay on the Treatment of African Slaves"):

> It is a point of honour among negroes of a high spirit to die rather than to suffer their glossy skin to bear the mark of the whip. Quashi had somehow offended his master, a young planter with whom he had been bred up in the endearing intimacy of a playfellow. His services had been faithful; his attachment affectionate. The master resolved to punish him, and pursued him for that purpose. In trying to escape Quashi stumbled and fell; the master fell upon him: they wrestled long with doubtful victory; at length Quashi got uppermost, and, being firmly seated on his master's breast, he secured his legs with one hand, and with the other drew a sharp knife; then said, "Master, I have been bred up with you from a child; I have loved you as myself: in return, you have condemned me to a punishment of which I must ever have borne the marks—thus only I can avoid them," so saying, he drew the knife with all his strength across his own throat, and fell down dead, without a groan, on his master's body.

That is, the modern reader would be troubled by any suggestion that the faultless slave, and not the unjust master, should have to make the supreme sacrifice on this occasion. It might not be enough for the modern reader to suggest, as the poet does, that the slave's "generous arm" had spared his "barbarous master."

VIII

However all this may be, it seems to be assumed by the poet that Africa should not be simply left alone by Europeans. It is not enough, it seems, simply to suppress the slave trade. Africa is in need of enlightenment, something (it seems to be assumed) it never had.

Particularly lacking, then, seems to be Christianity. Thus, Africa is in need of the guidance that only the Europeans can provide, but not the kind of influence supplied by the slave-traders. Would such guidance require much more self-sacrifice on the part of Europeans than that which may be supplied by the occasional missionary?

It might even be wondered whether the only practicable way that More's benighted Africans would likely become "civilized" in the European mode would be by way of enslavement in places such as the United States. Thus, African Americans would become equipped to guide Africans into the modern world. Of course, the Southern slaveholders in this country did not recognize what they were really doing, which made them reluctant to give up their slaves even after they had become remarkably "Americanized."

IX

We have noticed that the more "Americanized" those slaves became, the harder it became to justify their continued enslavement. Also, the more "Americanized" they became, the harder it was to keep them "in their place," whether or not emancipated. The supposed economic interests of Southern whites, as well as their self-esteem, made it difficult for them to face up to reality.

Among the anti-slavery poems produced in this country is an ode (inscribed to W. H. Channing) published by Ralph Waldo Emerson in 1847. The central stanza of the ode includes the observation,

> Things are in the saddle,
> And ride mankind.

We can see here, as in Hannah More's poem, how supposed economic self-interest can lead to disregard of the demands of justice and simple humanity.

Certainly, it is well to be aware of the limits of economic explanations in such matters. Thus, Adam Smith argued, in *The Wealth of Nations* (published a dozen years before Hannah More's poem), that neither the colonies nor the slavery of his day really served the economic interests of rulers, whether countries or masters. Rather, in both cases, Smith suggested, the desire to exercise control over others was the main attraction, something that may be appreciated by those (whether poets or literary critics or even scholars) who strive to understand the subjects they undertake to study at considerable cost to themselves and with no serious prospect of material rewards.

12. Suppression of the International Slave Trade

I

Traditional features of a bill of rights may be found in Section 9 of Article I of the Constitution of 1787. These include assurances about "the Writ of Habeas Corpus," about "Bill[s] of Attainder and ex post facto Law[s]," and about "Title[s] of Nobility." But preceding this enumeration in Section 9 is, we have seen, a provision protecting temporarily the international slave trade from substantial restraint by the General Government.

Of course, we have also seen, this provision avoids, as is done throughout the Constitution of 1787, any use of the terms "slave" and "slavery." It is said at the outset of Section 9, just after the extensive enumeration in Section 8 of many of the powers of Congress,

> The Migration or Importation of such Persons as any of the States now existing shall think proper to admit, shall not be prohibited by the Congress prior to the Year one thousand eight hundred and eight, but a Tax or duty may be imposed on such Importation, not exceeding ten dollars for each Person.

This assurance, we recall, is said to have been conceded in deference to the indications from South Carolina and Georgia that they would not ratify the Constitution without it.

This permission for continued importation of slaves from Africa offended sensibilities that had developed among European countries. That this permission was grudgingly granted is indicated, we have seen as well, by a further assurance that its advocates evidently insisted upon, the provision in Article V (where the amending process is laid out) that the 1808 Clause could not "in any Manner" be affected by an amendment to the Constitution. This reflects an awareness of the abhorrence with which the international slave trade had come to be generally regarded in the Western world.

II

This abhorrence contributed to the determination by Congress to attempt to do what it could to suppress the international slave trade as soon as it could. Congress was urged to act here by President Thomas Jefferson in his Annual Message to Congress in December 1806. He, although himself a slaveholder, was moved to want to prohibit "all further participation [by Americans] in the violation of human rights which have been so long continued on the unoffending inhabitants of Africa, and which the morality, the reputation, and the best interests of our country have long been eager to proscribe."

There was enacted, on March 2, 1807, an "Act to prohibit the importation of Slaves into any port or place within the jurisdiction of the United States, from and after the first day of January, in the year of our Lord one thousand eight hundred and eight." Thus, there was put in place a prohibition upon the international slave trade that would take effect as soon as the Congress was empowered to provide it. Those who have doubted the power of Congress to act as it did in 1807 have never had much support among students of the Constitution.

After all, the restraint on Congress until 1808 implies that without such a restraint Congress would have been able at once to prohibit the importation of slaves, perhaps by using its commerce power. It is also implied by the Section 9 restraint that Congress can otherwise place such "a Tax or duty . . . on such Importation" as would effectively suppress it. The 1808 prohibition by Congress did not interfere with the power of the states to allow the shipment of slaves by sea from one state to another in the Union.

III

It has been wondered how effective the 1808 prohibition was in curbing the importation of slaves into the United States. We can be reminded of the difficulty, in our own time, of prohibiting the routine importation of tons of forbidden narcotics. We can be reminded as well of the considerable traffic suspected these days in undocumented aliens.

A curious feature of the 1808 prohibition, and of follow-up legislation in subsequent decades, is the uncertainty resulting as to what was to be done with any illegally imported slaves seized by the General Government. Some, it seems, were considered free men and women in the United States; some may even have been returned to Africa; and some, perhaps (it is said) even a majority, were sold as slaves, with the proceeds ending up in the treasuries of the United States and of the states. Perhaps the critical thing to notice here is that Africans thus intercepted were not routinely (or naturally) treated simply as human beings.

It is recognized in the *Encyclopedia of the American Constitution* that "[e]stimates regarding the numbers involved in the illegal slave trade varied." It is further recognized:

> In the decades following passage of [various prohibitory] acts, slavers easily evaded federal authorities, and enforcement received no more than lip service in Washington. In 1839 President Martin Van Buren called for revision of the laws covering the slave trade in order that "the integrity and honor of our flag may be carefully preserved." A decade later President Zachary Taylor invited the attention of Congress "to an amendment of our existing laws relating to the African slave trade, with a view to the effectual suppression of that barbarous traffic." Nothing happened, and the trade continued down through the Civil War.

It is then added in this *Encyclopedia* article by John Hope Franklin, "Because of its clandestine nature, precise figures are impossible; a recent student of the trade estimates that some 51,000 slaves were illegally imported by 1860."

IV

However limited the suppression of importations may have been, critical things *were* happening in the United States with respect to slavery. Thus, the law was, at least nominally, on the side of the opponents of the slave trade. And presidents could speak, and could be expected to speak, of it as "that barbarous traffic."

Even Southerners (such as Jefferson Davis) who were skeptical about the powers of Congress to regulate the international slave trade could come to oppose such trade as simply immoral. And it could be said of Davis himself (in the *Encyclopedia of the American Constitution*) that his own "plantation was a model, surpassed only by his brother's, for treating blacks with compassion and for giving them a great deal of self-government." Perhaps it can be said that the longer the slaves were here, the greater the opportunity their masters had to begin to see them as human beings.

Thus, although the international slave trade was not completely suppressed before the Civil War, the men and women who had been imported (and who hence were most obviously "African") were a small proportion of the total slave population in the United States. It is reported in the *Encyclopedia of the American Constitution*, "In 1860, the aggregate value of the nearly four million slaves was more than $3 billion—the equivalent of roughly $58 billion in 1998." But something else is also reported there which helps explain why it was difficult for Southerners (no matter how sensitive to world opinion and hence enlightened they became) to repudiate the system of slavery they had inherited: "Slaves [in 1860] constituted 44 percent of all the South's wealth, with real estate—land and buildings—amounting to only 25 percent."

V

The Congressional restraint, as of January 1, 1808, upon the international slave trade was followed, as we have seen, by other statutes. These statutes (reinforced by treaties among Western nations) eventually included the designation of such traffic as piracy, punishable by death. However limited the 1808 restraint may have been in practice, it seems to have been a significant step in the shaping of American public opinion with respect to slavery, especially since it was obvious that the millions of slaves in the United States had been secured by means that had come to be recognized as "barbarous."

Within eighteen months of the effective date of the 1808 prohibition, the two political leaders of the contending forces during the Civil War (Jefferson Davis and Abraham Lincoln) would be born (in Kentucky, one of the Middle States!). Much of what they did in their careers was dedicated to efforts to deal with slavery in ways they could consider both humane and prudent. The moral concerns that found expression in the 1808 restraint would necessarily continue to grow, encompassing not only the mode of acquiring slaves but also the indefinite continuation of the system thus supplied.

The abolitionism that became so disturbing to most Southerners (as well as to many apprehensive citizens in the North) must have been significantly encouraged by the 1808 prohibition. A letter of August 18, 1849, by Jefferson Davis to a fellow Mississippian includes a passage which reflects a fatal unease about slavery even among the most "committed" slaveholders:

> It is utterly untrue, that slavery in the [Southern] States is the creature of their enactment. It existed in the colonies and was regulated like other property by the common law of England. It existed before the colonies were founded. It is traced to the earliest period of history, and there we find laws prescribed for

> its government, as an existing institution. Its beginning is still further back, lost in the mists of a more remote antiquity. When our Northern brethren drove a profitable trade with the tribes of Africa, for their captive slaves, to be imported and sold in the Southern States, it was enough for them to know where their introduction was not prohibited. The discovery that property in the service of an African was of such peculiar character that it could only exist where it had been previously provided for by municipal law, was reserved for this age of sectional strife, pseudo philanthropy, speculative philosophy, and political prostitution to make.

An awareness of the vulnerability of slavery may be reflected in the instinctive desire to share with others the immorality that it depends upon and that it engenders.

VI

For Jefferson Davis to speak as he did of the origins and perpetuation of slavery can make one wonder what dubious enterprises one may in turn be trapped into defending against one's true interests. The steady decline in the defensibility of slavery continues to our day, with some contemporary champions of the Lost Cause even being moved to insist (we shall see in the last chapter in this volume) that the Civil War could never have been "about Slavery." They thereby recognize, that is, that "it never made sense."

Of course, it could be wondered as well whether it had made sense for the opponents of slavery to have insisted on measures which drove Southerners to resort to desperate measures. One measure that the opponents of slavery resorted to was the discouragement of the return of fugitive slaves to their masters. Such a "duty" to return slaves (as Ralph Waldo Emerson discovered) made it ever more difficult for Northerners to regard slavery as something going on "elsewhere."

But the South could probably have accommodated itself (by insurance or otherwise) to the costs of runaway slaves. A far more serious challenge (as we have seen) was the prospect of no new slave states in the Territories of the United States. What could—what should—the opponents of slavery have done to reassure Southerners fearful of the eventual loss of the "veto power" they had long had in the General Government?

VII

Of course, there had been, no matter what the *Dred Scott* Court said in 1857, the august precedent of the Northwest Ordinance of 1787 with its permanent prohibition of slavery in a substantial Territory of the United States. But precedent aside, should the power to exclude slavery completely from the remaining Territories have been insisted upon (as the Republican Party did in 1860)? Were other means available, that is, to make likely a steady decline in the influence of slavery in the United States?

Chance events (including technological developments) might have contributed to an amelioration of the slavery system in this country, an amelioration which could take advantage of a steadily growing disapproval of slavery, at least in the Western world. But the experience with the 1808 Clause may have made it more difficult for the opponents of slavery to give Southerners some of the access to the Territories they very much wanted. It must have seemed to some of the more vigilant opponents of slavery that something comparable to the importation of slaves until 1808 was being asked for by slaveholders.

Such opponents may have sensed, that is, that they were now being asked for the kind of accommodation to slavery that some of them had criticized their forebears for having made in 1787–1789. Those forebears had perhaps thought that slavery was indeed withering away and that temporary accommodations would be prudent. But was there not by, say, 1850, fewer indications of a likely decline in the appeal and vitality of slavery (especially in the South) than there had been in 1787–1789?

VIII

One disturbing sign in the 1850s was the agitation by some Southerners for a revival of the international slave trade. That this prospect also troubled some Southerners is indicated in the Confederate Constitution of 1861. It is there made explicit, and definite, that revival of the international slave trade was forbidden, in dramatic contrast to the comparable provision in the United States Constitution of 1787.

It can be wondered what developments might have led Southerners, even though still powerful in the Union, eventually to repudiate slavery without either secession or war. Would slavery have been virtually impossible to maintain indefinitely once the descendants of the kidnapped Africans had been thoroughly "Americanized"? And in what way (it must again and again be wondered) would this development have been affected by the steadily growing proportion of these descendants who shared more and more of their blood with their Caucasian masters?

It can also be wondered whether European opinion, and especially British opinion, might have made it more difficult for each generation of Southerners to "believe in" slavery. Would it have become ever harder to reconcile slavery with that principle of rational liberty at the core of Anglo-American constitutionalism? Southerners themselves had too many much-acclaimed champions of liberty in their own heritage to be permanently comfortable with the obviously despotic system they had inherited.

IX

These and like conjectures bear on perennial questions about how political leaders, North and South, conducted themselves in the quarter-century leading up to the Civil War. The decisive step, it can be seen in retrospect, may well have been the decision by Congress in 1807 to prohibit the international slave trade. That this prohibition had been suspended for twenty years (prior to 1808) testified in effect to the unreliable judgment (if not also to the unhealthy passions) of some of the proponents of slavery.

Another way of putting all this is to suggest that the Virginians of 1860–1861 simply should have known better. It was Virginia that President Lincoln, as a Constitutionalist, desperately tried, in his First Inaugural Address and thereafter, to reassure. Without Virginia, the secession movement could have reasonably been expected to collapse fairly soon.

If Virginians had recalled how their predecessors had been coerced, in the Constitutional Convention of 1787, to acquiesce in something so obviously indefensible as a continuation of the international slave trade, they might have reconsidered what the truly honorable course was for them in 1861. Thus, the firing on Fort Sumter could have been recognized by Virginians as something comparable to the rash threats that had led to the 1808 Clause. The 1787 capitulation took twenty years to recover from, while the 1861 capitulation still awaits (a century and a half later) the liberation of a full recovery, a recovery which requires the complete "Americanization" of those people who had for so long been subjected to an unbelievably "barbarous traffic."

13. John Quincy Adams and John C. Calhoun on the Abolitionist Petitions to Congress

I

We have seen that sensible leaders, North and South, could generally agree, during the opening decades of the nineteenth century, that the international slave trade should be suppressed. But what to do about slavery as it existed in the United States could provoke fierce debates. Particularly troubling, we have also seen, were questions about where slavery would be permitted in the Territories of the country, for that would help determine, eventually, control of the national government.

A particularly provocative challenge to slavery everywhere in the country was mounted by the abolitionist petitions submitted to Congress in the 1830s and thereafter. The abolitionists themselves have been described in this fashion by Mark Mayo Boatner's *Civil War Dictionary*:

> Group favoring the abolishment of slavery, characterized just prior to the Civil War by Harriet Beecher Stowe's *Uncle Tom's Cabin*, the Underground Railroad, [in support of fugitive slaves], and the Abolitionist Congressmen. The initial outcry against slavery came as early as 1624 in the Colonies, and this feeling gained enough adherents to bring about abolition [of slavery] in most of the Northern States before the Revolution.

After the Revolution, we are then told by the *Civil War Dictionary*, abolitionism grew steadily in the United States:

> Spurred by Great Britain's abolishing the [international] slave trade in 1807 and slavery in [its] colonies in 1833 . . . , the movement took the form of the American Anti-Slavery Society (1833). This unification of regional organizations was largely the result of work done by William Lloyd Garrison. At this period in the South [some leaders] agitated for a modified form of abolition, as opposed to the immediate, uncompensated emancipation demanded by Garrison [and others].

Illustrative of how the abolitionist petitions to Congress were regarded is how they were dealt with by two members of Congress who were of national stature. One of them was Representative John Quincy Adams of Massachusetts, who had been secretary of state and president of the United States. The other was Senator John C. Calhoun of South Carolina, who had been secretary of state and vice president of the United States.

II

Adams recorded in 1831 his first submission of abolitionist petitions to the House of Representatives. He had, earlier in his career, expressed sympathy for Southern grievances with respect to tariffs imposed by Congress. I have provided, in my *Constitutionalist* volume of 1971, an extended account of how Adams insisted, for a decade and a half, upon having the House receive the abolitionist petitions that had been sent to him for submission to the House.

The House refused to accept such petitions, condemning them as highly improper inasmuch as Congress was said not to have any power to deal with slavery. The House's routine tabling of these abolitionist petitions was regarded by Adams as an abridgment of his and his constituents' constitutional rights. The longer the House resisted, the greater the volume of petitions grew.

The Massachusetts Representative's persistence provoked, on more than one occasion, substantial efforts to have the House of Representatives censure him. Finally, in 1844, the by-then quite elderly Adams prevailed in his efforts to have the petitions received, perhaps because "the slavery element" could (upon having just elected a president) relax its vigilance. I added, to my 1971 account of this controversy in *The Constitutionalist*, a comment on Adams's noble folly:

> This story suggests to me that the most serious abuses of freedom of speech and of the press among us are likely to occur in circumstances where there is no safeguard but the good sense and self-restraint of the best citizens, of men who know when and how to use delicacy while "in pursuit of the public good." It is not enough to be right, in the strict constitutional sense. Rather, the good man should be concerned lest he deserve the rebuke that Cicero leveled against Cato: . . . "Cato means well, but he does hurt sometimes to the State; for he talks as if he were in the republic of Plato and not in the dregs of Romulus."

III

Calhoun opened a Senate speech, in 1837, with the request that a sample be read "of the mass of [abolitionist] petitions [that had been submitted to that body], in order that [the Senate] might know what language they hold towards the slaveholding States and their institutions." After the reading he could say, "Such is the language held towards us and ours." Thus, both Calhoun and Adams insisted upon respect being displayed for their constitutional rights, finding the efforts of their opponents to be insulting and destructive.

The South Carolinian describes at length how offensive he regards the abolitionist petitions to be. He begins with this assessment of the petitions just sampled:

> The peculiar institution of the South—that on the maintenance of which the very existence of the slaveholding States depends, is pronounced to be sinful and odious in the sight of God and man; and this with a systematic design of rendering us hateful in the eyes of the world—with a view to a general crusade against us and our institutions.

It can be wondered how Calhoun would have responded if reminded that the characterization of slavery as "odious" had been resorted to by so respectable a jurist as Lord Mansfield in his 1772 *Somerset* Opinion.

One consequence of the approach to these matters by someone as talented and influential as Calhoun was to discourage those leaders in the South who "agitated for a modified form of abolition." He finds intolerable the constraints placed upon him by abolitionists:

> [W]e, the representatives of twelve of these sovereign States against whom this deadly war is waged, are expected to sit here in silence, hearing ourselves and our constituents day after day denounced, without uttering a word, for if we but open our lips, the charge of agitation is resounded on all sides, and we are held

> up as seeking to aggravate the evil which we resist. Every reflecting mind must see in all this a state of things deeply and dangerously diseased.

In short, Calhoun, like Adams, was capable of noble folly in an insistence upon what were taken to be constitutional prerogatives.

IV

Ralph Waldo Emerson spoke of his fellow Massachusetts-man John Quincy Adams as "a man of audacious independence that always kept the public curiosity alive in regard to what he might do." He added (in this passage quoted in my *Constitutionalist*), "None could predict his word, and a whole Congress could not gainsay it when it was spoken." Much the same could be said about John C. Calhoun.

Both men had been prominent in the Executive Branch of the General Government, but their careers culminated in Congress. John Quincy Adams collapsed on the floor of the House of Representatives, dying within hours (in 1848). John C. Calhoun had to have his last speech read for him in the Senate by a colleague, dying thereafter within a month (in 1850).

We are reminded by the careers of these two men that the great constitutional and political debates of *their* time were carried on largely (if not even primarily) in Congress. One dubious consequence of the Civil War was to expand substantially the power of the Executive Branch of the General Government. If the men debating in Congress had been more prudent, would that war have been avoided, with one consequence being the continued preeminence of Congressional debate in the governance of the United States?

V

Calhoun, in his last speech (of March 4, 1850), recognizes that critical changes had taken place in the United States that made the cause of Unionism ever more difficult, if not even hopeless, in the South. He confronted the fact, as he put it, "that the equilibrium between the two sections [North and South], in the government as it stood when the Constitution was ratified and the Government put in action, has been destroyed." There is something pathetic in the need of the dying Calhoun to prepare "a last statistical statement, showing the relative weight of the two sections in the Government under the first census of 1790 and the last census of 1840."

In 1790, he reminds the Senate, of the total population of the United States (3,929,827), "the Northern States had 1,997,899, and the Southern 1,952,072, making a difference of only 45,827 in favor of the former States." In 1840, there had been this ominous count: "[T]he aggregate population of the United States amounted to 17,063,357, of which the Northern section contained 9,728,920, and the Southern 7,334,437, making a difference, in round numbers, of 2,400,000." Although the numbers of Senators had remained roughly the same, North and South, it was already evident what would likely happen in the governance of the country, with the presidency and the House of Representatives having already come under Northern control.

Critical to this shift, Calhoun argues, had been the legislation of the government, such as with respect to the allocations of federal funds and with respect to the status of slavery in the Territories of the United States. That is, he never seemed to recognize that slavery itself tended to discourage in the South the steady population growth (by immigration and otherwise) seen in the North. Of course, the election to the presidency of a Free Soil Republican in 1860 confirmed for the Calhounians the ominous tendency that had been all too evident in 1850 to Calhoun himself.

VI

Calhoun asks, as both he and his speech draw to an end, "How can the Union be saved?" His answer is firm:

> There is but one way by which it can [be saved] with any certainty, and that is, by a full and final settlement, on the principle of justice, of all the questions at issue between the two sections. The South asks for justice, simple justice, and less [than that] she ought not to take.

He then explains:

> The North has only to will it to accomplish it—to do justice by conceding to the South an equal right in the acquired territory, and to do her duty by causing the stipulations relative to fugitive slaves to be faithfully fulfilled—to cease the agitation of the slave question, and to provide for the insertion of a provision in the Constitution, by an amendment, which will restore to the South, in substance, the power she [once] possessed of protecting herself, before the equilibrium between the sections was destroyed by the actions of the Government.

Calhoun adds, "There will be no difficulty in devising such [a Constitutional amendment]—one that would protect the South." But he could never do more than barely notice one fact that no constitutional contrivance resorted to by desperate Unionists (North and South) could get around—the fact that informed Northerners were beginning to recognize not only that slavery was deeply wrong but also that they had long been complicit in the effort to maintain it. The most that such conscientious citizens in the North could say on behalf of slavery was that it should be eliminated in such a way as to do the least harm both to everyone involved in the slave system and to the country at large.

That is, Calhoun was somewhat in the position of a corporation executive who discovers that his principal product is something that systematically poisons its consumers. All kinds of solutions to the problems posed by such a discovery may be experimented with, including a conscientious search for effective antidotes. But may it not become obvious, to all but some of those trapped in such a corporation either as stockholders or as employees, that the only sensible solution is simply to abandon the principal product of the corporation?

VII

It may be a matter of chance who is trapped by what. Southern partisans sometimes sought solace, if not redemption, in the recognition that Northerners were often enslaved by an intense commercialization of their everyday lives which promoted a despicable avariciousness. It could even be pointed out that Northerners were far less conscientious than the typical Southern slave owner tended to be about taking care of the elderly laborers among them who could no longer work.

Critical to how these matters were assessed was the language that was employed. Thus, Calhoun (in his March 4, 1850, speech) could refer to the terms "slave territories" and "free soil" as "the slang of the day." It is evident that he and others like him preferred to speak instead (however awkwardly) of "slaveholding States" and "non-slaveholding States."

I have observed that Calhoun can do little more than notice that some Northerners had come to recognize slavery as deeply wrong. We should notice, in turn, how Calhoun dealt with such a state of affairs (to the extent that he did) (emphasis added):

> There is a question of vital importance to the Southern section, in reference to which the views and feelings of the two sections are as opposite and hostile as they can possibly be. I refer to the relation between the two races in the Southern section, which constitutes a vital portion of her social organization.

> Every portion of the North entertains views and feelings more or less hostile to it. Those most opposed and hostile regard it as a sin, and consider themselves under the most sacred obligations to use every effort to destroy it. Indeed, to the extent that they conceive they have power, they regard themselves as implicated in the sin, and responsible for suppressing it by the use of all and every means. Those less opposed and hostile, regard it as a crime—an offence against humanity, as they call it, and, although not so fanatical, feel themselves bound to use all efforts to effect the same objects; while those who are least opposed and hostile, regard it as a blot and stain on the character of *what they call the nation*, and feel themselves accordingly bound to give it no countenance or support. On the contrary, the Southern section regards the relation as one which cannot be destroyed without subjecting the two races to the greatest calamity, and the section to poverty, desolation, and wretchedness; and accordingly they feel bound by every consideration of interest and safety, to defend it.

It is far from clear what Calhoun expected conscientious Northerners to do if they indeed believed the slavery of their day to be either a grave sin or a serious crime, that slavery which seemed to require Northern cooperation one way or another in order to be maintained and perpetuated.

VIII

What *is* clear is that Calhoun found troubling the continual Northern agitation against slavery. Thus, it could be suggested by him, "The first organized movement towards [the destruction of the existing relations between the two races in the South] commenced in 1835." The agitation at that time included (and, indeed, was anticipated by?) the controversies we have noticed involving John Quincy Adams.

By the time of Calhoun's March 1850 speech the troubling agitation among Northerners included their concerns both about the surrender of fugitive slaves and about the expansion of slavery into the Territories of the United States. Calhoun recalls (in this 1850 speech) the offensive 1830s petitions in this fashion:

> At the meeting of Congress, petitions poured in from the North, calling upon Congress to abolish slavery in the District of Columbia, and to prohibit, what they called, the internal slave trade between the States—announcing at the same time, that their ultimate object was to abolish slavery, not only in the District, but in the States and throughout the Union. At this period, the number engaged in the agitation was small, and possessed little or no personal influence.

Thus, it can seem, one concern after another had been agitated by Northerners about various aspects of slavery.

Calhoun and his allies had insisted for decades that the proffered petitions were improper, addressing as they did matters beyond the authority of Congress to deal with. But, it seems, Southerners did expect Congress to legislate with respect to such matters as fugitive slaves, slavery in the Territories, slavery in the District of Columbia, the international slave trade, and the distribution of anti-slavery agitation in the mails. Calhoun insists, again and again, that justice be done to the South by the General Government, especially with respect to slavery-related issues, even as he also insists in effect that no one outside the South was either entitled or equipped to assess the risks and hence the justice of any serious slavery-related issues that were to be dealt with (one way or another) by Congress.

IX

Calhoun and others maintained, of course, that their slaves were justly treated, that the system of slavery, as administered in the South in their time, resulted in a "positive good" for everyone involved. They seemed to consider it improper, and an assault on their honor, for anyone to question this assessment. And, of course, they believed that their safety was threatened by any interference with their management of their slaves.

Southern grievances against outside interference with their "peculiar institution" was said by Calhoun to have originated even as the Constitution was being drafted:

> The first of the series of acts by which the South was deprived of its due share of the territories, originated with the Confederacy, which preceded the existence of this Government. It is to be found in the provision of the ordinance of 1787. Its effect was to exclude the South [that is, slavery] entirely from that vast and fertile region which lies between the Ohio and the Mississippi rivers, now embracing five States and one Territory.

Calhoun does not choose to recall here the significant part played by Thomas Jefferson, one of the most eminent of slaveholding Southerners, in preparing the ground for the prohibition of slavery in the Northwest Ordinance of 1787. We can recall as well that Jefferson engaged John Adams in a correspondence that graced their last years in retirement.

That Jefferson-Adams correspondence of 1812–1826 anticipated, in effect, the "correspondence" of 1835–1850 we have noticed between Calhoun and another Adams with respect to the propriety of slavery-related petitions to Congress. The deliberately elevated Adams-Jefferson discourse seems to provide a better guide to republican statesmanship than does the combative Adams-Calhoun discourse. Among the problems with the later discourse is that inability to agree even upon the vocabulary to be employed in dealing with the political challenges of the day, that inability reflected in John C. Calhoun's tacitly distancing himself (as we have seen) from the Unionists who (he says) purport to serve "what they call the nation."

PART TWO

~

1. The Fugitive Slave Laws (1793, 1850)

I

The enforcement of the Fugitive Slave Law of 1850 posed serious problems for both the North and the South during the generation preceding the Civil War. Resistance to enforcement of Congressional fugitive slave legislation had been growing steadily in the North for a quarter century. The legendary Underground Railroad was part of such resistance.

Also growing, of course, was Southern resentment at the failure of Northerners to be as respectful of their fugitive-slave obligations as slaveholders wanted them to be. Northerners were considered to have legal (if not also moral) obligations here that they were not living up to. These obligations, which echoed those in the relevant state legislation that emphasized the labor or service owed by or due from slaves, were not only being neglected; they were being disparaged more and more by influential Northerners.

All this dramatized political developments that did not bode well for the long-term influence of the South in the Union, especially with respect to slavery interests. We have seen that the power of the South in the government of the Union was steadily eroding as the population in the North was growing faster than that in the South. Reinforcing these ominous developments for Southern leaders (we have also seen) was the Northern insistence that no new slave states should be expected to be created out of the remaining Territories of the United States.

II

There had been no obligation imposed in the Articles of Confederation for the return of fugitive slaves. The division between free and slave states was not yet as clear as it would be even only a decade later, when the Constitution of 1787 was drafted. Besides, the association governed by the Articles of Confederation was regarded by many as more like a league than like a country.

Still, the Congress authorized by the Articles of Confederation not only opened the way (and otherwise provided) for the establishment of the Constitution of 1787 but it also enacted the Northwest Ordinance. That 1787 legislation, which was reenacted by the First Congress in 1789, provided for the organization of the Northwest Territory, then the principal Territory of the United States. We have noticed that this was to lead, during the following half-century, to five new states in the Union.

The Northwest Ordinance included a provision that the Articles of Confederation did not have, the obligation of states to return fugitive slaves. Even more significant, of course, was the prohibition in the Ordinance of '87 of slavery in the Northwest Territory. This prohibition turned out to be critical for the fate of the Nation, not least with respect to the outcome of the Civil War.

III

The Northwest Ordinance provision with respect to a duty to return fugitive slaves was included in Article IV of the Constitution of 1787. Also provided in Article IV was the duty to return a fugitive from justice to the state demanding him. A harbinger of things to come, about how slavery would come to be widely regarded, *was* the refusal of the Constitutional Convention to use language which suggested that fugitive slaves should also be regarded as "fugitives from justice."

An emphasis is in effect placed instead upon the fact that one is a slave only pursuant to the laws of a state. Of course, fugitives from justice are also identified as such by the criminal laws of a state. But those criminal laws usually confirm, so to speak, the judgments people generally make about conduct they consider reprehensible.

An Act of 1793 implemented the Article IV provisions with respect both to fugitives from justice and to fugitive slaves. Roughly the same amount of space was devoted to each of these two kinds of fugitives in this two-page statute. It is, for us, a curious coincidence (in a minor mode) that this Act of

Congress was enacted on February 12, 1793, sixteen years to the day before Abraham Lincoln was born.

IV

The fugitive-slave provisions of 1793 did not seem to arouse much concern or controversy when they were enacted. Some, perhaps many, Americans tended to believe about slavery, when they did think about it, that it was not to be a major concern of the country over the long term, that it might even wither away. Besides, there were pressing concerns, about getting the new government soundly established, that evidently dominated people's attention.

Responses to the growing pains of the new country, including the challenges posed by the War of 1812, did not leave much public energy for dealing with slavery-related issues. But such concerns developed when it became evident, especially (it is said) as the profits grew from the cultivation of cotton, that slavery would not gradually disappear. These Northern concerns were matched by those in the South promoted by the fierce battles, in the French colonies of Santo Domingo and Haiti, between former slaves and former masters.

Once the country settled down under the Constitution, abolitionist sentiment in the North developed steadily, drawing in part on the principles of the Declaration of Independence and Anglo-American constitutionalism, and in part on Christian sensibilities. Abolitionism had already contributed to the European suppression of the international slave trade, a development for which there was considerable support even in the Old South. But we have noticed that there also developed in the South, in opposition to all this, the opinion that slavery was to be regarded *not* as "a necessary evil" but rather as "a positive good."

V

Declining Northern cooperation with Southern efforts to reclaim fugitive slaves led to the 1850 statute, supplementing the 1793 statute, with the later enactment making much more of fugitive slaves than of fugitives from justice. Particularly aggravating the problem had been the resort in Northern states to "personal liberty" laws, described in this way by the *Encyclopedia of the American Constitution*:

> Between 1826 and 1858, all the free states east of Illinois enacted "personal liberty laws" providing one or more procedural remedies to persons seized as

> fugitive slaves. These included the writs of *habeas corpus* and personal replevin. Some personal liberty laws also provided jury trial to alleged fugitives; prohibited kidnaping or enticement of black persons out of state; imposed more stringent state procedures for recaptions; or provided the services of state's attorneys to alleged fugitives. The Vermont Freedom Act of 1858 declared every slave who came into the state free. In *Prigg* v. *Pennsylvania* (1842), Justice Joseph Story held that state statutes interfering with recaptures under the 1793 Fugitive Slave Act were unconstitutional. But in *obiter dictum* unique to him, Story stated that state officials need not participate in a recapture under federal authority. This spurred enactment of statutes prohibiting state officials such as judges and sheriffs from participating in fugitive recaptures and prohibiting the use of state facilities such as jails to slave-catchers trying to hold runaways. Proslavery spokesmen tirelessly denounced the personal liberty laws. In his last annual message, President James Buchanan blamed the crisis of 1860 on them. South Carolina cited the laws as justification for its secession.

The 1850 law was a measure which obliged Northerners to cooperate much more in sustaining the Southern slavery system than they had ever had to do before.

Indicative of how much of a challenge all this was to Northerners, who were willing to tolerate (if not even to profit from) slavery at a distance, not cooperate with it up close, are the defiant speeches it provoked from an apolitical Ralph Waldo Emerson (perhaps the leading American "intellectual" of his day). This 1850 Fugitive Slave Law added fuel to the fire of sectional strife. We can be reminded, by the harsh measures resorted to in the effort to curb fugitive slaves, of the grimness of the Berlin Wall erected by the Soviets in 1961.

In short, the 1850 statute forced Northerners to cooperate in returning fugitive slaves—or, at least, to become more consciously acquiescent in the Southern slavery system. Only those Southerners eager to precipitate a crisis that might lead to secession could have been happy with the controversy aroused by the 1850 statute. It was a controversy, routinely calling vital Southern institutions into question, that could leave Southerners feeling insulted and threatened by an ever more powerful North.

VI

An alternative approach to the 1850 statute would have been for Southerners to consider slaves who could manage to flee North as permanently lost. Such steady seepage could have been regarded as among the costs of doing business. It could even have been argued that an enduring slavery system was better off with the removal from it of the more disaffected *and* enterprising slaves, those who dared to run away.

Continued Northern acquiescence depended, in any event, on Northern ignorance. That is, slavery is something that does take getting used to. The worst of it, at least on this side of the Atlantic, was to be seen when the hunters of fugitive slaves prowled across Northern states, a spectacle that was considered particularly offensive by observers such as Emerson.

What may have made matters even worse was that the men and women being rounded up and dragged back to the South were slaves who *had* been most stirred by the lure of liberty. That is, they were people who had done what most white Americans would have also wanted to do in like circumstances. The plight of such fugitives, we can recall, could be dramatized effectively in the phenomenal best seller, Harriet Beecher Stowe's *Uncle Tom's Cabin*.

VII

However all this may have been, we have noticed, the longer slavery lasted in the United States, the harder it was to justify. Especially was this so when the supply of new slaves was pretty much cut off after January 1, 1808. The slaves all became ever more "Americanized" as the decades rolled by, sharing with their masters their language, religion, and even moral principles.

All this was reinforced (we have seen) by more and more sharing of blood between masters and slaves. It must have been evident that there would come a day when there would be large families of slaves and free men who would look and sound alike. Chance events, like John Brown's venture in 1859, could remind Southerners of how much they depended on the acquiescence, if not even the loyalty, of their slaves.

Besides, the "better opinion" of the age did seem to be against the perpetuation of chattel slavery. Thoughtful Americans, South as well as North, recalled that the 1772 *Somerset* case had reminded everyone of how much English constitutionalism assumed and promoted liberty. Even someone such as Patrick Henry (we have also noticed) could depend on his fellow slaveholders to be stirred by his declaration against "enslavement" by the British, "Give me liberty, or give me death!"

VIII

No one, we have noticed as well, could defend after 1808 how slaves had been originally acquired on the coast of West Africa. So abhorrent had this practice become that it was explicitly forbidden in the Confederate Constitution of 1861. We have recalled (in the preface to this volume) that Thomas Jefferson had even attempted to include, as a grievance in the Declaration of Independence, the complaint that the British had foisted the international slave trade upon their unwilling American colonies.

The hunting down of escaped slaves in Northern states must have reminded sensitive souls of what had been done on the African coast in the original seizure of slaves for the Americas. It could be wondered why there were not supposed to be in the United States procedural safeguards that suspected fugitives from labor or service could invoke. The law was, in various ways, far more protective of those fugitives accused of serious crimes in their home states.

All this is to make us suspect, once again, that the Africans thus being dealt with were not regarded as truly, or fully, human. I have suggested that this approach may have seemed plausible, or at least somehow endurable, so long as slaves did consist of people so obviously different in many ways as were the men and women recently kidnapped in Africa and their immediate descendants. The 1793 Act had not "needed" such an infamous provision as that found in the 1850 Act: "In no trial or hearing under this act shall the testimony of such alleged fugitives [from owed service or labor] be admitted in evidence."

IX

The deeply lamentable failings of gifted leaders such as John C. Calhoun could be seen in their refusal to plan to phase out an institution that was obviously becoming more and more vulnerable worldwide. A profound unease with slavery (we have noticed) is suggested by the unwillingness to use the words "slave" or "slavery" even in those instruments—such as the Constitution of 1787 and the Fugitive Slave Laws of 1793 and 1850—which attempt to protect it. It turned out that decent legislators (as least in the North) could use the words "slave" and "slavery" in constitutional documents only when they tried to suppress slavery, as in the Northwest Ordinance of 1787 and in the Thirteenth Amendment of 1865.

These terms *are* used in the Confederate Constitution of 1861, where an indefinite continuation of slavery is insisted upon. But this is an act of defiance, part and parcel of the secession that was being attempted. It is not insignificant that this movement, explicitly endorsing slavery in perpetuity, was led by the "leaders" of the two states which had insisted, in 1787, that they had to be able to keep importing slaves from Africa for another twenty years.

Of course, each side in the great controversy over slavery and secession believed it had a critical right on its side. One side made much of *contract law*, the other more of *natural right*. It can be said to be natural that the more sensitive descendants of the secessionists today (those still dedicated to the Lost Cause) cannot bear the thought that their forebears had sacrificed as much as they did in order to perpetuate slavery indefinitely, preferring instead to see something like an insistence upon self-determination as more critical, a laudable preference that the "Americanized" fugitive slaves would have endorsed.

~

2. Frederick Douglass and *Uncle Tom's Cabin* (1852)

I

William Rives, a Virginia Democrat in the United States Senate, regarded slavery as an evil. John C. Calhoun, of South Carolina, conceded (in the course of an 1837 Senate debate) that evil is something that *is* to be resisted. But, it is recorded,

> He [Calhoun] did not admit [slavery] to be an evil. Not at all. It was a good—a great good.

This exchange between Rives and Calhoun is drawn on in this way in William Lee Miller's *Arguing About Slavery*:

> Mr. Calhoun complained of having been misrepresented. Again [he] denied having pronounced slavery in the abstract a good. All he had said of it referred to existing circumstances, to slavery as a practical, not as an abstract thing.

Slavery, it was then argued by Calhoun, "was good where a civilized race and a race of a different description were brought together, . . . where two races coexisted." Calhoun thereafter observed, in the Miller account,

> The gentleman from Virginia [Rives] held [slavery] an evil. . . . Surely if it was an evil, moral, social, and political, the Senator, a wise and virtuous man, was bound to exert himself to put it down. This position, that it was a moral evil, was the very root of the whole system of operations against it. That was the

spring and wellhead from which all these streams of abolition proceeded—the effects of which so deeply agitated the honorable Senator [from Virginia].

We can see illustrated here the struggle for the soul of the South between Virginia (whose most famous son had freed his slaves at his death) and South Carolina, that struggle which was to determine how formidable any secessionist effort might be. We can also see here, in the Calhoun concession about the obligation to put down whatever *is* identified as evil, that all human beings naturally seek the Good. It was critical, therefore, how slavery should be understood—and it is that understanding to which Harriet Beecher Stowe's *Uncle Tom's Cabin* contributed for multitudes in this country and abroad.

II

The publishing history of *Uncle Tom's Cabin* was simply phenomenal. The novel is introduced in this way by Edmund Wilson in his 1962 *Patriotic Gore* volume:

> This novel by Harriet Beecher Stowe was one of the greatest successes of American publishing history as well as one of the most influential books—immediately influential, at any rate—that have ever appeared in the United States. A year after its publication in March 20, 1852, it had sold 305,000 copies in America and something like two million and a half copies in English and in translations all over the world. As for its influence, it is enough to remember the greeting of Lincoln to Mrs. Stowe when she was taken to call on him at the White House: "So this is the little lady who made this big war."

It can be questioned whether President Lincoln had indeed spoken thus to Mrs. Stowe, but it cannot be doubted that her book had a great influence, putting human faces (so to speak) on the reports that people in the North and elsewhere had long been hearing about the chronic abuses of the slavery system in the South.

That the novel came to be regarded almost as a journalistic account of slavery is suggested by the subtitle provided it in an 1852 printing in England (instead of *Life Among the Lowly*): *Negro Life in the Slave States of America.* We recalled that the English Parliament had, in 1833, provided for mandatory (compensated) emancipation in its colonies in North America. Perhaps the Dickensian elements in *Uncle Tom's Cabin* (which, like some of Charles Dickens's fiction, had first appeared in serial form) reinforced the appeal of Mrs. Stowe's story.

A particularly significant assessment of the Stowe novel was provided by the ex-slave Frederick Douglass in chapter VIII of his autobiographical *Life and Times*:

> In the midst of [the] fugitive slave troubles came the book known as *Uncle Tom's Cabin*, a work of marvelous depth and power. Nothing could have better suited the moral and human requirements of the hour. Its effect was amazing, instantaneous, and universal. No book on the subject of slavery had so generally and favorably touched the American heart. It combined all the power and pathos of preceding publications of the kind, and was hailed by many as an inspired production. Mrs. Stowe at once became an object of interest and admiration. She had made fortune and fame at home, and had awakened a deep interest abroad. Eminent persons in England, roused to anti-slavery enthusiasm by her *Uncle Tom's Cabin*, invited her to visit that country.

The way Douglass spoke of this novel is in a far different spirit from the way that some African Americans speak today who ridicule the determinedly Christian (as well as Gandhian?) Uncle Tom as unduly obsequious. More in the Douglass spirit was that ardent abolitionist, Senator Charles Sumner of Massachusetts, who could (in 1852) liken Harriet Beecher Stowe ("inspired by Christian genius") to Joan of Arc.

III

However saintly Uncle Tom was, especially in his dealings with the murderous Simon Legree (an immigrant to Louisiana *from the North*), that could not be said of Frederick Douglass himself. He had not only escaped from slavery (unlike Uncle Tom) but he had even provided a refuge to fugitive slaves who had killed someone pursuing them. He did not, however, endorse all forms of resistance to slavery, as may be seen in his unwillingness to support (at least publicly) the notorious John Brown expedition to Harpers Ferry in 1859.

Even so, Douglass encouraged the use of force in some circumstances, not least in the Union efforts during the Civil War. One of his most memorable pre-war addresses was his 1852 Independence Day oration, in Rochester, New York, "What to the Slave is the Fourth of July?" Much of this speech, especially at its outset, reminded his audience of how their ancestors had justified *their* armed resistance to English tyranny.

He recalled, as an example of that resistance, that their ancestors had "bared [their] bosoms to the storm of British artillery, to throw off a threepenny tax on tea." Perhaps his most telling comparison of the manly heroism of the past with the unseemly passivity of the present is the following:

> You declare, before the world, and are understood by the world to declare, that you *"hold these truths to be self evident, that all men are created equal, and are endowed by their Creator with certain inalienable rights; and that, among these are, life, liberty, and the pursuit of happiness;"* and yet, you hold securely, in a bondage, which according to your own Thomas Jefferson, *"is worse than ages of that which your fathers rose in rebellion to oppose,"* a seventh part of the inhabitants of your country.

Douglass's use here of "you hold securely, in a bondage" suggested that non-slaveholding Northerners (if not personally actively anti-slavery) were cooperating in a system that held more than three million men and women of African descent in slavery in the United States.

IV

The Stowe book was, in effect, a new Declaration of Independence for many in this country. After all, it provided, in memorable scenes, the grievances that the slaves of North America were enduring. This recital of grievances proved remarkably effective.

Perhaps the most offensive feature of the slavery system (aside from how slaves were originally acquired by the international slave-traders) was the forced breakup of enslaved families. It is this which is drawn upon in the opening scene of *Uncle Tom's Cabin.* A slave trader is shown pressing a financially distressed plantation owner not only to separate Uncle Tom from his family but also to deprive a mother of her child.

The desperation of the mother, fleeing with her child, is dramatized by her jumping from one block of ice to another in crossing the Ohio River from enslavement in Kentucky to the freedom of Ohio. The reader is obliged to cheer on Eliza, especially in staged presentations of this episode in which pursuing bloodhounds were introduced. It is in the course of this flight that a quite respectable Ohio state senator is shown sacrificing his professional law-abidingness when he confronts an attractive mother in need of help if she is to escape the cruel fate that would follow upon her return to slavery.

V

Concerns about slavery had been steadily growing for decades in the free states of pre–Civil War America. The more slavery was known nationwide, the more resistance it encountered. Stories such as *Uncle Tom's Cabin* suggested to Northerners that they themselves were partly responsible for slavery in the South.

A serious tactical error had been made by those who insisted on the Fugitive Slave Act of 1850. Consider how Mrs. Stowe talks about it in the concluding chapter of her novel (which is reminiscent of how Ralph Waldo Emerson also responded to that act):

> For many years of her life, the author avoided all reading upon or allusion to the subject of slavery, considering it as too painful to be inquired into, and one which advancing light and civilization would certainly live down. But, since the legislative act of 1850, when she heard, with perfect surprise and consternation, Christian and humane people actually recommending the remanding escaped fugitives into slavery, as a duty binding on good citizens,—when she heard, on all hands from kind, compassionate, and estimable people, in the free states of the North, deliberations and discussions as to what Christian duty could be on this head,—she could only think, These men and Christians cannot know what slavery is; if they did, such a question could never be open for discussion. And from this arose a desire to exhibit it in a *living dramatic reality*. She has endeavored to show it fairly, in its best and its worst phases. In its *best* aspect, she has, perhaps, been successful; but oh! who shall say what yet remains untold in that valley and shadow of death, that lies the other side?

Thus, the Fugitive Slave Act had forced Northerners who preferred to ignore slavery to cooperate personally in its maintenance.

Perhaps, it can be said, the ultimate indefensibility (that is, irrationality) of chattel slavery had made it likely that its defenders would resort to more and more foolish, self-defeating measures on its behalf. It is those defenders that Mrs. Stowe appeals to in her concluding chapter when she says,

> To you, generous, noble-minded men and women, of the South,—you, whose virtue, and magnanimity, and purity of character are the greater for the severer trial it has encountered,—to you is her appeal. Have you not, in your own secret souls, in your own private conversings, felt that there are woes and evils, in this accursed system, far beyond what are here shadowed, or can be shadowed? Can it be otherwise? Is *man* ever a creature to be trusted with wholly irresponsible power? And does not the slave system, by denying the slave all legal right of testimony, make every individual owner an irresponsible despot? Can anybody fail to make the inference what the practical result will be? If there is, as we admit, a public sentiment among you, men of honor, justice, and humanity, is there not also another kind of public sentiment among the ruffian, the brutal, and debased? And cannot the ruffian, the brutal, the debased, by slave law,

> own just as many slaves as the best and purest? Are the honorable, the just, the high-minded, and compassionate, the majority anywhere in this world?

Particularly troubling for some defenders of slavery must have been the recognition of how many guarantees of personal liberty "had" to be denied to purported fugitive slaves in order to make the system "work," guarantees such as the right to trial by jury, the right to testify on one's behalf, and even the right to a presumption of innocence.

VI

A critical issue is raised, especially by critics of *Uncle Tom's Cabin*, about what Africans are truly like, and especially what life in Africa had been like. That there are important differences among peoples, or races, seems to be casually conceded by Frederick Douglass, as when he can observe, in chapter VII of his *Life and Times*,

> The black man (*un*like the Indian) loves civilization. He does not make very great progress in civilization himself, but he likes to be in the midst of it, and prefers to share its most galling evils, to encountering barbarism.

Critics of "racism" today would take issue also with Douglass's ambiguous stance toward "blackness," as may be seen in his Independence Day observation (emphases added), "The oath of any two villains is sufficient, under this *hell-black* enactment [the Fugitive Slave Law of 1850], to send the most pious and exemplary *black* men into the remorseless jaws of slavery!"

Vital differences between races are emphasized by the particularly instructive critique of *Uncle Tom's Cabin* in the January 1853 issue of the *Southern Quarterly Review* by Louisa S. McCord (1810–1879), a remarkably well-read Southerner of considerable talent. Mrs. McCord, like Mrs. Stowe an incipient feminist (but with different opinions about where the power of women was truly to be found and how it was to be used), comments in this fashion on the decision of the financially pressed Shelby family to sell the beloved Uncle Tom and Eliza's child to a slave-trader who means to take both of them to the New Orleans Market:

> [T]he "good-natured and kindly" Mr. Shelby determines to sell the child in a quiet way, to avoid the *screechin'*, by stealing it away from its mother. Upon this very probable and natural incident . . . turns the principal romance of the story. The woman runs away with her child, and after adventures infinite, finally arrives among the Quakers and in Canada, etc. In the next scene, the

authoress introduces us to one of her high and noble characters—one of those whose hearts, uncontaminated by the debasing effects of our system, rise above it. We will see whether she understands this class better than the gentlemanly, "good-natured and kindly:" "Mrs. Shelby was a woman of a high class, both intellectually and morally;" with "magnanimity and generosity of mind,"— "high moral and religious sensibility and principles, carried out with energy and ability into practical results." This very sensible, moral and religious lady, when made acquainted with her husband's brutal conduct, is very naturally distressed at it. But what remedy does she find? Does she consult with him as a wife should consult? Does she advise as a woman can advise? Does she suggest means and remedies for avoiding such a crisis? Does she endeavour to show her husband the folly and madness, as well as the wickedness, of his course? No. After a few remonstrances, feebly advanced, she, too, (the high intellectual woman!) seems to be struck dumb with the insurmountability of that terrible debt which is to be paid by the sale of *one elderly man and a little child*; she, too, seems to think there is no imaginable way for a comfortable farmer or planter to get round that enormous sum of one thousand dollars or thereabouts; and neither she nor her good-natured and kindly husband, seem to imagine or to care, whether it might not be possible—quite as easy perhaps—(should they be forced to part with a negro or two) to dispose of them in families to some humane neighbour (such servants as these are described to be, seldom go begging for owners), instead of tearing them apart and selling them to a brutal slave-dealer, whom Mr. Shelby himself describes as "cool and unhesitating, and unrelenting as death and the grave." No; she thinks she fulfills her Christian duty much better, by letting the "faithful, confiding, excellent creature, Tom," who is willing "to lay down his life" for his master, "be torn in a moment" from all he holds dear, the petted and delicate child, from its petted and delicate mother, while she, the magnanimous woman, who carries out her high principles with energy into practical results, bursts out into a tirade, which, if anything could, might excuse the cold brutality of her husband, by the supposition that the poor man had gone crazy under similar lectures: "This is God's curse on slavery!—a bitter, bitter, most accursed thing!—a curse to the master and a curse to the slave! I was a fool to think I could make anything good out of such a deadly evil. It is a sin to hold a slave under laws like ours—I always felt it was." "Abolitionist! If they knew all I know about slavery they might talk!" etc.

The Shelby family is considered "incomprehensible" because it does not do what can properly be done to avoid the abuses of which the slavery system (or any other social arrangement?) is capable.

The system of African slavery in the United States is believed by Mrs. McCord to have been ordained by both God and nature. She anticipates the dreadful consequences if the abolitionists should succeed in disrupting even more than they had already done the proper, mutually beneficial relations between masters and slaves in this country:

> Make a law perverting nature by which (as our woman's rights reformers would have it) woman and man are equal, and created with similar rights, and what ensues but bloody barbarity and tyrannic force, trampling to earth the beneficent, though often abused relations, which now exist between them? Make a law by which (because the parent sometimes abuses his authority) the child shall become the free and equal competitor for that parent's privileges, to aim at a general home democracy, and on true free soil principle, to take what suits him of house or land; and what again follows, but the extinction of all affection; the early murder of infants; the reign of blood and brute force, instead of charity, affection, beautiful dependence, and christian love? Make your laws to interfere with the God-established system of slavery, which our Southern States are beautifully developing to perfection, daily improving the condition of the slave, daily waking more and more the master to his high and responsible position; make your laws, we say, to pervert this God-directed course, and the world has yet to see the horrors which might ensue from it. The natural order of things perverted, ill must follow. The magnitude of that ill, may heaven protect us from witnessing! Mrs. Stowe has seen, on the border lands, where something of a clash has arisen between the rival powers of abolitionism and slavery, a shadow of those evils which would result to the slave, when the natural boundaries of the system being broken down, the master would retain the powers without the affections belonging to his position. These evils her imagination has multiplied an hundred fold; but yet are to be depicted those scenes, when the slave, struggling with his destiny, shall force into opposition the rival might of civilization and barbarism, of brute force and intellectual power. Imagination has not yet depicted *those*. She threatens us with a second Haytien tragedy. Hayti! She knows not of what she talks. As the ocean to the wave—as the rill to the torrent—as the zephyr to the whirlwind—would any such scenes, if possible among us, be to those of Hayti, fearful as they were [in 1791]; as an ocean's gulf to a rain-puddle, would be the ensuing barbarism. Mrs. Stowe has a fertile imagination, and has got up quite a respectable collection of "tales of wonder," which would rival in horrors those of Monk Lewis; yet, though she should go on, and on, and on, till even *her* thought should quail, and even *her* heart sink at the fearful picture, yet will she not have touched, yet can she not have began to imagine, the fearful penalties which indignant nature would attach to her so outraged laws. "Thus far shalt thou go, and no farther," that God said, not to the great ocean only, when he chained it within its bed, but equally to every creature within the limits of its uses and its intelligence. To the white man, he has given *his* place; to the negro, *his*. The white man who abuses his God-given power, is indeed criminal, both to God and to man. Hitchings there are, and disorders numberless, in the great world-system

> of machinery, which Omniscience has not seen fit to make perfect; but what are these, compared to the general crash which would follow, should man, with his tinkering, upset the whole fabric, that he may rectify its errors by his puny wisdom? The civilized world must totter to its foundations, when, if ever, African slavery in America ceases to exist.

We can wonder how Mrs. McCord, who is obviously sincere and high-minded (and who is troubled by the plight of mulattoes), understood the disturbing social relations reflected in the observation by Frederick Law Olmstead (said to be one of the most trustworthy observers of life in the antebellum South), who quotes a Louisiana planter as having told him,

> There is not a likely looking black girl in this State that is not the paramour of a white man. There is not an old plantation in which the grandchildren of the owner are not whipped in the field by his overseer.

VII

Mrs. McCord, in challenging the accuracy of Mrs. Stowe's accounts of Southern ways, can fault her novel from its outset:

> The book opens with the introduction of "*two gentlemen*," seated at a table in a house, of which the general style "indicated easy and even opulent circumstances." The master of the house is one of the "gentlemen." The other, "when *critically* examined, did not seem, *strictly* speaking, to come under the species." This gentleman, who proves to be a slave-trader, but who must be so *critically* examined to discover that he is not *strictly a gentleman*, seems, however, quite at his ease, and rattles his watch-seals like a man of consequence,—hale fellow well met with the opulent signor, whom he constantly and familiarly terms Shelby, (leaving off the form of Mr.,) and occasionally slaps on the back, to make his conversation more impressive. Into what society can Mrs. Stowe have been admitted, to see slave-traders so much at their ease in gentlemen's homes? We have lived at the South, in the very heart of a slave country, for thirty years out of forty of our lives, and have never seen a slave-trader set foot in a gentleman's house.

Abraham Lincoln, too, noticed (in the 1850s) that Southerners tended to shun not only slave-traders but also their children. Did Mrs. McCord recognize what this social ostracism of the slave-trader revealed about a perhaps instinctive awareness among Southerners about the ultimate dubiousness of a system which relied upon the services of such socially unacceptable men?

The role of chance in determining the allegiance one has may be seen in the career of Mrs. McCord herself. She, a lady who had disdained the efforts of abolitionists who aided fugitive slaves to avoid the service "owed" by them to their masters, is said to have considered herself entitled, after the Civil War, to flee (for awhile) to Canada rather than take the required oath of allegiance to her new master, the government of the United States. It would be quite instructive to develop a conjecture of how Louisa McCord and Frederick Douglass (who also once fled to Canada) might have discussed the implications of such radical changes in circumstances and in the duties and entitlements to be acknowledged by those who resist the authority of one's time and place.

The role of chance in these matters included not only the caliber of the master that a slave had but also whether one's family had been kidnapped by slavers in Africa. And the allegiance of someone such as Louisa McCord also probably depended in large part on chance. Indeed, considering her capacity for literary expression, her considerable intelligence, and her eye for telling details, one can imagine her even writing a novel like *Uncle Tom's Cabin* if she had happened to settle in Massachusetts instead of in South Carolina.

VIII

Christianity can be invoked by both slaveholders and abolitionists in developing their respective positions. But (as we have seen) by the middle of the nineteenth century, Christian sentiment worldwide had mostly turned against slavery, and not only against the international slave trade. The mobilization of such sentiment against slavery in the United States culminated in the deliverance (by another woman!) of "The Battle Hymn of the Republic" in 1862.

Certainly, the author of *Uncle Tom's Cabin* considers her position grounded in Christianity—and in a sound morality. This may be seen in the appeal (quoted above) that she makes, in the concluding chapter of her novel, to the "generous, noble-minded men and women of the South" about the abuses inherent in "the slave system." In short, she implores Southerners to hearken to their nobler instincts, however threatening both to security and to economic interests the abandonment of slavery may appear to be.

By the middle of the twentieth century, as the Civil Rights Movement developed, the "Southern" apologists found little comfort in religion (however many crosses had been burned by their extremists). Martin Luther King, Jr., for example, was very much a "Reverend" appealing to the best in Southerners. Whatever the long-standing, if not even the natural, limitations of traditional African life, it had become evident by then that African Americans had become among the most "Christianized" (and hence, in their Protestantism, among the most "Americanized"?) ethnic groups in this country.

IX

The steady "Americanization" of African slaves in this country bears on a critical issue dividing Frederick Douglass and Harriet Beecher Stowe, that with respect to the colonization of emancipated slaves. One of the heroes of *Uncle Tom's Cabin*, George Harris (Eliza's husband), is destined to take his considerable talents to Liberia. Douglass, on the other hand, insists that the Africans in this country are Americans now who are obviously here to stay, something testified to for us today by the "phenomenon" of having had two African Americans serve, in succession, as our secretary of state and thereafter another as president of the United States.

The remarkable changes in race relations we have seen in recent decades are anticipated perhaps in the very title of the Stowe novel. A slave, it seems, could be thought of as *having* a *cabin* (and all the relations and privileges implied in that institution), however vulnerable such "ownership" may always be to the vagaries of the system. It would not make sense or have much of an appeal, on the other hand, to christen the story of another much-loved character, *Black Beauty's Stable*.

The merits of Mrs. Stowe's novel are recalled by Edmund Wilson in a *Patriotic Gore* essay, an essay written at a time when few in this country still read the Stowe book:

> To expose oneself in maturity to *Uncle Tom* may prove a startling experience. It is a much more impressive work than one has ever been allowed to suspect. The first thing that strikes one about it is a certain eruptive force. This is partly explained by the author in a preface to a late edition, in which she tells of the oppressive silence that hung over the whole question of slavery before she published her book. "It was a general saying," she explains, "among conservative and sagacious people that this subject was a dangerous one to investigate, and that nobody could begin to read and think upon it without becoming practically insane; moreover, that it was a subject of such delicacy that no discussion of it could be held in the free states without impinging upon the sensibilities of the slave states, to whom alone the management of the matter belonged." The story came so suddenly to Mrs. Stowe and seemed so irresistibly to write itself that she felt as if some power beyond her had laid hold of her to deliver its message, and she said sometimes that the book had been written by God. This is actually a little the impression that the novel makes on the reader. Out of a background of undistinguished narrative, inelegantly and carelessly written,

> the characters leap into being with a vitality that is all the more striking for the ineptitude of the prose that presents them. These characters—like those of Dickens, at least in his early phase—express themselves a good deal better than the author expresses herself. The Shelbys and George Harris and Eliza and Aunt Chloe and Uncle Tom project themselves out of the void. They come before us arguing and struggling, like real people who cannot be quiet. We feel that the dams of discretion of which Mrs. Stowe has spoken have been burst by a passionate force that, compressed, has been mounting behind them, and which, liberated, has taken the form of a flock of lamenting and ranting, prattling and preaching characters, in a drama that demands to be played to the end. Not, however, that it is merely a question of a troubled imagination and an inhibited emotional impulse finding vent in a waking fantasy. What is most unexpected is that, the farther one reads in *Uncle Tom*, the more one becomes aware that a critical mind is at work, which has the complex situation in a very firm grip and which, no matter how vehement the characters become, is controlling and coordinating their interrelations.

Even so, it can be said that our impressive 1852 authors prepared the way for even more accomplished successors. Harriet Beecher Stowe was succeeded by Mark Twain (especially in *The Adventures of Huckleberry Finn*) and Frederick Douglass was succeeded by Abraham Lincoln (especially in the Second Inaugural Address, a statement that Douglass himself was inspired to acclaim as "sacred").

3. Chief Justice Taney and the *Dred Scott* Case (1857)

I

The *Dred Scott* case is generally regarded as one of the most momentous in the annals of the United States Supreme Court. Abraham Lincoln rose to national prominence in large part because of his reasoned opposition in 1858 to the doctrines advanced by the Supreme Court in *Dred Scott*. Particularly influential for the Lincoln career were his much-publicized differences with Stephen A. Douglas in response to this case.

Here, with my bracketed additions, is how the case is introduced these days in the *Encyclopedia Britannica*:

> *Dred Scott* decision (March 6, 1857), ruling of the U.S. Supreme Court that made slavery legal in all the territories [of the United States], thereby adding fuel to the sectional controversy and pushing the nation along the road to civil war. The decision—only the second time in the nation's history that the Supreme Court declared an act of Congress unconstitutional [the first time had been *Marbury* v. *Madison* (1803)]—was a clear victory for the slaveholding South. Southerners had argued that both Congress and the territorial legislature [empowered by Congress] were powerless to exclude slavery from a territory. Only a state could exclude slavery, they maintained. Dred Scott was a slave whose master, in 1834, had taken him from Missouri (a slave state) to Illinois (a free state), then into the Wisconsin Territory (a free territory under the provisions of the Missouri Compromise [and of the Northwest Ordinance]), and finally back to Missouri. In 1846, with the help of anti-slavery lawyers, Scott sued for his freedom in the Missouri state courts on the grounds

> that his residence in a free state and a free territory had made him a free man. The Missouri Supreme Court overturned *an initial ruling by a lower court which had declared Scott free* [emphasis added], and the case, then, began a long sojourn up to the U.S. Supreme Court.

The *Britannica* entry on the *Dred Scott* decision continues in this fashion (again with my bracketed addition):

> Chief Justice Roger B. Taney, one of the seven justices denying Scott his freedom (two dissented), declared that a Negro could not be entitled to rights as a U.S. citizen, such as the right to sue in federal courts. In fact, Taney wrote, Negroes "had no rights which any white man was bound to respect." The decision might have ended there, with the dismissal of Scott's appeal. But Taney and the other justices in the majority went on to declare that the Missouri Compromise of 1820 (which had forbidden slavery in that part of the Louisiana Purchase north of the latitude 36° 30', except for Missouri) was unconstitutional because Congress had no power to prohibit slavery in the territories. Slaves were property, and masters were guaranteed their property rights under the Fifth Amendment. Neither Congress nor a territorial legislature could deprive a citizen of his property without due process of law. As for Scott's residence in a free state, Illinois, the majority said that Scott had still been subject then to Missouri law. [In *Marbury* v. *Madison*, too, the court "went on to declare" far more than it needed to do in disposing of *that* case.]

The *Britannica* author then recalls how the disposition of this case was regarded in various circles:

> The *Dred Scott* decision seemed a mortal blow to the newly created Republican Party, formed to halt the extension of slavery into the western territories. . . . President James Buchanan, the South, and the majority of the Supreme Court hoped that the *Dred Scott* decision would mark the end of antislavery agitation. Instead, the decision increased antislavery sentiment in the North, strengthened the Republican Party, and fed the sectional antagonism that burst into war in 1861.

At the very least, one's response to *Dred Scott* provided a ready indication of where one stood on the slavery issue in the United States. Certainly, it seems, the case did not provide the calming effect, with respect to the slavery issue, that the Chief Justice had evidently expected. That the Taney career should be blighted by his expectations with respect to *Dred Scott* is symptomatic of how the better element in the South had been corrupted by the slavery regime they had inherited and somehow felt obliged to perpetuate and to defend.

II

Lord Charnwood, a remarkably sensitive biographer of Lincoln, has spoken thus of the *Dred Scott* case:

> Chief Justice Roger Taney [of Maryland] may be seen from the refined features of his portrait and the clear-cut literary style of his famous judgment [in *Dred Scott*] to have been a remarkable man. He was now eighty-three, but in unimpaired intellectual vigour. In a judgment, with which five of his colleagues entirely concurred and from which only two dissented, he decided that Dred Scott was not [and never could be] a citizen, and went on [to say] that Dred Scott was not free, because the Missouri Compromise [of 1820] had all along been unconstitutional and void.

The vocabulary of the slaveholders and their champions reflects their dependence on a constitutionalism of sorts. Particularly significant is how "the United States" was regarded by them.

That is, critical to their constitutionalism was a severely limited range of powers assigned to the United States government by the Constitution. The state governments were considered by the slaveholders and their champions to have a far greater range of powers than did the United States with respect to the existence and governance of slavery. Indeed, each of the states could even be regarded by the slavery camp as being closer than the United States to a fully sovereign political association.

Some of the slaveholders' champions (such as Chief Justice Taney) were inclined to see the states, not the United States, as countries or nations. They anticipated the emphasis placed, in the eleven Ordinances of Secession of 1860–1861, on the Constitution of 1787 as a *compact*. The states were thus more apt, than the United States, to be spoken of by them as *countries* and *nations*.

III

The limited scope of the powers of the United States government under the Constitution is suggested by what Chief Justice Taney says about the lack of Congressional authority for the Missouri Compromise of 1820. Particularly vulnerable, he argues, is the assumption that the Constitution authorizes Congress to determine where slavery may be permitted in the Territories of the United States. Such an unauthorized determination may be seen in the attempted 1820 Congressional exclusion of slavery from the Louisiana Purchase Territory north of 36° 30'.

The great precedent here had been what the Articles of Confederation Congress had done in its Northwest Ordinance of 1787 (which was confirmed by the First Congress in 1789). But, the Chief Justice argued, the Confederation Congress had far greater power in 1787, at least with respect to slavery, than Congress was to have in 1820. This was a curious line of argument in the light of what both slave holders and free staters had considered themselves able to agree to in 1820 in order to settle a threatening controversy.

Counsel for Dred Scott, the Chief Justice notices, had "laid much stress upon that article in the Constitution which confers on Congress the power 'to dispose of and make all needful rules and regulations respecting the territory or other property belonging to the United States.'" But the Chief Justice then draws in *Dred Scott* a remarkable distinction:

> [T]hat provision [just quoted] has no bearing on the present controversy, and the power there given, whatever it may be, is confined, and was intended to be confined, to the territory which at that time belonged to, or was claimed by, the United States, and was within their boundaries as settled by the treaty with Great Britain, and can have no influence upon a territory afterwards acquired from a foreign Government. It was a special provision for a known and particular territory, and to meet a present emergency, and nothing more.

This suggests that the United States can acquire territories that neither it nor the states can govern fully (as Territories), especially with respect to the status there of slavery.

IV

All this also suggests that the Articles of Confederation Congress could seem to be regarded by the Chief Justice as significantly more powerful than the Congress authorized by the Constitution. One can see here, as elsewhere, the curious contrivances that had to be resorted to by those who championed the indefinite continuation of slavery in this country. Among those contrivances was the insistence that the United States was not truly a *country* or *nation* but rather no more than an association or confederation for limited, specified purposes.

It is emphasized by the Chief Justice that "the rights of private property" are protected by the Constitution. "Thus," he argues, "the rights of property are united with the rights of persons, and placed on the same ground by the fifth amendment to the Constitution, which provides that no person shall be deprived of life, liberty, and property, without due process of law." It follows then, the Chief Justice argues, that "an act of Congress [such as the Missouri Compromise of 1820] which deprives a citizen of the United States of his liberty or property, merely because he came himself or brought his property into a particular Territory of the United States, and who had committed no offence against the laws, could hardly be dignified with the name of due process of law."

Of course, the property thus protected could include the slaves one owned, those slaves who can be referred to more than once in the Constitution as *persons*. Placing restrictions on the ownership and movement of slaves is condemned as an obvous violation of due process of law. But no "offence against the laws"—divine, natural, or man-made—is seen in rules which can systematically and permanently deprive persons of their liberty if they or their forebears had been kidnapped on the coast of Africa.

V

The Chief Justice, when he developed here his apparent reliance on "due process of law," shifted from his uses of "person" in the passage just quoted to his use of "citizen." That must have made it easier to invoke "dignity" here, considering what he says elsewhere in his *Dred Scott* Opinion about the inability of people of African descent ever to become citizens of the United States. Thus, the rights of citizens can be championed, even when those rights take the form of the permanent subjugation of persons who have committed no offense against any laws of the United States or of any of the states thereof.

It is noticed in the *Encyclopedia of the American Constitution* that *Dred Scott* was "the first instance in which a major federal law [the 1820 Missouri Compromise legislation] was ruled unconstitutional." Indeed, it can be argued with considerable plausibility that the exercise of judicial review of *Acts of Congress* during the century and a half since *Dred Scott* has not generally advanced the causes either of liberty or justice. The risks of reliance on judicial review, when a judge's passions do not have to be moderated by the consideration that practicing politicians usually have to defer to somewhat, may be seen in the characterization in the *Encyclopedia of the American Constitution* of the Taney Opinion in *Dred Scott*:

> Throughout the entire document, [the Chief Justice] made not a single concession to antislavery feeling but instead committed the judicial power of the United States totally to the defense of slavery. Behind his mask of judicial propriety, the Chief Justice had become privately a fierce Southern

sectionalist, seething with anger at "Northern insult and Northern aggression." His flat legal prose does not entirely conceal the intensity of emotion that animated his *Dred Scott* opinion.

What, it may well be asked, was at the root of the intense anger exhibited by the more passionate Southerners in response to "Northern insult and Northern aggression"? The legal principles resolutely invoked by the Chief Justice were themselves grounded in those standards of liberty and justice vital to Anglo-American constitutionalism, standards which (as *Somerset* v. *Stewart* [1772] reminded the thoughtful student of law) called into question any system of chattel slavery. Southerners may have sensed, that is, that their Northern critics were fundamentally correct, however imprudent they may have sometimes been in mounting their criticisms of the slavery of their day.

VI

It was because African slaves were human beings that they could be regarded as eminently useful by Southerners. But their humanity had to be minimized if continued enslavement was to be justified. This process of depreciation is evident in how Chief Justice Taney could speak repeatedly of the African race as degraded, so much so (Southerners had been arguing for a generation) that slavery was good for those held in the United States.

Moral judgments were to be minimized in assessing where and how slaves might be used in the United States. Thus, the Chief Justice could challenge the self-proclaimed moral superiority of Northerners in this fashion:

> It is very true, that in that portion of the Union where the labor of the negro race was found to be unsuited to the climate and unprofitable to the master, but few slaves were held at the time of the Declaration of Independence; and when the Constitution was adopted, [slavery] had entirely worn out in one of them, and measures had been taken for its gradual abolition is several others. But this change had not been produced by any change of opinion in relation to this race; but because it was discovered, from experience, that slave labor was unsuited to the climate and production of these States; for some of the States, where it had ceased or nearly ceased to exist, were actively engaged in the slave trade, procuring cargoes on the coast of Africa, and transporting them for sale to those parts of the Union where their labor was found to be profitable, and suited to the climate and productions. And this traffic was openly carried on, and fortunes accumulated by it, without reproach from the people of the States where they resided. And it can hardly be supposed that, in the States where it was then countenanced in its worst form—that is, in the seizure and

> transportation—the people could have regarded those who were emancipated as entitled to equal rights with themselves.

In this, and other ways, it was argued by the Chief Justice that when the Framers of the Declaration of Independence proclaimed that "all Men are created equal," this was intended to have a limited (if any) application with respect to those of African descent.

It is recognized, of course, that the international slave trade had been generally regarded as horrendous, something that was evident even in the concession made to South Carolina and Georgia in the 1808 provision in the Constitution. Still, the Chief Justice argued, it had long been generally understood that Africans were "beings of an inferior order, and altogether unfit to associate with the white race, either in social or political relations." It should not be surprising that one critical consequence of these assessments was the insistence that neither those "imported as slaves, nor their descendants, whether they had become free or not," had any rights "which the white man was bound to respect."

VII

All this is not to deny that there were Southerners, perhaps most of them, who insisted that slaves should be treated humanely. And, it should be remembered, the Confederate Constitution of 1861 included an unequivocal prohibition of the international slave trade, a trade which had been generally condemned by Europeans for at least half a century. Southerners probably appeared at their worst when they chanced to show up in Northern communities intent upon recovering slaves who had presumed to escape the "Service or Labour" authorized by the laws of some States.

Chief Justice Taney (born in 1777), who had been in his judicial post since 1836, was very much an old man in the way he responded to the *Dred Scott* challenge. This may be implicit in the way he can be described by his biographer in the *Encyclopedia of the American Constitution*:

> Constitutional problems related to slavery combined with Taney's personal failings to blight his reputation and eclipse his real achievements. *Dred Scott* remains a monument to judicial hubris, and all the slavery cases that came before the Taney Court bear the impress of Taney's determination to bend the Constitution to the service of sectional interest. Though he manumitted nearly all his own slaves and was in his personal relations a kind and loving man, Taney as Chief Justice was immoderate and willful when the times called for judicial caution.

It is then suggested, "It is the tragic irony of Taney's career that his virtues were so closely linked to his faults, especially in their results."

A somewhat technical instance of the partisan service in which Taney enlisted his considerable talent and prestige may be seen in how he could speak of the powers provided to the General Government by the Constitution. Again and again he seemed inclined to suggest that that government had only the powers "expressly" granted to it, resurrecting thereby the restrictive spirit of Article II of the Articles of Confederation. Whatever necessary implications of powers there may be suggested in the Constitution were grudgingly recognized by him—and limited to their narrowest scope.

VIII

We have noticed that the Chief Justice presented himself as a defender of due process of law. This defense included, for him, considerable respect for the common law. One consequence of such a dedication is respect for property, not least that property in slaves upon which the South very much depended.

At the foundations of the Anglo-American respect for law and property are such pronouncements as Magna Carta. A particularly strong application of the principles of liberty may be seen in *Somerset*. We have several times noticed that this is made even more striking in that it came from a great commercial law judge, Lord Mansfield, who was at least as conservative and as dedicated to the law as Chief Justice Taney.

Somerset reminded students of the law how local, and precarious, the claims of slaveholders tended to be. There could be seen in *Dred Scott* the challenges to continued enslavement whenever a slave was moved by his master from those states in which the legal system had been thoroughly fashioned to perpetuate slavery. It is a feature of Anglo-American constitutionalism (sustained, in part, by respect for the venerable writ of *habeas corpus*) that slavery (or any other kind of extended subjugation) can only be justified (if at all) on the basis of special, usually local or temporary, circumstances.

IX

Anyone familiar with the political debates of 1857–1860, and especially the dramatic Lincoln-Douglas Debates of 1858, can notice in the Chief Justice's *Dred Scott* Opinion issues and arguments that became ever more intense as the Civil War approached. Thus, the Chief Justice noticed the insistence in the Declaration of Independence that "all Men are created equal." The Chief Justice then attempted to explain away these words in this fashion:

> The general words above quoted would seem to embrace the whole human family, and if they were used in a similar instrument at this day would be so understood. But it is too clear for dispute, that the enslaved African race were not intended to be included, and formed no part of the people who framed and adopted this declaration; for if the language, as understood in that day, would embrace them, the conduct of the distinguished men who framed the Declaration of Independence would have been utterly and flagrantly inconsistent with the principles they asserted; and instead of the sympathy of mankind, to which they so confidently appealed, they would have deserved and received universal rebuke and reprobation. Yet the men who framed this declaration were great men—high in literary acquirements—high in their sense of honor, and incapable of asserting principles inconsistent with those on which they were acting. They perfectly understood the meaning of the language they used, and how it would be understood by others; and they knew that it would not in any part of the civilized world be supposed to embrace the negro race, which, by common consent, had been excluded from civilized Governments and the family of nations, and doomed to slavery. They spoke and acted according to the then established doctrines and principles, and in the ordinary language of the day, and no one misunderstood them. The unhappy black race were separated from the white by indelible marks, and laws long before established, and were never thought of or spoken of except as property, and when the claims of the owner or the profit of the trader were supposed to need protection.

This kind of talk was probably critical for the determined equanimity of conscientious Southerners trapped in the system of slavery that they had inherited. Also critical was the determination of what should be the authoritative account of when the current United States began. The Supremacy Clause of the Constitution of 1787 is drawn on by the Chief Justice in an effort to justify the widespread Southern insistence that the now-relevant Union began with the Constitution, *not* with the Declaration of Independence:

> [The Supremacy Clause] provides that "all debts, contracts, and engagements entered into before the adoption of this Constitution, shall be as valid against the United States under this Government as under the Confederation." This provision, like the one under consideration, was indispensable if the new Constitution was adopted. The new Government was not a mere change in a dynasty, or in a form of government, leaving the nation or sovereignty the same, and clothed with all the rights, and bound by all the obligations of the preceding one. But, when the present United States came into existence under the new Government, it was a new political body, a new nation, then for the first time taking its place in the family of nations. It took nothing by succession from the Confederation. It had no right, as its successor, to any property or rights of property which it had acquired, and was not liable for any of its obligations. It

> was evidently viewed in this light by the framers of the Constitution. And as the several States would cease to exist in their former confederated character upon the adoption of the Constitution, and could not, in that character, again assemble together, special provisions were indispensable to transfer to the new Government the property and rights which at that time they held in common; and at the same time to authorize it to lay taxes and appropriate money to pay the common debt which they had contracted; and this power could only be given to it by special provisions in the Constitution. The clause in relation to the territory and other property of the United States provided for the first, and the clause last quoted provided for the other. They have no connection with the general powers and rights of sovereignty delegated to the new Government, and can neither enlarge nor diminish them. They were inserted to meet a present emergency, and not to regulate its powers as a Government.

All this is to be contrasted with the language used, not only in the Gettysburg Address but also in such dating as that found in the Constitution of 1787, which places the origins of the United States (and its "perpetual union") in 1776. Even so, is there not something reassuring about the (not altogether sane?) "rationalizations" resorted to by Chief Justice Taney and his Southern allies? They testify to the desire, indeed even the natural compulsion, of all human beings (however trapped they may be in their circumstances) to aim somehow at the Good.

4. The *Dred Scott* Case Dissenters (1857)

I

"Antislavery critics," we are told in the article on *Dred Scott* v. *Sandford* (1857) in the *Encyclopedia of the American Constitution*, "made good use of the [two *Dred Scott*] dissenting opinions in launching an angry, abusive attack upon the [Supreme] Court majority and its judgment." We are also told, in this *Encyclopedia* article,

> The dissenting Justices, John McLean and Benjamin R. Curtis, rejected [Chief Justice] Taney's blanket exclusion of Negroes from citizenship. Having thus affirmed [Dred] Scott's capacity to bring suit in a federal court, [the two dissenters] proceeded to the merits of the case while denying the right of the Court majority to do so [once that majority had ruled as it had on Scott's standing to sue].

We are then told,

> [Justices McLean and Curtis] upheld the constitutionality of the Missouri Compromise restriction [declared unconstitutional by the Taney Court] by interpreting the Territory Clause, in Republican style, as an express and plenary delegation of power to Congress. They went on to maintain that antislavery law, state or federal, dissolved the legal relationship between any master and slave coming within its purview [when a slave is taken into a free State or Territory], thereby working irrevocable emancipation.

The two *Dred Scott* dissenters were at quite different stages of their respective careers. Justice Curtis was to serve less than a decade on the Supreme Court, before retiring to a quite successful private legal practice for almost two decades. The end of his judicial career is described thus in a *Dictionary of American Biography* entry which further suggests the slavery-related passions of the times:

> Curtis's best-known association with the Supreme Court was connected with his leaving it. In the famous Dred Scott case . . . , argued on behalf of the negro by Curtis's brother, . . . he was one of the two dissenting judges, and urged in a long opinion that residence of a slave with his owner on free territory conferred freedom which the slave could vindicate in the courts on his return to the owner's domicile in slave territory. Curtis also claimed that the Court could not proceed, as it did, to decide the case on the merits after it had ruled that a slave was not a citizen, and was without capacity to sue. This opinion was given to the newspapers in advance of official publication. To meet its arguments, Taney revised the opinion which he had read from the bench. An unpleasant correspondence between Curtis and Taney ensued, Taney objecting to newspaper publication of Curtis's opinion and Curtis objecting to the revision of Taney's opinion after it had been delivered. At the close of the correspondence Curtis resigned from the Court, assigning as a reason the smallness of the salary he received as a judge, but admitting to his friends that he could not "again feel that confidence in the Court and that willingness to cooperate with them which was essential to the satisfactory discharge of my duties." . . . After Taney's death [in 1864] Curtis delivered, at a meeting of the Boston bar, a generous tribute to his service.

Justice McLean had been appointed to the Supreme Court by President Andrew Jackson in 1829. It is noticed in his *Dictionary of American Biography* entry,

> During his term on the bench, he was frequently mentioned as a possible candidate for the presidency. . . . His name was considered by the convention of "Free Democracy" in 1848 and was before the Whig Convention in 1852. In the Republican Convention of 1856 he received 196 votes, and, although seventy-five years of age, he still hoped for the nomination in the Republican Convention of 1860 [the year before he died].

This entry includes a brief reference to the *Dred Scott* case, recalling that Justice McLean "held that slavery had its origin merely in force and was contrary to right, being sustained only by local law."

II

The McLean position about the origins of and authority for slavery was substantially that relied upon by Lord Mansfield in *Somerset* v. *Stewart* (1772). The Mansfield position was drawn on, in effect, in what Justice McLean had said, fifteen years before *Dred Scott*, in *Prigg* v. *Pennsylvania* (1842). The *Prigg* case dealt with the indictment in Pennsylvania of a Maryland citizen of a charge of kidnapping after he had "forcibly taken and carried away [from Pennsylvania] to the state of Maryland a negro woman . . . with the design and intention of her being held, sold, and disposed of as a slave for life, contrary to a [1826] statute of Pennsylvania."

The McLean Opinion in *Prigg* included these observations: "In a state where slavery is allowed, every coloured person is presumed to be a slave; and on the same principle, in a non-slaveholding state, every person is presumed to be free without regard to colour." One question before the Court was whether the Maryland authorities were correct in relying as they did on the 1793 Fugitive Slave Law to justify their refusal to deliver up Prigg as a fugitive from Pennsylvania justice. The Maryland authorities were vindicated by the United States Supreme Court which said, in an Opinion delivered by Justice Joseph Story,

> [T]he act of Pennsylvania upon which this indictment [of Prigg] is founded, is unconstitutional and void. It purports to punish as a public offence against that state, the very act of seizing and removing a slave by his master, which the Constitution of the United States was designed to justify and uphold.

Although the Maryland authorities prevailed in this case, Chief Justice Taney was troubled by the recognition in the Story Opinion for the Court of a paramount Congressional power to deal with these matters. Thus, the Chief Justice argued in a Concurring Opinion in *Prigg*, well before *Dred Scott*,

> The opinion of the Court maintains that the power over this subject [of the recovery of fugitive slaves] is so exclusively vested in Congress, that no state, since the adoption of the Constitution, can pass any law in relation to it. In other words, according to the opinion just delivered, the state authorities are prohibited from interfering for the purpose of protecting the right of the master and aiding him in the recovery of his property. I think the states are not prohibited; and that, on the contrary, it is enjoined upon them as a duty to protect and support the owner when he is endeavouring to obtain possession of his property found within their respective territories.

In *Dred Scott*, of course, the Chief Justice went even further, recognizing critical powers in slaveholders that extended not only into the free states (as in *Prigg*) but also into the Territories of the United States, no matter what Congress attempted to do in determining the status of slavery in such Territories.

III

In this and other ways, the spirit of *Somerset*, with its presumption of freedom, was routinely repudiated by Southern sympathizers. This may have been inevitable if the system of slavery in any part of a federation was to be effectively sustained. It is that system which Justices McLean and Curtis challenged in their *Dred Scott* Dissenting Opinions.

Justice McLean recalled that, in "the dark ages of the world," white men were also made slaves. "All slavery," he argued, "has its origin in power, and is against right." He could speak of "the mercenary spirit [having] introduced the infamous traffic in slaves."

The international slave trade, he notices, "is now declared to be piracy, and punished with death by Christian nations." It had been "the commercial colonies and States," not the Southern communities alone, who had been engaged in the system of traffic in slaves. And Justice McLean recalls that that system had been "imposed upon our colonial settlements by the mother country," something that Thomas Jefferson had attempted to add as a grievance in the Declaration of Independence (as we have seen in the preface to this volume).

IV

Both dissenting justices in *Dred Scott* draw on the Declaration of Independence in their efforts to counter what the Chief Justice was doing to the power of Congress to restrict the spread of slavery into the Territories of the United States. Justice Curtis argues that the "created equal" language of the Declaration included "the African race." This argument had already encountered such a response as that which Stephen A. Douglas was to make much of thereafter in the Lincoln-Douglas Debates of 1858, that Southern patriots could not have conducted themselves (as slaveholders and otherwise) if they had truly believed (at the time of the Declaration of Independence) that the "created equal" language included "the African race."

Justice Curtis invokes considerations of prudence in his effort to explain why the authors of the Declaration of Independence conducted themselves as they did. Thus, he observes,

> My own opinion is, that a calm comparison of these assertions of universal abstract truths, and of their own individual opinions and acts, would not leave these men under any reproach of inconsistency; that the great truths they asserted on that solemn occasion [in 1776], they were ready and anxious to make effectual, wherever a necessary regard to circumstances, which no statesman can disregard without producing more evil than good, would allow, and that it would not be just to them, nor true in itself, to allege that they intended to say that the Creator of all men had endowed the white race, exclusively, with the great natural rights which the Declaration of Independence asserts.

Here, as elsewhere, Justice Curtis questions the justice of the anthropology that the Chief Justice and his slaveholding constituency relied upon.

Undergirding the Declaration of Independence and American political institutions, for Justice Curtis, was Magna Carta, the principles of which had been "brought to America by our ancestors, as part of their inherited liberties, and has existed in all the States, usually in the very words of the great charter." These considerations underlie the Curtis insistence, "Nor . . . will the position, that a [Congressional] prohibition to bring slaves into a Territory [of the United States] deprives any one of his property without due process of law, bear examination." Here, as elsewhere, Justice Curtis indicates that the Court's approach to these matters in *Dred Scott* is "as impracticable in fact, as it is . . . monstrous in theory."

V

The spirit of *Somerset* is evident throughout the McLean Opinion in *Dred Scott*. The natural condition of human beings is freedom, which means that restrictions such as slavery are regarded as so unnatural that they can be maintained only by positive law. Thus, for example, a fugitive slave need not be returned by any sovereignty that does not recognize slavery, unless there is a prior obligation (such as that in Article IV of the Constitution of 1787) for it to do so.

Perhaps at the heart of the distinctively Western respect for human rights are the dictates of the Bible. Thus, Justice McLean could say in his *Dred Scott* Dissenting Opinion,

> A slave is not a mere chattel. He bears the impress of his Maker, and is amenable to the laws of God and man; and he is destined to an endless existence.

It is this sentiment that underlies the appeal of the remarkable best seller of that day, *Uncle Tom's Cabin*.

Somewhat comparable to the general presumption against slavery, among civilized people everywhere since the eighteenth century, is the presumption against capital punishment that has developed in the Western world since the Second World War. This may be seen in the refusal of European nations to extradite fugitives from justice to the United States until assurances are given that capital punishment will not be imposed in any trial that may follow for them. And, of course, it is hardly fashionable today to *admit* to a systematic reliance on torture by any country that purports to be respectable, whatever may have been the provocation.

VI

We have seen again and again that very much a concern of slave states during the decade before *Dred Scott*, and certainly to the eve of the Civil War, was that fugitive slaves be returned to their masters by free state authorities. The Fugitive Slave Law of 1850 was designed to reassure slave owners at a time when abolitionist sentiment was steadily growing. Complicating the problems here was any disinclination on the part of some state courts to recognize the emancipation effected by a master's taking his slave into a jurisdiction where slavery was not sanctioned, a disinclination ratified, in effect, by the ruling in *Dred Scott*.

Justice McLean observed in that case, "Illinois has declared in the most solemn and impressive form that there shall be neither slavery nor involuntary servitude in that State, and that any slave brought into it, with a view of becoming a resident, shall be emancipated." An exception seemed to have been made with respect to slaves accompanying masters in transit across the state. But (Justice McLean further observed) the Missouri Supreme Court refused to consider Dred Scott emancipated, even though he had been "brought from Missouri to Rock Island, in the State of Illinois, and . . . retained there as a slave for two years, and then taken to Fort Snelling [in Wisconsin Territory], where slavery [was] prohibited by the Missouri Compromise and . . . detained there for two years longer in a state of slavery."

"I am not able," Justice McLean said, "to reconcile this result [in the Missouri Supreme Court] with the respect due to the State of Illinois." It seemed to him that "the principle [evidently endorsed by *Dred Scott*] will enable the people of a slave State to introduce slavery into a free State, for a longer or shorter time, as may suit their convenience." It should not be surprising, therefore, that Abraham Lincoln could insist during the Lincoln-Douglas Debates of 1858 that *Dred Scott* meant, in effect, that slavery was about to be made, if it was not already, a nationwide institution, in marked contrast to the Founders' expectation that it had been placed by them "in the course of ultimate extinction."

VII

We are not apt to take seriously today the Taney contention that Congress had never been authorized to legislate with respect to slavery in the Territories of the United States. After all, if Congress could not deal with this matter, how could it empower its Territorial governments to do so? And yet it could be wondered with what reasonable expectations with respect to slavery would settlers from both free states and slave states come into a Territory, expectations grounded in some official policy.

Even so, would it be simply a matter of chance whether slavery prevailed in a particular region? Was it also largely a matter of chance whether particular persons of African descent were considered slave or free? Complicating these issues is the maxim, "Once free, always free" (which Justice McLean attributes to the Maryland authorities).

The irrationality at the core of the slavery system, at least in modern times, is suggested by the refusal to recognize that people of African descent had been "once free" before they were kidnapped on behalf of European and American slave-traders. The problem of rationality here was dramatized by the difficulty we have noticed that defenders of slavery had in talking about their "peculiar institution." Thus, more and more, as the Civil War approached, it seemed that such defenders preferred to speak of "slaveholding states" and "non-slaveholding states," *not* of "slave states" and "free states."

VIII

The more strained the arguments of the Court in *Dred Scott*, the more ominous for the South was the success of the Republican Party in national politics. One consequence of such success to be feared by Southerners would be the eventual reshaping of the United States Supreme Court. That, in turn, could affect how the powers of the Congress were regarded, especially with respect to slavery.

Those powers would include, of course, the governance of the Territories of the United States. We have seen that it was already understood that the Republicans were determined that there should be no more slave states. And as the number of free states grew, Southerners could well wonder how much they could rely upon Republican assurances that slavery would be allowed to continue undisturbed wherever it had been long established.

Thus, it could be wondered how a Republican-controlled Congress might use its commerce power to discourage reliance on slave labor. Would, for instance, the shipment of slaves from one slave state to another continue to be permitted? Even more troubling (for the more apprehensive Southerners) would have been the prospect of Congressional regulation of shipments among the states of the products of slave labor.

IX

These were speculations that could indeed be troubling. Stephen Douglas, for example, tried (in effect) to get Abraham Lincoln to say, in 1858, whether the commerce power of Congress might be used to regulate the slave-based economy of the South. It was becoming apparent, we have noticed, that the significantly higher rate of population growth in the North threatened the continuing ability of the South to protect, in the Senate and hence in the Supreme Court, what it considered its vital interests.

Perhaps even more threatening was the growing awareness, in the North and worldwide, if not yet in the South, that chattel slavery was simply indefensible. The Chief Justice could suggest, in various ways, that Africans were naturally inferior, if not even in need of enslavement. But Justice Curtis drew on what was coming to be gradually recognized, at least in the Western world, that slavery was "contrary to natural right," a proposition that Lord Mansfield had built upon three-quarters of a century before in *Somerset* (where he had called slavery "odious").

Justice Curtis, in his *Dred Scott* Dissenting Opinion, had invoked William Blackstone for the proposition that "the common law . . . adopts, in its full extent, the law of nations, and holds it to be a part of the law of the land." Justice Curtis also cited *Swift* v. *Tyson* (1842) in support of the proposition that "principles of universal jurisprudence" should govern, as much as possible, the decisions of State courts. The Civil War accelerated the jurisprudential development espoused by Justices McLean and Curtis, as may be seen in an account provided by the *Encyclopedia of the American Constitution*:

> The constitutional effect of the [*Dred Scott*] decision . . . proved to be slight, especially after the outbreak of the Civil War. The wartime Union government treated *Dred Scott* v. *Sandford* as though it had never been rendered. In June 1862, Congress abolished slavery in all the federal territories. Later that same year, [President] Lincoln's Attorney General issued an official opinion holding that free men of color born in the United States were citizens of the United States. The Thirteenth Amendment (1865) and the Fourteenth Amendment (1868) completed the work of overthrowing [Chief Justice] Taney's decision.

5. Abraham Lincoln in Cincinnati (1859, 1861)

I

Abraham Lincoln opened his September 17, 1859, speech in Cincinnati with the observation, "This is the first time in my life that I have appeared before an audience in so great a city as this." This appearance anticipated the critical speech he was to give the following February at the Cooper Union in New York City. These, and like, speeches were part of the astute Lincoln campaign that was to secure for him in Chicago the Republican Party nomination for the presidency in the summer of 1860.

The Cincinnati speech was one of a series given by Lincoln in Wisconsin, Indiana, and Ohio, as well as in Illinois (that is, throughout much of that area once known as the Northwest Territory). These 1859 speeches exploited, and attempted to consolidate, the national reputation that Lincoln had earned the year before because of the campaign he had run against Stephen A. Douglas in the Illinois Senatorial contest. People seem to have been interested in seeing the remarkable orator from Illinois who had handled himself well during the encounter with the formidable Douglas, the likely Democratic candidate for the Northern Democrats in the then-forthcoming presidential election.

Lincoln makes much of the fact that there are numerous Kentuckians in his Cincinnati audience. Thus, it is an audience that is partly "Southern" in its sympathies, permitting Lincoln to show how cosmopolitan the Prairie Lawyer could be. In short, he is now in the Big Leagues, having distinguished himself in the Minor Leagues.

II

Critical to Lincoln's emergence as a national figure had been his 1858 Springfield, Illinois, House Divided Speech, in which he had "declared it as [his] opinion that this government cannot 'endure permanently half slave and half free, that a house divided against itself cannot stand.'" Senator Douglas took issue with this sentiment, insisting that this was (on Lincoln's part) a declaration of war between the free and slave states. Indeed, Douglas brought up the House Divided Speech during each of his half-dozen Illinois debates with Lincoln in 1858 as well as elsewhere.

In proceeding thus, Douglas appealed to the Unionists in the North. He attempted to identify Lincoln as an abolitionist who cared more for the slaves than for the Union. Lincoln's response (he recalls in Cincinnati) was calculated to assure worried Unionists without alienating sympathetic abolitionists:

> I told him [Senator Douglas] that I had not said I did not expect any peace upon this question until Slavery was exterminated; that I had only said I expected peace when that institution was put where the public mind should [once again] rest in the belief that it was in course of ultimate extinction [as it had been] from the organization of our government, until a very recent period of time.

Lincoln's language, in his "house divided" imagery, had been Biblical. Although the House Divided Speech had helped distinguish Lincoln from other Republicans, he was careful not to appear to be too far out in front of his party. Thus, he noticed at times (as in Cincinnati) that other respectable Republicans, such as Governor William Henry Seward of New York, had (with his "Irrepressible Conflict" talk) expressed similar sentiments (although on other occasions Lincoln tried to distinguish himself from Seward).

III

Lincoln not only identified his policy with that of various other respectable Republicans. He also insisted that it was a policy that revived what the Fathers of the Country had done. That is, they, too, had so acted as to assure the public that slavery "was [indeed] in course of ultimate extinction."

Thus, Lincoln read the Constitution as exhibiting no more than a reluctant accommodation to slavery where it already existed in 1787. He noticed on various occasions the reluctance of the Framers of the Constitution even to refer to slavery explicitly. That reluctance becomes dramatically apparent to anyone who studies the Confederate Constitution of 1861, which insists (as we have seen) upon explicitly recognizing slavery again and again.

Particularly revealing for Lincoln of the Fathers' expectations with respect to slavery in the United States is (as we have also seen) what was done in the Northwest Ordinance of 1787, the statute providing for the future of what was then the largest Territory of the United States. The dramatic prohibition there of slavery suggested the way of the future, beginning with the prospect of the five free states expected to be formed out of that Territory. The complications engendered by the acquisition in 1803 of the vast Louisiana Purchase Territory, in part of which slavery was already established, seem not to have been provided for by the Fathers.

IV

There was the sense, in what Lincoln and his allies were saying, that the distinction between free states and slave states was not as clear as it might have seemed. That is, there was the sense that the entire country was somewhat enslaved by the South's "peculiar institution." The obligations imposed upon free states by the controversial Fugitive Slave Law of 1850 could remind some of this nationwide enslavement.

The entire country, somehow enslaved, could be affected by the chronic insecurity of the South. That insecurity is reflected in the panic that someone such as John Brown could provoke, however puny his immediate effect was in arousing slaves. Southerners, we again notice, *could* be fearful lest their slaves be moved to do to their masters what those masters would want to do to anyone who treated *them* as they had long treated their slaves.

Southern insecurity is exploited by Lincoln in his Cincinnati speech by his somewhat playful recognition that Stephen Douglas had not been pro-slavery enough (with his popular sovereignty position) to suit Southern sensibilities and policies, even though Douglas had gone as far as he could on behalf of slavery without losing his Illinois supporters. It was becoming evident, that is, that the division between Northern and Southern Democrats could cost Douglas the presidency. Perhaps Lincoln, with his "advice" to Southerners that Douglas was really their man, was suggesting to Northern abolitionists that they should not make demands of the Republican Party that would split it as the Democratic Party was being split.

V

Of course, Lincoln's career as Douglas's campaign manager is not without reservations. Thus, he can develop this proposition:

> Douglas' Popular Sovereignty as a principle, is simply this: If one man chooses to make a slave of another man, neither that other man or anybody else has a right to object.

This formulation was, we are told, greeted by cheers and laughter.

Lincoln indicated several times in his Cincinnati speech that he, as a so-called "Black Republican," "think[s] Slavery is wrong, morally, and politically." It is apparent that this judgment is at the heart of the critical issues that divide the country. It is a judgment developed in this way further on as Lincoln's 1859 Cincinnati speech draws to a close:

> I think that we want and must have a national policy in regard to the institution of slavery, that acknowledges and deals with that institution as being wrong. (Loud cheering) Whoever desires the prevention of the spread of slavery and the nationalization of that institution, yields all, when he yields to any policy that either recognizes slavery as being right, or as being an indifferent thing. Nothing will make you successful but setting up a policy which shall treat the thing as being wrong.

Lincoln goes on to concede, "[W]e must not interfere with the institution of slavery in the states where it exists, because the Constitution forbids it, and the general welfare does not require us to do so." He then speaks to a particularly controversial issue of the day: "We must not withhold an efficient fugitive slave law because the Constitution requires us, as I understand it, not to withhold such a law." To this concession (for which there was no applause recorded), there are added proposals that were much more popular with abolitionists (and for which there *was* applause):

> [W]e must prevent the overreaching of the institution [of slavery], because neither the Constitution nor [the] general welfare requires us to extend it. We must prevent the revival of the African slave trade and the enacting by Congress of a territorial slave code. We must prevent each of these things being done by either Congresses or courts. The people of these United States are the rightful masters of both Congresses and courts not to overthrow the Constitution, but to overthrow the men who pervert that Constitution.

VI

Lincoln argues for a return to the original intention about the long-term prospects of the phasing out of slavery in the United States. In support of his argument is his invocation of notable Southerners—George Washington, Thomas Jefferson, and James Madison. He thus attempts to recall Southerners to a nationwide heritage that regarded slavery as an inherited evil that was to be steadily curtailed until it could be completely eliminated.

He also attempts to counter those arguments on behalf of slavery which invoke the Bible. He reminds his audience that the slavery justified by the Bible "was the Slavery of the *white* man—of men without reference to color." That kind of slavery, he indicates, is hardly what the contemporary promoters of American slavery had in mind.

Essential for modern slavery (unlike that in the ancient world, which evidently depended, as we have seen, much more [but not exclusively] on prisoners of wars) was the African slave trade. The systematic kidnapping upon which that transatlantic trade depended had proved so horrendous that virtually all civilized nations (including the United States) had legislated against it. In addition, Lincoln argued, American slavery repudiated the principles of the Declaration of Independence, as they had been originally understood, before Africans began to be spoken of by some Southern apologists as a permanently degraded race.

VII

Lincoln takes issue with the proposition, attributed to Stephen Douglas, that there was a "line drawn by the Almighty across the continent, on the one side of which the soil must always be cultivated by slaves." Cincinnati was a particularly apt place for Lincoln to put the following questions to his Ohio audience:

> Pray, what was it that made you free? What kept you free? Did you not find your country free when you came to decide that Ohio would be a Free State?

He then reminds his audience:

> Kentucky is separated by this river Ohio, not a mile wide. A portion of Kentucky, by reason of the course of the Ohio, is further north than this portion of Ohio in which we now stand. Kentucky is entirely covered with slavery—Ohio is entirely free from it. What made that difference? Was it

> climate? No! A portion of Kentucky [is] further north than this portion of Ohio. Was it soil? No! There is nothing in the soil of the one more favorable to slave labor than the other. It was not climate or soil that caused one side of the line to be entirely covered with slavery and the other side free of it. What was it? Study over it.

Lincoln continues, "Tell us, if you can, in all the range of conjecture, if there be anything you can conceive of that made that difference, other than that there was no law of any sort keeping it out of Kentucky, while the Ordinance of '87 kept it out of Ohio?" He may not have considered it prudent to add that when the relevant law of a place is like that applied almost a century before by Lord Mansfield in *Somerset's* case (1772), the fugitive slave may be automatically emancipated upon crossing a border (as happened when a slave from the South entered Canada). It is evident here that morality can be legislated on a large scale.

Daniel Webster had noticed that one-third of the people of Ohio had come from the South or were descendants of those who had done so. In various ways, then, it is evident that the law with respect to slavery that one becomes accustomed to (and even considers "natural"?) may be very much a matter of chance. It may also be a matter of chance, not of nature or of divine ordination, whether one lives in a time or place that contributes to one's enslavement.

VIII

A recognition of such variables supported Lincoln's repeated observation that how one regarded slavery usually depended on where one lived. Of course, decisions as to where one did live might depend on such factors as how ordinary labor is regarded. Slavery, Lincoln observed, tends to demean labor, for it comes to be regarded in a slave state as something that slaves do.

We have seen that this had contributed (since the Founding) to the steady growth of the North, in population and hence politically, compared to the South. Immigrants, that is, tended to go where the laboring force was respected. Lincoln's own career testified to the opportunities available in a system dominated by free laborers.

He observed in a fragment of text that may have been part of his Cincinnati speech, "We know, Southern men declare that their slaves are better off than hired laborers amongst us." But domestic slavery does depend on a system of inherited inequality. It is a dramatic kind of inequality which can find much milder expression in those titles of nobility that both the United States and the states are forbidden by the Constitution of 1787 to grant.

IX

Lincoln, in his 1859 Cincinnati speech, reports, "I often hear it intimated that [Southerners] mean to divide the Union whenever a Republican, or anything like it, is elected president of the United States." He then addresses the Kentuckians in his audience (eliciting considerable applause and laughter, presumably from the Ohioans present):

> Well, then, I want to know what you are going to do with your half of [a divided United States]? . . . Are you going to build up a wall some way between your country and ours, by which that moveable property of yours [that is, slaves] can't come over here any more, to the danger of your losing it? Do you think you can better yourselves on that subject, by leaving us here under no obligation whatever to return those specimens of your moveable property that come hither? You have divided the Union because we would not do right with you as you think upon that subject; when we cease to be under obligations to do anything for you, how much better off do you think you will be?

Thus, the troubling losses Southerners are already suffering because of the fugitive slaves would become much greater, an observation that Lincoln develops in his First Inaugural Address.

He asks, "Will you [then] make war upon us and kill us all?" His remarkably tactful answer anticipates what did happen in the Civil War:

> Why, gentlemen, I think you are as gallant and as brave men as live; that you can fight as bravely in a good cause, man for man, as any other people living; that you have shown yourselves capable of this upon various occasions; but, man for man, you are not better than we are, and there are not so many of you as there are of us. You will never make much of a hand at whipping us. If we were fewer in numbers than you, I think that you could whip us; if we were equal it would likely be a drawn battle; but being inferior in numbers, you will make nothing by attempting to master us.

A critical concern of President Lincoln during the Civil War was to find tough-minded generals willing and able to take advantage of the substantial Northern superiority in numbers.

The next time Abraham Lincoln spoke in Cincinnati after his September 1859 speech was when he passed through the city, on February 12, 1861, on his way to Washington for his Inauguration. On that occasion he urged all citizens—North and South, Democrats and Republicans—to close ranks behind the duly elected president. The Jeffersonian appeal he made then, developed further in his First Inaugural Address the following month, was designed for obviously desperate times:

> I hope that, although we have some threatening National difficulties now—I hope that while these free institutions shall continue to be in the enjoyment of millions of free people of the United States, we will see repeated every four years what we now witness. In a few short years, I and every other individual man who is now living will pass away. I hope that our national difficulties will also pass away, and I hope we shall see in the streets of Cincinnati—good old Cincinnati—for centuries to come, once every four years her people give such a reception as this to the constitutionally elected President of the whole United States. I hope you shall all join in that reception, and that you shall also welcome your brethren far across the river to participate in it. We will welcome them in every State of the Union, no matter where they are from. From away South we shall extend them a cordial good will when our present differences shall have been forgotten and blown to the winds forever.

6. Stephen A. Douglas in Montgomery (November 1860)

I

Stephen A. Douglas, on the eve of the November 1860 presidential election, appeared in Montgomery, Alabama. He was aware, because of early returns from Indiana and Pennsylvania, that Abraham Lincoln would likely be elected president of the United States. He was also aware that this would be, for all too many of his fellow Democrats in the South, the signal for secession.

Douglas filled his Montgomery speech of November 2 with affirmations of a national orientation. This note is struck in his opening sentence, which begins with "Fellow citizens of Alabama" and closes with "our common country." He says at the outset of his speech:

> The Republic is now involved in darkness, and surrounded with those elements of discord which inspire the patriot's heart with dread. I sincerely cherish the hope that the light of reason and patriotism will enter the hearts of our countrymen, and guide their action in such direction as will save the Republic from this threatened disaster. I believe that if we are faithful to the Constitution, as our fathers made it, there is no grievance of which any portion of our people complain, but what can be remedied under the Constitution and within the Union. I regard this Union as the greatest blessing ever conferred upon a free people. I know but one mode by which this Union can be preserved, and that is by maintaining inviolate every provision of the Constitution. Every right secured by that instrument, every obligation imposed by it must be protected and performed in good faith.

It is evident, both from this speech and from the vigorous schedule that Douglas would maintain in the coming months, that the Senator was desperate in his concerns about the future of the Republic. His exhausting schedule, which continued into the opening months of the Civil War, may have contributed to the condition that made him susceptible to a fatal typhoid infection in June 1861. It was obvious that he, like many other Northerners, cared more about the preservation of the Union than about the abolition of slavery.

II

It is appropriate that we should be particularly interested in a speech given in the city where (in the coming months) a constitution would be drafted for the Confederate States of America. We have seen that Douglas insisted, at the outset of this speech, "Every right secured by [the Constitution], every obligation imposed by it must be protected and performed in good faith." The obligation he was most concerned about, on the eve of Lincoln's likely victory, was that of respecting the outcome of a fairly conducted presidential election.

But Douglas, in order to secure the cooperation here of his Alabama audience, had to remind them of his respect for other obligations imposed by the Constitution, obligations dear to the heart of Southerners. These were obligations with respect both to the return of fugitive slaves and to the eligibility of slaveholders for a role in the Territories of the United States. He displays himself as having been as firm here for Southern interests as any Northern politician could be in his circumstances.

Again and again, he condemns Northern abolitionists as irresponsible, if not even as traitors. The more he says against them, the better qualified he seems to be to condemn Southern fire-eaters as irresponsible as well. And, he can argue, if the secessionist fire-eaters do *not* get their way, the forthcoming Lincoln administration would be prevented by Congress from disregarding Southern rights with respect to slavery.

III

However important the fugitive slave issue was, it was apparent that the Territorial issue was far more important. What was done with the Territories, we have noticed, would determine by whom the United States would be governed in the coming decades. Critical here, we have also noticed, was the identification of the Republican Party as vigorously "Free Soil."

Douglas did not have to spell out for Southerners what would happen to the balance of power (between North and South) in Washington if slavery was to be excluded from all future states admitted to the Union. The continuing population shift in favor of the North was already evident in the ascendancy of the Republican Party with respect to both the presidency and the House of Representatives. The Territorial policy that was followed would determine, in turn, who controlled the Senate.

Much is made by Douglas, in his 1860 Montgomery speech, of respect for the courts. The 1857 *Dred Scott* decision had been very much relied upon by Southerners eager to shape Territorial policy in accordance with what they considered their long-term interests. But if the Senate, along with the presidency, came to be controlled by Northerners, then the United States Supreme Court could not (as new justices were appointed and confirmed) continue to be relied upon with respect to supposed Southern slavery interests.

IV

Much of Douglas's speech is designed to remind Southerners of how respectful *he* had been of their interests during his service in Congress. He indicates again and again that he had gone as far as he could, on behalf of slavery interests, without losing the support he needed in his Northern constituency (including, of course, Illinois). He must have wondered at times whether Southerners appreciated the political risks he had taken on their behalf.

The secession that he dreaded had been anticipated by what had happened that year to his presidential ambitions. That is, part of the Democratic Party that he had relied upon had seceded from its Douglas wing. It was this that made it highly likely that the Lincoln Republicans would prevail in the impending presidential election.

The political problems faced by Douglas are suggested by the entry about him in the *Encyclopedia of the American Constitution*:

> Throughout his career Douglas attempted to finesse the issue of slavery in the territories while supporting territorial acquisitions and western settlement. . . . The key to [his] program was *popular sovereignty*, which would allow settlers to decide the slavery issue for themselves, and thus not require Congress and the national Democratic Party to take a position on slavery in any particular territory.

But, it turned out, Douglas had to contend with a tacit alliance between abolitionists and pro-slavery advocates, with both factions agreeing that one should not remain as neutral on the slavery issue as Douglas attempted to be. "By 1858," the *Encyclopedia* recalls, "Douglas discovered he could not satisfy the voters at home [in Illinois] and remain a viable Presidential candidate in the South."

V

There can be found, at the heart of Douglas's Montgomery speech, his account of that split in the Democratic party which had doomed his campaign for the presidency. He had had to take issue with such Southerners as Jefferson Davis. Critical to the Douglas position was an insistence that the Union "could only be preserved on the basis of non-intervention by Congress with slavery in the States or in the Territories."

Douglas takes comfort from the fact that his Congressional "non-intervention" policy had been vigorously attacked both in the North and in the South:

> It is funny to hear these Southern and Northern interventionists talk on this question. The Abolitionists of the North say that if you allow the people to decide the question they will be sure to adopt slavery everywhere in the Territories, and the Southern interventionists say that if you allow the people to decide it they will be sure to abolish and prohibit slavery everywhere in the Territories.

Douglas did not seem to recognize, however, that there were involved here fundamental moral issues that moved both abolitionists and slaveholders. His approach must have seemed unnatural to the partisans on either side of this great controversy.

Douglas did attempt, however, to ground himself in nature. This he did by repeated variations upon this argument:

> [The] question of slavery is one of political economy depending upon the laws of climate, production and self-interest. You cannot compel slavery to exist in a cold, Northern latitude any more than by an act of Congress you can make cotton grow upon the tops of the Rocky Mountains. Whenever you make up your minds to maintain slavery in those cold Northern regions, where the people do not want it and will not have it, you must first get an act of Congress compelling cotton, rice, sugar and tobacco to grow there, and then you can have negroes.

This and like comments were greeted with laughter and applause by his Montgomery audience.

VI

Douglas, in this Montgomery speech, had already endorsed "the true Democratic doctrine as affirmed in [Party] platforms in 1848, 1852, 1856, and 1860." That doctrine was, he insisted, "the true doctrine of the Constitution, the great fundamental principle of free government the world over, [which] is that every people on earth shall be allowed to make their own laws, establish their own institutions, manage their own affairs, take care of their own negroes and mind their own business." There can be heard here echoes of the Declaration of Independence.

But, somehow or other, "every people on earth" still does not seem to include Africans; they, it seems, are not entitled to "establish their own institutions, manage their own affairs"; the most the Africans are entitled to do is to supply "negroes" to be managed by others. It is evident, here as in other speeches, that Douglas was in favor of humane treatment of slaves (as was, say, Jefferson Davis), but he refused, as during the 1858 Lincoln-Douglas Debates, to concede that Africans were to be regarded as fully human. We have seen that this meant, among other things, that they were not intended to be included in the proposition that "all Men are created equal."

In this and other ways Douglas considered his position consistent with the intentions of the Founders. Those intentions, he argued at Montgomery as elsewhere, included the expectation that slavery would be left to the states to be dealt with, that it was not a proper concern of the government of the United Slates (beyond the obligation to see that fugitive slaves could be recovered). The most that the Congress could properly do, it had already done, when it abolished (as of January 1, 1808) the importation of slaves from abroad.

VII

The Douglas insistence upon the virtual neutrality of the Founders with respect to slavery depends not only on a determined repudiation of the proclamation that "all Men are created equal." It depends as well on an evident determination to ignore the apparently reluctant deference to slavery in the Constitution. Thus, we again recall that the deference to South Carolina and Georgia seen in the slave-trade permission until 1808 even had to be protected by the assurance in Article V that that permission would not be amended out of the Constitution (that is, after South Carolina and Georgia had dared to subject themselves to the document).

It has been noticed, furthermore, how carefully Douglas, in his Montgomery speech and elsewhere, ignored the dramatic anti-slavery provision in the

Northwest Ordinance. That pre-Constitution ordinance, it should never be forgotten, was reenacted by the First Congress. Thus, the Congress took a decidedly anti-slavery position with respect to what was then the major Territory of the United States.

Abraham Lincoln, in his 1859 speech in Cincinnati, had reminded his Ohio audience that they chanced to have the same geographical conditions as the Kentuckians across the Ohio River—and yet they had no slavery. This was, he reminded them, only because of the Northwest Ordinance that the government of the United States had enacted and enforced. And, he argued, again and again, this testified to the Founders' expectation that slavery was "in the course of ultimate extinction."

VIII

Douglas was vigorous, in Montgomery as elsewhere, in condemning the abolitionists. They had, for several decades, stirred up national controversies that threatened the continuation of the Union as established by the Fathers. It was (we have seen) the Union that seemed to matter more to Douglas than did all the other issues of the day.

His repeated attacks on abolitionists permitted him to deal severely with even more ominous elements, the fire-eaters. They were agitating for "Southern disunion." That Douglas was particularly concerned about this agitation is indicated by an editorial comment accompanying the Montgomery speech in the 1939 *Journal of Southern History*:

> Douglas went that night by boat to Selma, and after speaking there, went on to Mobile, where the evening before the election, "a large crowd cheered his plea, that Alabama had more security within than without the Union." Next day, he heard the news of the election in the [newspaper] office of . . . the Unionist Mobile *Register*.

Douglas recognized that he had, in his Montgomery speech, said harsh things about the fire-eaters who were pushing for secession. His political instincts are evident in the concluding remarks he makes:

> I do not know how to express to you the gratitude I feel for the patience and kindness with which you have listened to me. It is due to those who differ with me in opinion—and I take it for granted there are some, perhaps many in this large crowd of that class—to say, that while they may take a course which I deeply lament as destructive of our government, they know when they go to a public meeting how to conduct themselves as gentlemen. They have certainly

> done so on this occasion. While I always express my opinions with entire freedom, and without the slightest reservation or concealment, it is never my purpose to wound the sensibilities of any one, much less to say that which shall give just cause of offence. I always speak freely, boldly and unequivocally when I speak at all, but I recognize those courtesies and proprieties of life which a gentleman never forgets. I thank you all.

These remarks are said to have elicited "tremendous applause by the assembled multitude" as he retired.

IX

These gracious remarks followed upon perhaps the harshest language in this speech, after which he observes, "I believe there is a conspiracy on foot to break up the Union." This is what the fire-eaters insisted was called for if Lincoln should be elected. But, Douglas observes (not without some bitterness), "If Lincoln is elected, he owes it to [those men who split the Democratic Party], and then they tell us, after having tried to secure that result by dividing the [Democratic] Party, that if he is elected they are going to dissolve the Union."

"There is," Douglas insists, "no living man who would do more to defeat Lincoln than myself." "And," he adds, "I would have no trouble in beating him to death, but for the support given him by [those who had split the Democratic Party]." He then counsels, "If Lincoln is elected, he must be inaugurated," after which he can be legally held to account "if he attempts to violate any man's rights, or the Constitution of the country."

Further on, as Douglas prepares to close, he makes much of *country* as he had done at the outset, as he urges respect for constitutional processes: "I hold that the election of any man on earth by the American people, according to the Constitution, is no justification for breaking up this government." This is a sentiment that could be heard four months later in Lincoln's Inaugural Address. On that occasion, it is reported, Senator Douglas held the president's hat while he spoke.

~

7. The Ordinances of Secession (1860–1861)

I

The Southern Ordinances of Secession began with an enactment in South Carolina in 1860 and ended with an enactment by Tennessee in 1861. The Boatner *Civil War Dictionary* provides this roster of "Secession Sequence and Dates":

> South Carolina, 20 December 1860; Mississippi, 9 January 1861; Florida, 10 January 1861; Alabama, 11 January 1861; Georgia, 19 January 1861; Louisiana, 26 January 1861; Texas, 1 February 1861. After the fall of Fort Sumter: Virginia, 17 April 1861; Arkansas, 6 May 1861; North Carolina, 26 May 1861; and Tennessee, 8 June 1861.

Substantial factions in two other states (Missouri and Kentucky) attempted to get their states to join the eleven "seceding" states.

It can be said that it was "natural" for South Carolina to lead the secessionist movement. The influence there of John C. Calhoun (who had died in 1850) was still considerable. The Boatner *Civil War Dictionary* records this anticipation of the 1860–1861 secessionist movement:

> [Calhoun] was [James] Monroe's Secretary of War in 1817 and Vice-President of the United States 1824–32. During the protective tariff dispute in the latter year he resigned his office [of vice president] to be elected to the Senate and defend his theory of nullification, i.e., that a state has the right to declare null and void and to set aside any Federal law that violates the compact of Union

> which was voluntarily accepted by the state. That was the first hint of secession, but upon adoption of a compromise tariff the matter subsided.

The Calhoun nullification doctrine and the South Carolina secession doctrine had been anticipated by the Virginia and Kentucky Resolutions in response to the Alien and Sedition Acts of 1798. The 1860–1861 actions took the form of Ordinances of Secession by eleven states (which were reinforced by Declarations of the Causes of Secession issued by four of these states: South Carolina, Mississippi, Georgia, and Texas). The text of the ordinance "to dissolve the union between the state of South Carolina and other states united with her under the compact entitled 'The Constitution of the United States of America'" is the shortest of the eleven Ordinances of Secession in 1860–1861 (and was "Done at Charleston the twentieth day of December, in the Year of our Lord one thousand eight hundred and sixty"), reading,

> We, the People of the State of South Carolina, in convention assembled, do declare and ordain, and it is hereby declared and ordained, That the ordinance adopted by us in convention on the twenty-third day of May, in the year of our Lord one thousand seven hundred and eighty-eight, whereby the Constitution of the United States of America was ratified, and also all acts and parts of acts of the General Assembly of this State ratifying amendments of the said Constitution, are hereby repealed; and that the union now subsisting between South Carolina and other States, under the name of the "United States of America," is hereby dissolved.

II

The Ordinances of Secession of eight of the eleven states (as well as the two attempted ordinances) repeatedly speak of the Constitution of the United States as a "compact." That is, it is insisted that a contractual relation was once entered into, a contractual relation that can be dissolved if a party to it does not live up to its obligations. Such a violation, by the General Government of the Union, it alleged by one state after another.

The Constitution of 1787 is treated in these Ordinances of Secession as substantially like the Articles of Confederation. Related to this emphasis on the tentative character of the 1787–1789 association is the use, in two of the Ordinances (Virginia and Tennessee), of the term *Federal*, a term that is *not* used in the Constitution of 1787 but that is used several times in the Confederate Constitution of 1861. The United States is *not* called a *nation*, even though that designation can be appropriated for Florida in its Ordinance of Secession.

The Southern federation to be developed will not be a *nation* either. Rather, the Mississippi Ordinance of Secession announced, "[T]he people of the State of Mississippi hereby consent to form a federal union with such of the States as may have [already] seceded or may [hereafter] secede from the Union of the United States of America." It is indicated here as elsewhere, by the seceding states, that a substantial part of the Constitution of 1787 should be adapted for use in a newly fashioned compact for the new confederation.

III

We have noticed that it is argued that violations of the compact by the General Government (at the behest of various Northern states) free the seceding states from any obligation under the Constitution of 1787. Therefore, a state may (as is said in the Mississippi Ordinance of Secession) "resume all the rights, functions, and powers [that had been] conveyed to the government of the said United States." That is, it is suggested, a properly seceding state can "resume" the status of an independent state.

But how should such "resumption" be understood for more than half of the seceding states? Only four of the eleven had been states in 1776–1789, and hence (in the view of some) possibly independent of the United States. One other, Texas, had briefly been an independent state before it joined the Union in 1845.

The other six seceding states had been created as states by the Congress of the United States. What status should *they* have been understood to "resume" upon leaving the Union? That is, did most of the seceding states (created out of the Territories of the United States) risk the impiety of repudiating their parentage?

IV

Secessionism may have been years, if not even decades, in the making. But, as we have seen, it was triggered to make its decisive move by the 1860 presidential election. This kind of response, we have also seen, had been anticipated for some months before that election.

Alabama, in its Ordinance of Secession (of January 11, 1861), explained (as fourth in line) that

> the election of Abraham Lincoln and Hannibal Hamlin to the offices of president and vice-president of the United States of America, by a sectional party, avowedly hostile to the domestic institutions and to the peace and security of

> the people of the State of Alabama, preceded by many and dangerous infractions of the constitution of the United States by many of the States and people of the Northern section, is a political wrong of so insulting and menacing a character as to justify the people of the State of Alabama in the adoption of prompt and decided measures for their future peace and security.

This was two months before the new president was to be inaugurated. That is, this decision to secede did not depend on anything *done* by the new administration.

After Inauguration Day, the Arkansas convention (as ninth in line) spoke out "against the sectional party, now in power in Washington City, headed by Abraham Lincoln." By the following October, would-be secessionists in Missouri could provide a series of grievances against the seven-month-old Republican Party Administration in Washington:

> [T]he Government of the United States, in the possession and under the control of a sectional party, has wantonly violated the compact originally made between said Government and the State of Missouri, by invading with hostile armies the soil of the State, attacking and making prisoners the militia while legally assembled under the State laws, forcibly occupying the State capitol, and attempting through the instrumentality of domestic traitors to usurp the State government, seizing and destroying private property, and murdering with fiendish malignity peaceable citizens, men, women, and children, together with other acts of atrocity, indicating a deep-settled hostility toward the people of Missouri and their institutions.

The following month would-be secessionists in Kentucky complained in a similar fashion about the atrocities of the Lincoln administration which had "turned loose upon [Kentuckians] the unrestrained and raging passions of mobs and fanatics."

V

We have noticed that the January 1861 Alabama Ordinance of Secession had declared that the Republican Party (about to take power in Washington) was "avowedly hostile to the domestic institutions" of the state of Alabama. Those "domestic institutions"—that is, slavery—are explicitly referred to in other Ordinances as well. Thus, both the Texas and the Virginia secessionist conventions refer in their ordinances to "slave-holding States" that are under attack by the Republican Party.

The Alabama Convention makes it clear that it is slavery that singles out fifteen states as likely victims of the administration scheduled to be inaugurated in March 1861. This leads the Alabamans to issue this invitation:

> [A]s it is the desire and purpose of the people of Alabama to meet the slaveholding States of the South . . . in order to frame a provisional as well as a permanent Government upon the principles of the Constitution of the United States, Be it resolved by the people of Alabama in convention assembled, That the people of the States of Delaware, Maryland, Virginia, North Carolina, South Carolina, Florida, Georgia, Mississippi, Louisiana, Texas, Arkansas, Tennessee, Kentucky, and Missouri, be and are hereby invited to meet the people of the State of Alabama, by their Delegates, in Convention, on the 4th day of February, A.D., 1861, at the city of Montgomery, in the State of Alabama, for the purpose of consulting with each other as to the most effectual mode of securing concerted and harmonious action in whatever measures may be deemed most desirable for our common peace and security.

This call for the fifteen slaveholding states to meet in Montgomery can be considered equivalent to the call from Annapolis in 1786 for the Constitutional Convention that was to meet the following spring in Philadelphia.

Eleven of the fifteen designated states did eventually join the secessionist movement. Secessionists in two of them (Missouri and Kentucky) were stymied; and those in another two (Delaware and Maryland) came quite early under Union military domination and hence were obliged to remain "loyal." Did the Alabama draftsmen sense that four of the fifteen slaveholding states would be hardest to secure and therefore exposed them to special view (to be "worked on"), listing two of them (Delaware and Maryland) at the beginning of this enumeration and two of them (Kentucky and Missouri) at the end?

VI

We have noticed that only four of the eleven states attempting to secede had been states when the Constitution of 1787 was ratified. We have also noticed that only two of these four acted before the Inauguration of Abraham Lincoln. It should not be surprising that those two were South Carolina and Georgia.

We again recall that these were, after all, the states that had, in the 1787 Constitutional Convention, most dramatically identified themselves with slavery interests. For it had been these two states that evidently threatened, in 1787, to withhold their ratifications of the proposed Constitution if the international slave trade could not be continued by them for twenty years. Virginians, such as James Madison, were evidently distressed by the accommodation that "had" to be made in this way to South Carolina and Georgia.

We have noticed as well that the Southern secessionists were careful *not* to refer to the United States as a *nation*. This care had evidently become standard among Southerners who were sensitive to the vocabulary they used. Such sensitivity may be seen as well in the Lincoln emphasis at Gettysburg upon the United States as a *nation*—and, indeed, a "nation" which had been "brought forth" in 1776.

VII

More should be said, when the four Declarations of the Causes of Secession are examined in my next chapter, about the use in 1860–1861 of terminology and related matters. The Ordinances themselves do refer to causes as well. We have noticed the critical bond among secessionists provided by their dependence upon slavery.

We should once again notice that the states that insisted upon slavery were themselves in critical respects enslaved. And yet they could see themselves as particularly dedicated to the Cause of Liberty, including the liberty (emphatically insisted upon) to deny that "all Men are created equal." This, too, is dramatically contradicted by Lincoln at Gettysburg.

Thus, personal enslavement in the South extended far beyond those who chanced to be of African descent, as is suggested by statistics provided by the Boatner *Civil War Dictionary*:

> By 1861 one third of the 12,000,000 population of the South were Negro slaves who were owned by but 384,000 whites, and only about 1800 of this number owned 100 or more.

That is, must not many whites in the South have felt themselves trapped in and exploited by a system evidently geared to keep so many potentially dangerous slaves in check, slaves who were owned (it is said) by only one-twentieth of the whites? Did the white majority ever wonder what their long-term interests truly were, however much satisfaction many of them may have derived from the recognition that at least they were better off than the slaves among them?

VIII

All this is not to deny that the pro-slavery interests in Southern states could muster broad support at the polls. Three of the eleven Ordinances of Secession were put to statewide votes. They were ratified decisively by referenda in those states (46,153 to 14,747, in Texas, 132,201 to 37,481, in Virginia, and 104,471 to 47,183, in Tennessee).

One can be reminded of the enthusiasm with which various peoples in Europe went to war in 1914, a war which proved so disastrous for Western civilization—so disastrous that it can even be wondered about that war whether anyone "in charge" knew what he was doing. A similar question can be asked about many of the leaders, South and North, during the Civil War. At the root of the problem of the rationality of Southern leaders was the question of whether slavery was morally defensible as a permanent institution.

The effort by the slave-owning minority in a state to impose its will not only on slaves but also on the population at large is suggested by the group of Kentuckians styling itself as a "Convention of the People of Kentucky." This group condemned the unconstitutional edicts of "a factious majority" of the state legislature. That Kentucky legislative *majority* is vigorously condemned (on November 20, 1861) for its determination not to allow the state to secede from the Union.

IX

The group styling itself as a "Convention of the People of Kentucky" said that it spoke for the people at large of the state. It condemned the legislative majority for having "violated their most solemn pledges made before the election, and deceived and betrayed the people." It can be seen, again and again, that would-be secessionists (and not only in Kentucky) presented themselves as champions of constitutionalism, liberty, and a sense of humanity.

The complaints against "the majority of the Legislature of Kentucky" include the objections that they have "invited into the state the organized armies of Lincoln, have abdicated the Government [of the state] in favor of a military despotism which they have placed around themselves, but cannot control, . . . and have thrown upon [the] people and the state the horrors and ravages of war, instead of attempting to preserve the peace." Furthermore, the legislative majority had "voted men and money for the war waged by the North for the destruction of [the] constitutional rights [of Kentuckians].” Such destruction included the suspension of the writ of *habeas corpus*, by the Union government, “without an effort [by the Kentucky legislature] for its preservation.”

Thus, the Kentucky secessionists offer themselves as vigilant in the “cause for civil liberty and constitutional governments against a sectional [that is, a Northern] majority against the people and institutions of fifteen independent states of the old Federal Union.” The Lincoln administration is condemned for having “substituted for the highest forms of natural liberty and constitutional government a central despotism founded upon the ignorant prejudices of Northern society.” It can be somehow reassuring, for a long-term redemption of the American Republic, to observe that even those who sought to perpetuate the institution of chattel slavery were repeatedly obliged to speak the language of constitutional liberties.

8. The Declarations of Causes Issued by Seceding States (1860–1861)

I

If one has any doubt about the slavery issue being decisive for the outbreak of the Civil War, it should be removed upon recalling the precipitating cause of the secessionists' moves in 1860–1861. That cause was, of course, the election to the presidency of a "Free Soil" Northerner. Seven of the eleven seceding states had so declared themselves before Abraham Lincoln could be inaugurated.

All eleven of these states (usually identifying themselves as "in Convention assembled") enacted the Ordinances of Secession that we have examined. Four of these states also promulgated Declarations of the Causes of Secession. The total length of these four Declarations was twice that of the total length of the eleven Ordinances.

The South Carolina Declaration (of December 24, 1860), the first of four such declarations, explains that that state had anticipated these revolutionary developments a decade earlier:

> The People of the State of South Carolina, in Convention assembled, on the 26th day of April, A.D., 1852, declared that the frequent violations of the Constitution of the United States, by the Federal Government, and its encroachments upon the reserved rights of the States, fully justified this State in their withdrawing from the Federal Union; but in deference to the opinions and wishes of the other slave-holding States, she forbore, at that time, to exercise this right. Since that time, these encroachments have continued to increase, and further forbearance ceases to be a virtue.

It is evident, at the outset of these historic movements of 1860–1861, that those considered most sympathetic to secession were the "slave-holding States." The relevant states could also be identified with respect to the "Mason and Dixon Line," which has been described in this way by the Boatner *Civil War Dictionary*:

> Symbolic border between the North and South that originated as a line surveyed in 1763 and 1767 to settle boundary differences between the Penn family of Pennsylvania and the Calverts of Maryland. The line goes along the parallel 39 degrees, 42 minutes, 23.6 seconds. In the antebellum era it was understood to be the dividing line between slave and free territory and was the boundary between Pennsylvania to the north and Delaware, Maryland and West[ern] Virginia to the south.

II

The 1860 presidential election confirmed, for Southern states, the steady "encroachments upon the reserved rights of the States." For the first time, it was said, a "sectional" party had prevailed in such an election. It was generally known that what made that party distinctive was, as we have seen, its clearly proclaimed determination that there should be no new slave states created out of the Territories of the United States.

This kind of policy had been troubling enough, for some in the South, when it led to the permanent exclusion of slavery in 1787 from the Northwest Territory by the Articles of Confederation Congress. It cannot be too often recalled that that exclusion, with respect to what was then the principal Territory of the United States, was confirmed in 1789 by the First Congress under the Constitution of 1787. A further exclusion was dictated, in the Missouri Compromise of 1820, for that part of the vast Louisiana Purchase Territory (aside from Missouri itself) which lies north of 36 degrees, 30 minutes latitude.

Such limitations, especially if they should be applied as well to the territories acquired because of the Mexican War, very much troubled some in the South, especially when reinforced by growing abolitionist sentiments in the North. It could be anticipated, that is, that "the slave-holding States" would become vulnerable as such. A sobering indication of what was to be expected could be seen by some in the growing difficulty Southerners were experiencing in recovering their fugitive slaves (even after the enactment of the troubling Fugitive Slave Law of 1850).

III

South Carolina had declared herself seceded in its Ordinance of December 20, 1860. Four days later, on Christmas Eve, there was issued (by the South Carolina Convention) a "Declaration of the Immediate Causes Which Induce and Justify the Secession of South Carolina from the Federal Union" (a document from which we have already quoted the opening paragraph). The argument then developed includes the insistence that South Carolina had been (before its ratification of the Constitution of 1787) a sovereign state, so much so that it can be several times indicated that South Carolina had once been one of the "nations" of the world, something that is never said about the federation organized pursuant to the "compact" known as the Constitution of the United States.

The South Carolina Declaration, as the first of the four seceding states' Declarations of Causes of 1860–1861, is distinctive in the number of uses it makes of the *language* of the Declaration of Independence. Among such uses is an adapted quotation from the 1776 document seen in the insistence that "whenever any form of Government becomes destructive of the ends for which it was established, it is the right of the people to alter or abolish it, and to institute a new Government." Conspicuously absent from this and the other state Declarations of Causes of Secession of 1860–1861 is, of course, any recollection of the insistence in the Declaration of Independence that "all Men are created equal."

The implications of a compact theory of the Constitution are suggested in this passage from the South Carolina Declaration of Causes (emphases added):

> In 1787, Deputies were appointed by the States to revise the Articles of Confederation, and on the 17th September, 1787, these Deputies recommended, for the adoption of the States, the *Articles of Union*, known as the Constitution of the United States. The parties to whom this Constitution was submitted, were the *several Sovereign States*; they were to agree or disagree, and when nine of them agreed *the Compact* was to take effect among those concurring, and the General Government, as the *common agent*, was then to be invested with their authority. If only nine of the thirteen States had concurred, the other four would have remained as they then were—*Separate, Sovereign States*, independent of any of the provisions of the Constitution. In fact, two of the States did not accede to the Constitution until long after it had gone into operation among the other eleven; and during that interval, *they each exercised the functions of an Independent Nation.*

In short, for a few years Rhode Island was an "Independent Nation," something that the United States never had been, according to the secessionists. Abraham Lincoln, on the other hand, several times insisted that the Union was older than the states, which *could* mean, among other things (I venture to suggest), that Rhode Island and North Carolina could have been considered virtually Territories of the United States once the Constitution was ratified and set into motion without them, and certainly not as "Independent Nation[s]."

IV

The second state to adopt an Ordinance of Secession was Mississippi, three weeks after South Carolina. It, too, issued "A Declaration of the Immediate Causes which Induce[d] and Justif[ied]" secession. Particularly striking is the fact that virtually all of the Mississippi Declaration (in the opening weeks of the Great Rebellion) is devoted to a condemnation of various Northern assaults upon the institution of slavery.

The list of "the prominent reasons which [had] induced" the course followed by Mississippi begins thus:

> Our position is thoroughly identified with the institution of slavery—the greatest material interest in the world. Its labor supplies the products which constitute by far the largest and most important portions of commerce of the earth. These products are peculiar to the climate verging on the tropical regions, and by an imperious law of nature, none but the black race can bear exposure to the tropical sun. These products have become necessities of the world, and a blow at slavery is a blow at commerce and civilization. That blow has long been aimed at the institution, and was at the point of reaching its consummation. There was no choice left us but submission to the mandates of abolition, or a dissolution of the Union, whose principles had been subverted to work out our ruin.

The slaveholding states are depicted here as benefactors of "commerce and civilization" worldwide. And it is indicated in several ways that "the black race," too, is benefited by the institution of so useful a system of slavery.

The Mississippi Declaration includes the complaint that "[t]he hostility to this institution [of slavery] commenced before the adoption of the Constitution, and was manifested in the well-known Ordinance of 1787, in regard to the Northwestern Territory." It also seems to be complained that the international slave trade had been curtailed by the government of the United States. Northern hostility to the institution of slavery threatens Southern life in various ways:

It has invaded a State [Virginia], and invested with the honors of martyrdom the wretch [John Brown] whose purpose was to apply flames to our dwellings, and the weapons of destruction to our lives. . . . Utter subjugation awaits us in the Union, if we should consent longer to remain in it. It is not a matter of choice, but of necessity. We must either submit to degradation, and to the loss of property worth four billions of money, or we must secede from the Union, framed by our fathers, to secure this as other species of property. For far less cause than this, our fathers separated from the Crown of England.

V

It is several times indicated in the four Declarations of Causes of 1860–1861 that the right of revolution was being invoked by the seceding states, just as it had been invoked against the Crown of England in 1776. It is also several times indicated that slave uprisings were promoted by Northern abolitionists. Such interference with the "social system" of the South is exhibited by those who are determined to "excite and inflame with prejudice" "the whole popular mind of the North."

The nefarious measures taken against the "social system" of the South are described in some detail in the four Declarations of Causes. But there is a profound silence (here as elsewhere) about how the slaves, vital to that "social system," were acquired in the first place. That is, the systematic, centuries-long ravaging of the coast of Africa is never mentioned.

To what extent were the horrific measures employed in enslaving and transporting Africans acquiesced in because of the memories about how the native populations of the Western Hemisphere had themselves been steadily displaced (and pushed out of sight) since the sixteenth century by European immigrants? However that may have been, the descendants of kidnapped Africans remained very much in view—and hence remained a challenge to people nurtured by doctrines of liberty and equality. It could be particularly troubling, of course, when slaves even presumed to invoke the principles at the core of the people nourished by the Declaration of Independence and guided by the Constitution of the United States.

VI

The next Declaration of Causes to be surveyed here is that issued by Georgia on January 29, 1861. This appears the most scholarly of the four Declarations of Causes. Perhaps it reflects the influence of the most eminent Georgian of his day, Alexander H. Stephens, an anti-secession politician that Abraham Lincoln had respected ever since their two years together (decades earlier) in the House of Representatives.

Considerable space is devoted in this Declaration to "[t]he party of Lincoln, called the Republican party." It is reported that "[t]he prohibition of slavery in the Territories is the cardinal principle of this organization." This Declaration concludes with the explanation, "To avoid [the many] evils [enumerated,] we resume the powers which our fathers delegated to the Government of the United States, and henceforth will seek new safeguards for our liberty, equality, security, and tranquility."

It is again and again explained in the four Declarations of Causes of 1860–1861 that the Southern states must stand up for their liberty and equality, but it is never recognized of course that the Africans held as slaves should have these laudable objectives recognized for them as well. Thus, it is complained that the Fugitive Slave Clause "stands to-day a dead letter for all practicable purposes in every non-slaveholding State in the Union," so much so that "the unfortunate claimant [that is, the master of a fugitive slave] is everywhere met with fraud, with force, and with legislative enactments to elude, to resist, and defeat him." The treatment of "the unfortunate claimant" is lamented (he may even be "murdered with impunity" when he goes looking for his fugitive slave)—but there is never any serious concern expressed about the unfortunate fugitive who had considered himself so oppressed by slavery that he dared to risk the perils and punishment of a flight from his subjugation (a flight that would have been made much easier and safer for the fugitive, by the way, if the "Canadian" border had been moved south, in effect, to the Mason and Dixon Line, which it might well have been if the secession had been successful).

VII

It is evident *to us* that the champions of the North American slavery system simply did not hear what they said in these 1860–1861 Declarations. This may be seen, again and again, in the Texas Declaration of Causes, which includes such passages as this:

> [Abolition organizations] have for years past encouraged and sustained lawless organizations to steal our slaves and prevent their recapture, and have repeatedly murdered Southern citizens while lawfully seeking their rendition. They have invaded Southern soil and murdered unoffending citizens.

It would not take much adjustment to make such passages applicable to what had happened to "unoffending citizens" in one African community after another in order to supply "the slave-holding States" the system of slavery they considered themselves entitled not only to maintain but also to extend.

The Texas Declaration makes more than the others do of the propriety, if not even the necessity, of "the servitude of the African to the white race." Indeed, the Declaration of Independence seems to be deliberately challenged in this passage by the Texans:

> In all the non-slaveholding States, in violation of that good faith and comity which should exist between entirely distinct nations, the people have formed themselves into a great sectional party, now strong enough in numbers to control the affairs of each of those States, based upon an unnatural feeling of hostility to these Southern States and their beneficent and patriarchal system of African slavery, proclaiming the debasing doctrine of equality of men, irrespective of race or color—a doctrine at war with nature, in opposition to the experience of mankind, and in violation of the plainest revelations of Divine Law.

All this is reinforced by such sentiments as these (drawing, in effect, on the *Dred Scott* case [1857]):

> We hold as undeniable truths that the governments of the various States, and of the confederacy itself [the United States], were established exclusively by the white race, for themselves and their posterity, that the African race had no agency in their establishment; that they were rightfully held and regarded as an inferior and dependent race, and in that condition only could their existence in this country be rendered beneficial or tolerable. [We hold that] in this free government *all white men are and of right ought to be entitled to equal civil and political rights*; that the servitude of the African race, as existing in these States, is mutually beneficial to both bond and free, and is abundantly authorized and justified by the experience of mankind, and the revealed will of the Almighty Creator, as recognized by all Christian nations, while the destruction of the existing relations between the two races, as advocated by our sectional enemies, would bring inevitable calamities upon both and desolation upon the fifteen slave-holding states.

Texas was the only member of the emerging Confederacy which chanced ever to have had a "separate national existence," an existence which she "abandoned" with the understanding that she was to be "received as a commonwealth holding, maintaining and protecting the institution known as negro slavery—the servitude of the African to the white race, within her limits—a relation that had existed from the first settlement by the white race, and which her people intended should exist in all future time." Texas also chanced to be the only one of the seceding states that was moved to describe its vulnerability in this fashion:

> The Federal Government, while but partially under the control of these our unnatural and sectional enemies, has for years almost entirely failed to protect the lives and property of the people of Texas against the Indian savages on our border, and more recently against the murderous forays of banditti from the neighboring territory of Mexico; and when our State government has expended large amounts for such purpose, the Federal Government has refused reimbursement therefor, thus rendering our condition more insecure and harassing than it was during the existence of the Republic of Texas.

This suggests that Texas may also have been the only one of the seceding states able to appreciate the vulnerability of those African communities across the Atlantic that had been systematically and ruthlessly raided by "banditti" to supply the slave markets of the New World.

VIII

We have noticed, again and again, the inability of Southerners to recognize how the serious grievances they sincerely complained of in 1860–1861 often applied, usually with much greater force, to the grievances implicit in the histories of the lives of their slaves. Particularly striking, as indicative of their own sense of vulnerability, is how disturbed Southerners could become because of the raid of a dozen men at Harpers Ferry, Virginia, in 1859. What is it about our own sense of vulnerability, we may wonder, that has led us in turn to be as disturbed as we have been for a decade because of the raids of two dozen men in New York City and Washington in September 2001?

Monstrous as the September 11th attacks were, it is useful, if one is to understand them, to recognize the long-standing grievances "expressed" in this hateful fashion. How such grievances can fester is suggested by the recollections, in the Georgia Declaration of Causes, of the way that "the material prosperity of the North" had been developed at the expense of the South. There can be heard here the echoes of the fierce tariff debates in the United States Senate decades before the Civil War.

In what ways do our security-minded responses to the September 11th attacks resemble the self-defeating measures that Southerners relied upon in defense of what they considered their vital institutions? For example, what would be comparable today, in our efforts to secure ourselves, to the compensated gradual emancipation of slaves that Southern leaders evidently were not willing to consider seriously, even during a ruinous Civil War? A sense of proportion is essential in these calculations, something I suggested in a public address on September 12, 2001, entitled, "A Second Pearl Harbor? Let's Be Serious."

IX

Of the four 1860–1861 Declarations of the Causes of Secession that we have been examining, only one of them uses what may be called an old-fashioned mode of dating. That is the Texas Declaration, which concludes, "Adopted in Convention on the 2nd day of Feb[ruary], in the year of our Lord one thousand eight hundred and sixty-one and of the independence of Texas the twenty-fifth." One can be reminded here of that revealing mode of dating that had been used by the more illustrious predecessors of the drafts-men who had penned these four Declarations.

The Constitution of 1787, for example, was dated in this fashion: "[D]one in Convention by the Unanimous Consent of the states present the Seventeenth Day of September in the Year of our Lord one thousand seven hundred and Eighty-seven and of the Independence of the United States of America the Twelfth." This had been preceded by the dating of the Articles of Confederation: "Done at Philadelphia in the state of Pennsylvania the ninth day of July, in the Year of our Lord one Thousand seven Hundred and Seventy-eight, and in the third year of the independence of America." President Lincoln was in the spirit of these *identifications* of the country with that use at Gettysburg of "four score and seven years" which also took the founding of the United States back to 1776 and the Declaration of Independence.

We have seen that the Declarations of the Causes of Southern Secession, as well as their Ordinances of Secession and related statements, made much of "compacts" in the effort to deny that a country or nation had somehow taken root in 1776. In order to develop this denial these 1860–1861 polemicists had to ignore what had been said and meant in the Articles of Confederation about a "perpetual Union" and in the Constitution of 1787 about "a more perfect Union." It can be wondered, in short, to whom there should have been applied those words, in the Georgia Declaration of Causes, which referred to "[t]he faithless conduct of our adversaries."

9. The Confederate Constitution (1861)

I

A comparison of the Confederate Constitution of 1861 with the United States Constitution of 1787 (see Appendixes C, D, and E of this volume) can suggest critical differences between two ways of life. Among these differences are those which may be seen in how much more the power and authority of the states are recognized in the Confederate Constitution. This is dramatized by the provision therein which assigns to the states exclusive control of the process for amending the Confederate Constitution.

Even more dramatic, of course, is how much more is done with slavery in the Confederate Constitution. This includes a determination, on the part of its framers, to speak explicitly and frequently of slavery, quite unlike the much more reticent framers of the Constitution of 1787 in this respect. It is evident, in the 1861 instrument, that it was slavery, not (as in the 1780s) any Union, which was regarded as "perpetual."

What seems to be assumed about the conditions that are best for both maintaining and using the system referred to as "negro slavery"? And, conversely, what political/social system is likely to be encouraged and maintained when such slavery is depended upon? The relations here between social arrangements and slave institutions may have been such that only cataclysmic events could separate them, so much had the Southern way of life come (by 1860) both to promote and to depend upon slavery.

II

Various national controversies of the preceding half-century were addressed by the framers of the 1861 constitution. Principal among those, of course, were slavery-related issues. The *Dred Scott* case debate had been the most recent of the major issues (prior to the election of a Republican president) that had emerged to divide the country.

The 1861 Confederate Constitution takes the *Dred Scott* ruling even further than the United States Supreme Court had done in 1857. Thus, not only may slaves be taken into any territory of the Confederacy, but they may be taken as well into any state of the Confederacy, no matter how the people of that state may eventually come to feel about slavery. The Fugitive Slave Clause is reinforced, among the states of the Confederacy, however difficult it may thereafter prove to be to recover slaves who manage to cross over into what is left of the United States.

The tariff-related controversies of the preceding decades are also resolved, with the protection and encouragement of local industry placed beyond the authority of the government of the Confederacy. Even the postal system is expected to be self-sustaining. There is, in short, a repudiation of the dedication to sustained progress in industry and trade (or to "Commerce") that had been promoted for decades by Northern leaders such as Alexander Hamilton.

III

Language distinctly different from that used in the Constitution of 1787 reflects how the framers of the Confederate Constitution generally regarded government and social policy. An emphasis is placed in 1861 upon the local as both authoritative and healthier. The frequent uses of "slave" and "slavery" do reveal the frankness that the secessionists believed their circumstances and expectations both permitted and called for.

Less provocative are the uses of "federal," a term never used in the Constitution of 1787. This shift is heralded by what is done in the 1861 Preamble, with its "We the People of the Confederate States, each state acting in its sovereign and independent character." Thereafter it is indicated (in the Preamble) that "a permanent federal government" is anticipated.

The authority of the states is recognized and reinforced again and again, even in the ways that the Ninth and Tenth Amendments are modified in 1861. The power of localities is thereby sustained and protected against any tendencies toward domination that the officers of the Confederate government might improperly have. At the same time, an anticipated dominion over slaves is reinforced again and again, even as participation in the international slave trade is explicitly forbidden (whatever may have been contemplated about the extension of slavery into territory acquired thereafter by the Confederates in Cuba and Mexico).

IV

We have seen that it seems to have been widely believed, at least in the South, that the climate of that region required African labor for the agriculture that was most profitable. It seems also to have been believed, but not as widely, that slave labor could not be efficiently used for industrial development. Certainly, it could seem, industry and trade were considered unlikely to prosper where slaves made up much of the laboring class.

The steady industrial development in the North depended on a steady stream of immigrants from Europe. Such people (we have noticed) were not likely, as laborers, to prefer those places where routine manual labor was regarded as what slaves did. The tendency of European immigrants to prefer places where slavery was not permitted meant (we have also noticed) that the North would become ever more powerful, both economically and politically, compared to the South.

During the century when the transatlantic slave trade "prospered," Yankees were prominent in the racket of kidnapping, transporting, and selling African slaves. Even so, the principles of a commercial society seem to have been such that *liberty* meant more than *property*. This is reflected in the fact that even though much of the international slave trade was then probably being carried on in English ships, Lord Mansfield could say what he did, in *Somerset* v. *Stewart* (1772), about the incompatibility (at least in England) between the official recognition of *slavery* and a general *liberty*.

V

Slavery, it can seem, was considered particularly suited for a predominantly agricultural life, especially in warm climates. A different opinion may have prevailed when, as in European antiquity, slaves were much more apt to be prisoners of war, and hence much like their masters from the outset of their captivity. The Southern reliance on Africans for much of their labor meant that their slaves, at least in the founding generations, *could* appear as almost another species (as the Helots may have appeared to the Spartans).

This may have encouraged the tendency to exalt an aristocratic way of life grounded in the family, with recognized blood lines becoming ever more critical. There developed in the South an "aristocratic" sense of honor, something which could even have its devotees look down on trade and moneymaking. Such a sense of honor was not restricted to the more exalted socially, but rather could be appreciated and imitated by even those Southerners (the large majority of them) who did not rely directly on slaves.

This seems to have meant that the South *could* become rather feudal in character, even if not in law. This is reflected in the fact that sexual relations across racial lines could be developed by white males, not by white females bound by the dictates of honor. The feudal character of Southern life may be reflected as well in the greater proneness there to everyday violence, something evident (as noticed in the preface to this volume) in where official executions tend to prevail to this day in the United States.

VI

Slavery, as it developed in the United States, seems to have promoted an agricultural, and hence a rural, way of life. Industry and trade could come to be looked down upon. Southern sensibilities tended to be more genteel, at least in reputation, than those in the North.

One result of all this, with serious political consequences, was that the Southern population could be expected to be ever smaller than that of the North. The disparagement of trade meant, among other things, that industrial development, including with respect to modes of transportation, was less likely in the South. This also meant that social mobility was more restricted there than in the North.

Particularly threatening, of course, was any physical (as well as social) mobility of slaves. Southerners had come to believe that Northerners simply did not want to live up to their legal obligations to return fugitive slaves, with abolitionist publications (such as *Uncle Tom's Cabin*) being condemned for subverting long-standing constitutional relations. The extreme of such disturbances could be seen (perhaps even eagerly seen) in the futile but much-publicized attempt by John Brown in 1859 to promote a general uprising by slaves.

VII

A further indication of fundamental differences between North and South by the time of the Civil War is the invocation, in the Preamble of the Confederate Constitution, of "the favor and guidance of Almighty God." This is in marked contrast to the obviously secular spirit of the

Constitution of 1787. It might even be wondered whether systematic slaveholding was apt to promote some form of piety, especially when Biblical authority had to be relied upon as much as it was to justify the subjugation of specified peoples.

It may have been partly a matter of chance, however, how religion came to be used in pre–Civil War America. After all, many of the abolitionists considered slavery profoundly anti-Christian. Their sentiments could be reinforced by the authority of the proclamation that "all Men are created equal."

How dependent the influence of religion could be on chance is suggested, for example, by the considerable (even shocking) extent to which the Aztecs once came to rely on human sacrifice, something they evidently long considered necessary to insure divine favor, if not the very continuance of the world. The more conscientious Southerners, determined to perpetuate the system of slavery they had happened to inherit, could learn to speak (as John C. Calhoun and his disciples did) about "the positive good" of African slavery. All this was a far cry from the remarkable campaign against slavery developed, in the eighteenth century, by pious abolitionists such as John Woolman.

VIII

We have noticed that the framers of the Confederate Constitution were not squeamish about the use of "slaves" and "slavery." Even so, states could be referred to in that constitution as "slaveholding States," not as "Slave States." Particularly troubling for them, of course, would have been the suggestion that only the other states of the original Union were "Free States."

Southerners tended to insist that their way of life alone was truly free. That is, only such a way respected the naturally ordained, if not also the divinely required, relations between Caucasians and Africans, at least in the Western Hemisphere. These were relations that honor required that conscientious Southerners insist upon as called for by a long-established way of life.

Perhaps, it can be said, one distinctly Southern contribution to the Declaration of Independence had been the invocation, at its very end, of "sacred Honor." This, it can be argued, was not the language of businessmen, but rather of a tradition-bound community, part of which had accommodated itself to (among other things) the benefits and liabilities of slavery. Again and again, it can seem, there was indeed a reciprocal relation (for better and for worse) between slavery and distinctively Southern constitutional principles.

IX

Thus, it may have seemed to Southern leaders that their way of life absolutely required a system of chattel slavery. It may not have been as apparent to most of them that a system of slavery, at least in the modern world, may have required (or, at least, may have made more likely) a particular way of life. This meant (we have several times been obliged to notice) that Southerners had been enslaved, in turn, by the slaves they "controlled."

We have also noticed that Southerners had considered it necessary, in order to protect both slavery and their way of life, to make critical changes in 1861 to the Constitution of 1787. The more that changes were made by them on behalf of a slavery-oriented society, the more they conceded, in effect, that the 1787 Constitution had been anti-slavery in its ultimate orientation. We have seen again and again that this had been anticipated, even before the Constitutional Convention proposed its Constitution, by the decisive anti-slavery stance proclaimed in the Northwest Ordinance of 1787.

It might even be suspected, in short, that the secessionists of 1860–1861 did not truly understand what they were doing. Particularly sobering, we have also noticed, is the extent to which they themselves had been enslaved, and hence seriously misled, by the way of life they believed they controlled. They did not recognize, that is, how much it was ultimately in their interest that they too should become fugitives from slavery.

10. Abraham Lincoln, the Civil War Generals, and Slavery (1861–1865)

I

Abraham Lincoln had, throughout the Civil War, the problem of testing his generals in order to determine who could be used where, and how. The peacetime officer corps had been much smaller, with the more experienced of them (such as Ulysses S. Grant and Robert E. Lee) having gotten to know each other during the Mexican War (1846–1848). The limited scale of the peacetime army is suggested by the fact that Colonel (as he then was) Robert E. Lee had commanded the troops who moved in to suppress John Brown's 1859 raid at Harpers Ferry, Virginia.

The president's problem, as the commander ultimately in charge of military operations, was complicated by the considerable wartime expansion of the officer corps. This expansion included appointments influenced by political considerations. A modest instance of this may be seen in the career of Robert Todd Lincoln (1843–1926) who, after graduating from Harvard in 1864, was on Grant's staff for the remainder of the war.

The complexities here are suggested by the entry on "General Officers" in the Boatner *Civil War Dictionary*:

> In the Union Army 1,978 generals were appointed during and immediately after the war. Of this number, 1,700 held only the Brevet Rank of general; they are, therefore, classified in this book as "Union officers" and not [as] "Union generals." . . . In the United States Army [what we would call the Regular Army?] there were nine full Major Generals [with Grant eventually becoming

> a Lieutenant General], 152 Brevet Major Generals, two full Brigadier Generals, and 165 Brevet Brigadier Generals. In the United States Volunteers there were 71 full and 242 Brevet Major Generals, and 195 full and 1,140 Brevet Brigadier Generals.

The *Civil War Dictionary* entry on "Brevet Rank" suggests the confusion generated by the rapid expansion of the Union Army, an expansion complicated by the fact that it was being employed in a civil war:

> For practical purposes brevet rank can be regarded as an honorary title, awarded for gallant or meritorious action in time of war, and having none of the authority, precedence, or pay of real or full rank. There were occasions, however, when an officer could claim that his brevet rank be recognized as real rank. The regulations were so vague that controversies arose throughout the war.

It is added, in the "Generals" entry, that there were (according to one authority) "427 *bona fide* Confederate generals."

II

Lincoln had to supervise the appointment of officers, and especially those of the rank of general. Thereafter he had to learn what various of his generals could be relied upon to do. Almost legendary was the series of trials and errors that finally permitted him to settle on Grant as General in Chief of the Armies of the United States, someone Lincoln could praise as a general willing and able to fight.

Not only did Lincoln have to learn what his generals were capable of, but he also had to learn something still more important, what it was to be the Commander in Chief during a civil war. He even had to contend with members of his own Cabinet who believed at times that they were obviously better equipped than the president to lead the war effort. One Lincoln trait that helped him be as adept as he became was his ability to recognize his mistakes, as may be seen in Bruce Caton's account (in *U. S. Grant and the American Military Tradition*) of what happened after Grant had secured the surrender in 1863 of Vicksburg and thirty thousand Confederate soldiers:

> From President Lincoln, Grant got a letter: In his move east from the river Grant had been right and everybody in Washington (including the President himself) had been wrong, and Lincoln now wanted to make formal acknowl-

edgment of the fact—as heart-warming a letter, perhaps, as any American soldier ever got from his President.

The key issue for this president, in his effort to save the Union, was how the superior numbers and resources available to him could best be used to put down the attempted secession of eleven States. The *Civil War Dictionary*, in its "Slavery" entry, suggests (in a passage drawn on earlier in this volume) the enemy confronted by the president (at a time when the population of the entire United States was more than thirty millions): "By 1861 one third of the 12,000,000 population of the South were Negro slaves who were owned by but 384,000 whites, and only about 1,800 of this number owned 100 or more." So vigorous did Lincoln become in pressing the Union advantage that troubling questions have even been raised from time to time as to whether the devastating way that the Union Army dealt with Southern resistance violated the traditional norms of a just war.

III

A key issue, from early in the war, was how Union generals were to deal with the slaves of secessionists, especially those slaves who sought refuge in Union military camps. We have seen that the attempted secession had been precipitated (beginning with South Carolina in December 1860) by the election to the presidency of the candidate of a political party that insisted that there should be no new slave states. But Lincoln repeatedly insisted, during the first years of the war, that his was *not* a campaign to abolish slavery, but was rather an effort to preserve the Union.

That is, he was deeply concerned lest the war be seen from the outset as an abolitionist campaign, something that would lead to dangerous agitations in the four still-loyal (or, at least, not-yet-rebelling) slave states (Delaware, Kentucky, Maryland, and Missouri). He believed as well (we have noticed) that there were many more men in the North who were willing to fight to save the Union than there were to emancipate the slaves. Only after the dedication to the Union had been sealed by considerable Northern sacrifices in the first years of the war did it become widely recognized that an emancipation of slaves could be employed as a useful *military* measure.

Some Union generals with abolitionist sympathies (including John C. Fremont, the Republican candidate for president in 1856) had to be corrected by Lincoln when they resorted, prematurely, to emancipation decrees. Other generals, it could be feared by Lincoln, would resign their commissions before they would execute orders interfering with the lawful property of Southerners. After all, professional military officers are very much inclined to respect fixed and known rules, including regulations for dealing with slaves.

IV

Congress enacted, in 1861 and 1862, Confiscation Acts which provided for the emancipation of slaves used directly in the Confederate war effort. These two statutes do not seem to have had much effect, perhaps partly because of the difficulty of proving which slaves had been used where and how. Lincoln does draw on this legislation in his 1862–1863 Emancipation Proclamation, if only to suggest that his own more extensive measure was not without recent precedent.

It can be suspected, however, that slavery had been put at risk from the outset by the resort to secession—and that the wartime legislation and military measures were merely recognizing what was happening already. The transformation of Northern public opinion, with respect to slavery because of the war, is reflected in how anti-slavery songs such as "John Brown's Body" and "The Battle Hymn of the Republic" were invoked. This transformation may be seen as well in how Ulysses S. Grant came to regard slavery.

The Caton description of Grant's career includes this account of his last years in the pre–Civil War civilian life that followed the Mexican War:

> People who saw Grant during the last days in St. Louis remembered that he appeared sad and discouraged—and yet this, apparently, was less because of his own troubles than because he saw what other thoughtful men were seeing then: the approaching disruption of the Federal Union. He had voted for James Buchanan, the Democrat, in 1856, fearing that a Republican victory would goad the South into secession. He had followed the [1858] Lincoln-Douglas debates attentively, considering himself a Douglas Democrat, and he wrote that when he heard Southern friends discussing a breakup of the Union as casually as if they were talking about a tariff bill, "it made my blood run cold."

This account of Grant continues thus:

> Slowly his ideas were changing. He had lived in a slave state [Missouri], he despised abolitionists, his wife owned slaves given her by her father, he himself had acquired ownership of a field hand from [his father-in-law]. Yet in 1859, when he was giving up farming and was desperately pressed for money, and the one slave he owned could have been sold for a thousand dollars, he executed

> papers of manumission and gave the man his freedom. [Thereafter] he was living in Illinois, and the storm clouds were banked up black and ugly on the country's horizon.

Further on, Caton reports changes in Grant's thinking about slavery, changes which reflected that continuing shift in public opinion which Lincoln was able to take advantage of a year later when he developed the Emancipation Proclamation:

> [Grant] had thought long, since the war began, about slavery itself, the dark mystery that lay at the bottom of American life like an evil stain spread across the subconscious. He . . . had not [in civilian life] questioned the institution of slavery or voted for those who did question it. But while he was still at Cairo, [Illinois,] with all of his campaigning ahead of him, he began to see slavery in a new light. To his father, in the fall of 1861, he had written that he wanted to whip the Rebellion into submission, preserving all of the old institutions. And yet "if it cannot be whipped in any other way than through a war against slavery, let it come to that legitimately. If it is necessary that slavery should fall that the republic may continue its existence, let slavery go."

V

A critical issue here was what Grant's "legitimately" meant. The principal sources of guidance here for military officers were provided by the president, as Commander in Chief, and by the Congress as the shaper and supplier of military forces and even as the final arbiter as to whether a president remains in power. Congress also has a critical say, of course, about declarations of war, about the making of peace, and about the development of constitutional amendments.

The ultimate authority, it was generally understood, rested in the people. And the people's will was authoritatively expressed, from time to time, in the Constitution of the day. It was a Constitution, Lincoln had argued many times, that reflected the Framers' desire (in 1787) that slavery be obviously placed "in course of ultimate extinction."

How wars were to be conducted should, it was believed, be guided not only by what Congresses and presidents say but also by the law of nations and the generally accepted rules of war. Guidance is provided thereby as to how civilians, prisoners, and the property of the enemy should be treated. It was the law of nations, reinforced by various statutes (including American statutes), that had, decades before the Civil War, come to regard the international slave trade as piracy.

VI

By and large, then, military officers had to rely for the guidance they needed upon whatever was provided to them by their superiors. The Caton account of Grant includes this "creed of the regular army man":

> [I]t was not up to the soldier to say what the war aims ought to be. Just before Shiloh [in 1862, Grant wrote a Congressman]: "So long as I hold a commission in the army I have no views of my own to carry out. Whatever may be the orders of my superiors and the law, I will execute. No man can be efficient as a commander who sets his own notions above the law and those whom he has sworn to obey. When Congress enacts anything too odious for me to execute, I will resign."

Grant's own effectiveness as a general depended, in part, upon his being able to count on others to obey *his* orders, even when heavy casualties could be expected from a military operation.

Of course, orders alone (no matter how well conceived) cannot suffice. The rhetorical capacity of a leader can sometimes be critical, as may be seen in a now-famous letter of January 26, 1863, sent privately by President Lincoln to Major General Joseph Hooker:

> General. I have placed you at the head of the Army of the Potomac. Of course I have done this upon what appear to me to be sufficient reasons. And yet I think it best for you to know that there are some things in regard to which, I am not quite satisfied with you. I believe you to be a brave and skilful soldier, which, of course, I like. I also believe you do not mix politics with your profession, in which you are right. You have confidence in yourself, which is a valuable, if not an indispensable quality. You are ambitious, which, within reasonable bounds, does good rather than harm. But I think that during Gen. Burnside's command of the Army, you have taken counsel of your ambition, and thwarted him as much as you could, in which you did a great wrong to the country, and to a most meritorious and honorable brother officer. I have heard, in such way as to believe it, of your recently saying that both the Army and the Government needed a Dictator. Of course it was not *for* this, but in spite of it, that I have given you the command. Only those generals who gain successes, can set up dictators. What I now ask of you is military success, and I will risk the dictatorship. The government will support you to the utmost of it's ability, which is neither more nor less than it has done and will do for all commanders. I much fear that the spirit which you have aided to infuse into the Army, of criticizing their Commander, and withholding confidence from him, will now turn upon you. I shall assist you as far as I can, to put it down. Neither you, nor Napoleon, if he were alive

> again, could get any good out of an army, while such a spirit prevails in it. And now, beware of rashness. Beware of rashness, but with energy, and sleepless vigilance, go forward, and give us victories.

Even so, Hooker was relieved the following summer after his costly defeat at Chancellorsville, a defeat said to have been due in part to his unwillingness to be convinced (perhaps because of the "rashness" Lincoln feared?) that he was being endangered by a skillful enemy maneuver.

However this may have been, it is (according to the Boatner *Civil War Dictionary*) reported by John Nicolay and John Hay (in their biography of Lincoln),

> A friend to whom Hooker showed this [Lincoln] letter immediately upon reception, says it made a deep impression upon the general. While he was somewhat chagrined by its severe chiding, he was touched by its tone of mingled authority and kindness. "He talks to me like a father," [Hooker] said. "I shall not answer this letter until I have won him a great victory."

This story, whether or not true, does suggest the effect that Lincoln *could* have on some of his generals. In striking contrast is the impression made upon various observers by Jefferson Davis (as recorded by Boatner):

> Inaugurated provisional president [of the Confederate States of America] in February 1861 at Montgomery, he was elected to a six-year term and was [thereafter] inaugurated president of the permanent [Confederate] government at Richmond. . . . As the war progressed, [President Davis] took over more of the powers and became dictatorial and autocratic, a trend that ran counter to the states-rights philosophy of the seceding states. [The *Dictionary of American Biography*] speaks of his "imperious temper aggravated by ill health." [General P. G.] Beauregard succinctly summed up both Davis's and the Confederacy's problem when he said: "We needed for President either a military man of high order, or a politician of the first-class without military pretensions. The South did not fall crushed by the mere weight of the North; but it was nibbled away at all sides and ends, because its executive head never gathered and wielded its great strength under the ready advantages that greatly reduced or neutralized its adversary's naked physical superiority."

VII

The policies that leaders stood for and were able to implement depended, in part, on chance, including perhaps what both their temperaments and their circumstances happened to be. Consider, for example, critical shifts in Jefferson Davis's public positions (as recalled in the *Encyclopedia of the American Constitution*):

> In 1858 [Davis] said publicly [to Southerners] that if a Republican were elected [President in 1860] "I should deem it your duty to provide for your safety outside the Union." In 1859 he said that the John Brown raid meant that loyalty to the Constitution required secession. Even so, after Abraham Lincoln's election, Davis urged compromise, and served on the Committee of Thirty-Three. Only when the committee failed did he support secession. . . . He saw secession as a conservative measure to protect the Constitution from tyranny by Lincoln and the national government. But as Confederate president, Davis implemented conscription, suspension of *habeas corpus*, and impressment of supplies. A lifelong states' rights man, Davis was vilified by [Southern] politicians and governors as he sought, unsuccessfully, to create a Confederate national policy [which difficulties, we can notice, supported Lincoln's 1861 assessment of the secessionists' principles as anarchical].

We can see, in how Davis attempted to shape a viable war policy, the often similar problems that Lincoln faced in dealing with *other* Americans also at war.

Particularly instructive, with a view to understanding how slavery had to be dealt with by Abraham Lincoln at varying stages of the Civil War, is how Jefferson Davis himself dealt with slavery before and during that war. It is recorded in the *Encyclopedia of the American Constitution* (emphasis added),

> Davis was ambivalent in [this as in] other ways. He believed that blacks were inferior to whites, that Congressional prohibition of the African slave trade was unconstitutional, and that the federal government should not interfere with slavery. Yet his plantation was a model, surpassed only by his brother's, for treating blacks with compassion and for giving them a great deal of self-government. He opposed reopening the [international] slave trade on moral grounds and *in 1865 advocated emancipation [of Southern slaves] to save the Confederacy.*

The Davis advocacy of the use of emancipation *as a war measure* seemed to concede, in effect, the constitutional authority for Lincoln's Emancipation Proclamation two years before.

Of course, Davis's opinions on constitutionality cannot be accepted without careful examination, as may be seen if he did insist that "Congressional prohibition [as of 1808] of the African slave trade was unconstitutional." It is hard to deny the relevant Congressional power here when it *is* said, in Article I, Section 9 of the Constitution, "The Migration or Importation of such

Persons [that is, African slaves] as any of the States now existing shall think proper to admit, shall not be prohibited by the Congress prior to the Year one thousand eight hundred and eight, but a Tax or duty may be imposed on such Importation, not exceeding ten dollars for each Person." That is, is it not implied here that Congress, after 1807, could either directly prohibit the importation of "such Persons" or could impose so high a tax or duty on it as to amount to an indirect prohibition?

VIII

The issue of what was to be done by Union generals with the slaves of secessionists had to be repeatedly addressed by the Lincoln administration. On the one hand, as we have seen, were the abolitionists who (from the beginning of the war) wanted slaves emancipated wherever the Union army resumed control. On the other hand were those Unionists who had been taught that recognized property rights, including property in human beings, were virtually sacred.

The Emancipation Proclamation turned the advancing Union forces into armies of emancipation. The most controversial element of the Lincoln policy at *this* stage of the war was its willingness to use emancipated slaves as soldiers in Union armies. This was, in a way, the most critical step taken by the administration *toward* the permanent emancipation and eventual enfranchisement in this country of people of African descent (anticipating, in effect, the distinguished service of Japanese Americans in the United States Army in Italy during the Second World War, even as many of their relatives were confined in relocation camps in this country).

We have seen, both in the Lincoln letter to Hooker and in the Grant letter to a Congressman, that it was understood that the political control of military operations and their objectives rested ultimately with the president, subject to appropriate Congressional legislation. This understanding is reinforced by a Caton observation that "Grant never forgot who was boss," illustrating this by the following recollection:

> When Lincoln sent an officer down the valley to recruit Negro soldiers and bespoke Grant's help for the man, Grant wrote in reply, "You may rely upon it that I will give him [the recruiter] all the aid in my power. I would do this whether arming the Negro seemed to me a wise policy or not, because it is an order that I am bound to obey and I do not feel that in my position I have a right to question any policy of the government."

The Grant attitude exhibited here is in marked contrast to that of George McClellan, a much-celebrated general (and an ambitious prima donna) who found it difficult to respect the paramount duty of officers to obey the orders of their political superiors (anticipating thereby the troubling conduct almost a century later of Douglas MacArthur during the Korean War).

IX

A curious feature of Civil War polemics was that Southern secessionists repeatedly invoked the Constitution in judging Lincoln's actions. This reflected the Confederates' insistence that *they* had the true interpretation of the Constitution. Particularly outrageous for them was Lincoln's Emancipation Proclamation.

Also curious was the fact that secessionist leaders eventually found it "necessary" to resort to some of the measures that Lincoln had been condemned for using. This included, as we have seen, Davis's 1865 advocacy of an emancipation of Southern slaves (partly with a view to arming some of them?) in order to save the Confederacy. In short, both sides in this struggle were eventually moved to try to wage "total war."

Presidential management of military activities was more immediate and detailed during the Civil War than it had ever been. This was, in part, because of the telegraph that permitted Abraham Lincoln (and, to a lesser extent perhaps, Jefferson Davis) to stay in constant touch with commanders in the field. The war that ended the legal power of masters over slaves in this country expanded considerably the "acceptable" (or, at least, the accepted) power of the executive over the country itself, at least in time of war.

~

11. Ralph Waldo Emerson and the Emancipation Proclamation (1862)

I

Ralph Waldo Emerson introduces an October 12, 1862, talk on Abraham Lincoln's Preliminary Emancipation Proclamation with a recollection of key "step[s] in the history of political liberty." Every such step is, he says, "a sally of the human mind into the untried future, and has the interest of genius and is fruitful in heroic anecdotes." "Such [memorable] moments of expansion [of liberty] in modern history" were, he says,

> the Confession of Augsburg; the plantation of America; the English Commonwealth of 1648; the Declaration of American Independence in 1776; the British emancipation of slaves in the West Indies; the passage of the Reform Bill; the repeal of the Corn Laws, the magnetic ocean Telegraph; though yet imperfect, the passage of the Homestead Bill in the last Congress; and now, eminently, President Lincoln's Proclamation on the twenty-second of September [1862].

There are, we can notice, ten such remarkable "moments of expansion." We can suspect that this compilation echoes somehow the number used for the Ten Commandments. And we can notice that the ordering of these ten steps is more or less chronological.

These steps, it is suggested by Emerson, are critical to modern civilization with its dedication to political liberty. The Ten Commandments can be said to have been critical to the development of ancient civilization, at least in the Western world. The Emancipation Proclamation can thus be presented as the culmination of the modern development, at least for the time being.

II

The Emerson Decalogue begins with the Augsburg Confession of 1530. That statement is described thus in the *Encyclopedia Britannica*:

> [T]he 28 articles that constitute the basic confession of Lutheran churches, presented June 25, 1530, in German and Latin at the Diet of Augsburg to the emperor Charles V by seven Lutheran princes and two imperial free cities. The principal author was the Reformer Philipp Melanchthon, who drew on earlier Lutheran statements of faith. The purpose was to defend the Lutherans against misrepresentations and to provide a statement of their theology that would be acceptable to the Roman Catholics in the Holy Roman Empire. On August 3 the Catholic theologians replied with the so-called Confutation, which condemned 13 articles of the Confession, accepted 9 without qualifications, and approved 6 with qualifications. . . . The unaltered 1530 version of the Confession has always been authoritative for Lutherans.

The *Britannica* provides this further description of the Confession that had been presented at the Diet of Augsburg in 1530:

> The first 21 articles of the Unaltered Augsburg Confession set forth the Lutherans' overall doctrine in order to demonstrate that "they dissent in no article of faith from the Catholic Church." The remaining seven articles discuss abuses that had crept into the Western Church in the centuries immediately preceding the Reformation: Communion under one kind (the people received the bread only), enforced priestly celibacy, the mass as an expiatory sacrifice, compulsory confession, human institutions designed to merit grace, abuses in connection with monasticism, and the expanded authority claimed by the bishops.

The influence of the Augsburg Confession upon Anglo-Americans is suggested by the *Britannica* observation that "[t]he Confession was translated into English in 1536, and was a definite influence on the Thirty-nine Articles of the Anglicans and the Twenty-five Articles of Religion of the Methodists." A respect for the individual religious conscience may be seen here. It may be seen as well in the second and third memorable steps "in the history of political liberty" recorded by Emerson: "the plantation of America" (the Pilgrim landing in 1620) and Oliver Cromwell's "English Commonwealth of 1648."

Such moves, it can be said, opened the way to the modern world (including both to Science and to the Enlightenment). The *loosening* of the hold by multitudes of religious establishments may have been critical to the development of modern political liberty. This combination, with respect to both religious and political liberty, may be seen in the First Amendment to the Constitution of 1787, anticipated by the prohibition in the Constitution itself of any "religious Test . . . as a Qualification to any Office or public Trust under the United States."

III

The first half of Emerson's Decalogue of Political Liberty culminates in "the British emancipation of slaves in the West Indies." This development had been anticipated, it can be said, by Lord Mansfield's insistence in *Somerset* v. *Stewart* (1772) that slavery could not be legally recognized in England. Perhaps the spirit of the Declaration of Independence had contributed to the Parliamentary measure for the West Indies.

Emerson could have used *Somerset* in addition to, if not even in place of, the West Indian measure. But, it seems, he wanted an English measure of emancipation in parallel to that provided by Lincoln, which *is* the occasion of this talk. It also seems that Emerson even placed the West Indian action a little earlier than it was (that is, he placed that 1833 measure before the 1832 Reform Bill) perhaps in order to have it as the culmination of the first half of his Decalogue.

This points out, of course, the importance he sees in acts of emancipation. It testifies to the importance of liberty in that it has one people making sacrifices on behalf of the liberation of another people. Emerson can even be said to testify to the power of liberty in that he considers himself *not* to be bound more than is useful by the chronological discipline he had set for himself.

IV

The reader should not be surprised, therefore, to find the second half of Emerson's Decalogue of Political Liberty culminating in the emancipation of slaves in the United States. It might even be wondered whether the Homestead Bill (of 1862) did for Lincoln's Emancipation Proclamation what the Declaration of Independence might have done for West Indian emancipation. At the very least, the Homestead Bill favored the promotion of family farms that were quite different in spirit from plantations where slavery had "flourished."

The second half of Emerson's Decalogue, which culminates in the Emancipation Proclamation, makes much more of economic and technological developments than the first half of this Decalogue had. Such developments, it is indicated, make political liberty accessible to even more of the population of a country. The dignity of labor is thereby enhanced, counteracting the influence of slavery.

Perhaps there can be seen between the two halves of the Emerson Decalogue the movement that permitted, if it did not even encourage, American individualism. This can mean, among other things, an emphasis upon personal self-expression. It can also mean, therefore, a neglect of one's powers and duties as a citizen.

V

But such a decline in civic morale is not yet evident in Emerson's day. After all, it was a time of great sacrifice among his fellow citizens on behalf of the Union. Emerson's Decalogue celebrates a development of political liberty which culminates in the Emancipation Proclamation.

Both Northerners and Southerners stood for liberty during the Civil War, but with one critical difference. Southerners tended to believe that liberty was to be seen in the exercise of mastery by superiors over inferiors. Indeed, Southern citizens saw their liberty infringed by Northern interference with their institutions.

Religious liberty, or respect for the rights of the individual conscience, had been much more prominent in the early stages of the development recalled by Emerson. Once that liberty had contributed to the enhancement of political liberty, religion itself came to be taken less seriously in the community at large. An attempt to resurrect the Old Way may be seen in the pious stance taken in the Preamble of the Confederate Constitution of 1861, in marked contrast to the much more secular spirit of the Framers of the Constitution of 1787.

VI

The political liberty celebrated by Emerson is introduced as somehow worldwide. But once the Augsburg Confession is noticed, all the grand moments noticed by Emerson are Anglo-American. Did he expect that the most meaningful development of political liberty not only in his time but also in the century or two thereafter would be among the English-speaking peoples?

Another feature of the Emerson account is the lack of any recognition of scientific breakthroughs in the progress of the human species. A *technological* breakthrough *is* noticed, with the recognition of the importance of the development of the ocean telegraph. This particular development is part of a system of communication which permits more effective self-government by a populous state.

Technology itself can make possible the support of ever-larger populations. It can also make most chattel slavery obsolete. However that may be, once political liberty *is* established, an even more intensive economic development can follow, perhaps reinforcing the political development of a people, at least until technology promotes an unhealthy self-absorption, something that we may be seeing among ourselves these days.

VII

What, in these matters, is *cause* and what is *effect* can be uncertain. Also uncertain can be why there should have been many more memorable events in the history of political liberty during Emerson's lifetime than there had been before. After all, he had said that only "once in a century, if so often, a poetic act and record occur."

Did Emerson notice how far off the mark he was in his "count"? Or is it a matter of chance that there are so many more memorable liberty-related events now than there once were? Had his opening flourish been a rhetorical device designed to dramatize what had been happening in his own day?

The acceleration in emancipation that Emerson records may testify to his personal abhorrence of slavery. Thus, an elimination worldwide of slavery may be seen by him as so revolutionary as to distort the usual historical processes. The spirit here—and in this may be seen the Emersonian grounding of political liberty in the Augsburg Confession—is that of "The Battle Hymn of the Republic," which celebrates a political mission spiritualized.

VIII

What, it may well be wondered, was the status for Emerson of pre–Augsburg Confession developments? Has it been only in modern times that a concern for political liberty has been dominant? In what way have Christian aspirations, especially in their Protestant forms, contributed to this shift in emphasis?

The pre-modern ways may have been more concerned than we tend to be with virtue and citizenship. Those are ways grounded (at least in the

Western world) in Classical learning, in the Hebrew Bible, and in Roman civic-mindedness. Christianity, on the other hand, seemed to open the way for human beings to a meaningful (if not even eternal) personal existence independent of one's political and social relations.

The emancipation that Emerson celebrates may tend to liberate human beings from inherited social obligations. Emerson was an early American student of non-Western thought. Insofar as he was influenced by such thought, he would have recognized that there was something distinctively American, perhaps even parochial, in his celebration of the heroics of political liberty.

IX

The organization of European history as a campaign for political liberty is implicit, for Emerson, in his celebration of Lincoln's Emancipation Proclamation as a singular act of astutely developed statesmanship. The awfulness of slavery, especially in its modern form, had been brought home to Emerson by the Fugitive Slave Law of 1850. Even Boston, the proud champion of political liberty, had been dreadfully compromised by the hunters of runaway slaves who were said to have been empowered to prowl across Massachusetts.

There may be seen in Emerson's anti-slavery talks, especially since 1850, the passion drawn upon by Unionists during the Civil War. Even someone such as the obviously imprudent (if not even insane) John Brown can arouse his admiration. Did Emerson, in proceeding as he did, make more of exciting campaigns of liberation than of dedication to the discipline of an enduring liberty?

Still, the way that he organized his Decalogue of political liberty reflects the discipline that may be necessary for liberty to endure. It may reflect as well the dependence of a productive political order upon a sound mythic history. That is, Ralph Waldo Emerson, in his celebration of American Emancipation, may be very much the political poet, anticipating in this way Abraham Lincoln's Second Inaugural Address.

12. The Civil War Amendments (1865, 1868, 1870)

I

The Thirteenth Amendment was initiated by Congress even before the Civil War had ended. It provides most decisively, "Neither slavery nor involuntary servitude, except as a punishment for crime whereof the party shall have been duly convicted, shall exist within the United States, or any place subject to their jurisdiction." This unequivocal repudiation, nationwide, of chattel slavery has been cataclysmic both in its unanticipated presuppositions and in its challenging consequences, reflecting thereby the great civil war which culminated in this development.

This Amendment confirmed and extended President Lincoln's Emancipation Proclamation of 1862–1863. That executive order is made comprehensive and permanent in its nationwide application. The repudiation of slavery by the Thirteenth Amendment of 1865 could at last speak explicitly of that institution, unlike the determined reliance there had been upon euphemisms to provide for slavery in the Constitution of 1787.

After all, this decisive repudiation of slavery redeems, in effect, the assumptions about liberty, as well as about equality, implicit in the Declaration of Independence, if not also in Magna Carta. It had been such an assumption among the English-speaking people that had been built upon, for example, by Lord Mansfield in *Somerset* v. *Stewart* (1772). We have noticed that the reticence in 1787 about the use in the Constitution of the term *slavery* had been revealing for those sensitive to how uncomfortable thoughtful Americans, South as well as North, had become with the troubling servile institutions they had inherited.

II

The opening lines of Section 1 of the Fourteenth Amendment nullifies the demoralizing ruling in the *Dred Scott* case of 1857 about the permanently debased status in this country of people of African descent, a case which is believed to have contributed to the passions that led to the Civil War. Those opening lines read, "All persons born or naturalized in the United States and subject to the jurisdiction thereof, are citizens of the United States and of the State wherein they reside." A critical doctrine of *Dred Scott* was thereby buried with its author, the Chief Justice who had died in 1864.

Section 1 of the Fourteenth Amendment then goes on to provide, "No State shall make or enforce any law which shall abridge the privileges or immunities of citizens of the United States." This seems to reinforce the much-neglected Privileges and Immunities Clause in Article IV of the Constitution, which had also provided guidance for state governments. It is then provided, in the Fourteenth Amendment, "[N]or shall any State deprive any person of life, liberty, or property without due process of law, nor deny to any person within its jurisdiction the equal protection of the laws."

It does not seem to be generally recognized that Section 1 of the Fourteenth Amendment nullifies not only *Dred Scott* in a critical respect but also *Barron* v. *Baltimore* (1833). That is, it provides in effect that state governments are bound, by and large, by the traditional provisions on behalf of liberty that the government of the United States is also bound by. This would not have surprised those promoters of the Constitution who argued, during the 1787–1788 Ratification Campaign, that the new General Government (like all governments in the United States) would be bound to respect the traditional liberties of the English-speaking peoples, whether or not a bill of rights was added to the proposed Constitution.

III

One consequence of the emancipation of all slaves provided for in the Thirteenth Amendment is that the Southern states would be able to add such persons to those calculations with respect to population which form the basis for the various state entitlements to seats in the House of Representatives. Under the Constitution of 1787, we recall, states had been able to count only "three fifths of [such] Persons." The rebels who had been suppressed could even find themselves stronger politically after 1865 than they would otherwise have been.

It is this curious possibility that may have contributed to Section 2 of the Fourteenth Amendment. First, it is recognized, in effect, that the former slaves would indeed be counted in the allocation of House of Representatives seats. This is followed by the provision,

> But when the right to vote at any election for the choice of electors for President and Vice-President of the United States, Representatives in Congress, the Executive and Judicial officers of a State, or the members of the Legislature thereof, is denied to any of the male inhabitants of such State, being twenty-one years of age, and citizens of the United States, or in any way abridged, except for participation in rebellion or other crime, the basis of representation therein shall be reduced in the proportion which the number of such male citizens shall bear to the whole number of male citizens twenty-one years of age in such State.

It may be wondered how this penalty came to be used in determining the allocations of House seats. But it can assure us that the framers of the Fourteenth Amendment were at least aware of some dubious "unintended consequences" of the Union victory in the Civil War. A more direct way of trying to provide for a proper treatment politically of the emancipated slaves may be seen in the Fifteenth Amendment, which will be explained further on in this chapter.

IV

Sections 3 and 4 address how promises made in the political realm should be regarded. Section 3 deals with those who, although they had "taken an oath . . . to support the Constitution of the United States," had nevertheless "engaged in insurrection or rebellion against the [United States], or given aid and comfort to the enemies thereof." Such persons, unless rehabilitated by Congress, may never serve as "a Senator or a Representative in Congress, or elector of President and Vice-President, or hold any other office, civil or military, under the United States, or under any State."

Section 4 of the Fourteenth Amendment goes on to reinforce some "promises" (including public "debts incurred . . . in suppressing insurrection or rebellion"). But it invalidates other promises, those which took the form of "any debt or obligation incurred in aid of insurrection or rebellion against the United States." Thus, not all financial or other promises are to be regarded as equal.

Such deliberate repudiation of the obligations of rebels must have seemed, to some Southerners, as disturbingly consistent with the disregard by the North of the elements of the "compact" that they had considered the Constitution to be. These sections of the Fourteenth Amendment insist, that is, that obligations and immunities in the service of the Constitution of 1787 are to be respected. On the other hand, expectations resulting from service in rebellion against the Constitution and its institutions are systematically repudiated.

V

The Fifteenth Amendment, of 1870, provides, "The right of citizens of the United States to vote shall not be denied or abridged by the United States or by any State on account of race, color, or previous condition of servitude." This reinforces what is done in Sections 1 and 2 of the Fourteenth Amendment. People of African descent, no matter what *Dred Scott* had said, are to be fully members of the political order in this country.

Critical to this development, it seems, is the insistence upon being explicit about the slavery which is now so decisively repudiated. The language used in the three Civil War amendments—"slavery," "involuntary servitude," "emancipation of any slave," and "color, or previous condition of servitude"—is in marked contrast to the less-than-candid language that had had to be used in the Constitution of 1787, such as "Person[s] held to Service or Labour in [a] State, under the Laws thereof." That is, slavery and its presuppositions can now be brought out in full view and repudiated.

The Fifteenth Amendment is the last grand flourish of the Civil War. Much that has followed since, such as various Civil Rights measures, can be seen as implementation of the Civil War amendments. These amendments anticipate others (the Seventeenth, the Nineteenth, the Twenty-fourth, and the Twenty-sixth) that have the People of the United States repeatedly limiting what the states can do in managing the elections that they are depended upon to conduct.

VI

The Civil War amendments, especially the Fifteenth Amendment and Section 1 of the Fourteenth Amendment, have been implemented and reinforced by Congressional legislation. Particularly noteworthy have been various Voting Rights acts. The consequences of such effective enfranchisement of the descendants of slaves remain significant.

The right to vote, it can be argued, is, at least for any substantial minority among us, the ultimate safeguard of all other rights. A truly representative legislature (sensitive to the power of constituents) is likely to be more apt than judges and executives to be aware of, and to respond to, the interests and concerns of minorities. We can be reminded here of the difficulty inherent in attempts to distinguish between constitutional principles and political issues.

However this may be, interpretations by the United States Supreme Court of the Civil War amendments in the nineteenth century were inferior to the understanding of those amendments by the Congress. One of the most notable cases in the annals of the Supreme Court has been *Brown* v. *Board of Education* (1954), but that much-celebrated ruling may not have been necessary if the nineteenth-century Supreme Court had conscientiously followed the lead provided by post–Civil War Congresses attempting to implement the principles of the Fourteenth Amendment. What the post–Civil War Supreme Court did again and again was much more in the spirit of that *Dred Scott* Court which presumed to second-guess Congressional efforts (going back to the Northwest Ordinance) to restrict the extension of slavery in the Territories of the United States.

VII

Chance developments may have affected how the Civil War amendments were used in their early decades. *Perhaps*, for example, things would have been different if Abraham Lincoln had been able to serve out his second term. Chance can be seen as well in how the careers of men such as Thomas Jefferson and John C. Calhoun affected the development of slavery-related issues in this country.

It becomes convenient, if not even at times necessary, to accept "the way things are," however dubious the reasoning was that may have contributed to a questionable state of things. This may be seen in how we have had to accommodate ourselves to the practice of judicial review of all Acts of Congress for constitutionality. The constitutional authority for such a general (and often unhelpful) supervisory power remains questionable.

Accommodations may be seen as well to how an irregular way of "amending" the Articles of Confederation was resorted to in 1787–1789. Similarly, significant (that is, "theoretical") questions remain about how the Civil War amendments were ratified. And then there is the curious history, deliberately overlooked by the Congress, when it considered the (rather inconsequential) Twenty-seventh Amendment to have been ratified.

VIII

However all this may be, the legacy of slavery remains with us. It is likely that the adverse effects of that legacy will take at least several more generations to be corrected. The persistence of long-standing class distinctions in modern England can be instructive here.

Particularly troubling can be the "defeatist" factors among those who have been unjustly treated for generations, especially when those factors contribute to self-crippling resentment if not even to a determined resistance to salutary discipline. The difficulty of restoring healthy relations—for the benefit of both victims and their oppressors—is still another argument for conducting oneself justly "in the first place." Both the oppressors and their victims do have to live with a past that cannot be reformed out of existence.

Even so, it has been instructive—and perhaps a tribute to the natural human desire to aim at the Good—to see how the Fourteenth Amendment has been extended on behalf of others than our original freedmen, something that the Supreme Court was at first reluctant to do. This development was anticipated by how Magna Carta, forced by the barons from the king, came to be used by the subjects of the barons against their masters in turn. The rightness of things is hard to restrict indefinitely to only a few beneficiaries.

IX

All of the Civil War amendments conclude with a section similar to that found in the Fourteenth Amendment: "The Congress shall have power to enforce, by appropriate legislation, the provisions of this article." That kind of empowerment had not been seen theretofore in the amendments to the Constitution, not even in the Twelfth Amendment, with its revamping of the presidential electors processes. But, it might have been thought, Congress would be able to guide and supervise that process by using the powers already given it in Article II of the Constitution.

The Congressional-empowerment provisions in the Civil War amendments extend, in effect, the empowerment found at the end of Section 8 of Article I, where there is an extensive enumeration of Congressional powers. That Article I empowerment, which reinforces more than the powers found in Section 8, is a prudent precaution, reinforcing in still another way the differences between the Articles of Confederation and the Constitution of 1787. It is, of course, what we honor as the Necessary and Proper Clause, which reads,

> To make all Laws which shall be necessary and proper for carrying into Execution the foregoing Powers, and all other Powers vested by this Constitution in the Government of the United States, or in any Department or Officer thereof.

Such provisions both in the original Constitution and in some of the amendments can remind us of the ultimate Congressional dominance, among the branches of government, taken for granted in the Constitution. Even more authoritative, of course, is that form of legislating exercised by the people both in originally establishing the Constitution and thereafter in amending it from time to time. This should remind us of the standards by which even constitutions may be judged, standards which have at last made chattel slavery *appear* (at least in the Western world) as questionable as it always was.

~

13. The Lost Cause Transformed

I

There was issued, in April 2000, a five-page "Statement of College and University Professors in Support of the Confederate Battle Flag Atop the South Carolina Statehouse." This was in response to a press conference by academicians (held March 31, 2000, in Columbia, South Carolina). That press conference had offered a two-page statement, "The Flag Controversy and the Causes of the Civil War—A Statement by Historians."

The statement by the "Historians," in opposition to an official South Carolina State House display of a Confederate flag, had suggested,

> The crux of the present controversy is not in the flag itself but in conflicting interpretations of the meaning of the Civil War. Some South Carolinians deny that the Civil War was fought over slavery, maintaining that it was fought [instead] over the rights of the states to control their own destinies. Slavery, they believe, was incidental.

These "Historians" (evidently based for the most part in South Carolina schools) concluded their challenging statement with this argument:

> After the war had been lost, and the Lost Cause was in need of justification, [Jefferson] Davis and [Alexander H.] Stephens [who had been president and vice president, respectively, of the Confederate States of America] backed away from their original statements [candidly acknowledging that their new nation was created for the specific purpose of perpetuating slavery], casting the

> cause of the war [instead] in the context of "states' rights." Their revisionist interpretation, in which slavery became not the cause but merely the "question" resolved on the field of battle, still misleads many South Carolinians. The historical record, however, clearly shows that the cause for which the South seceded and fought a devastating war was slavery.

A nineteenth-century quarrel was thereby brought into the twenty-first century.

This is an instructive exchange primarily because of what the Champions of the Lost Cause, who identify themselves as mostly descendants of Civil War Southerners, were provoked to say on this occasion. They challenge at the outset of their statement those "professional historians" who avow that the Confederate battle flag "represents only the evil waging of war against the United States in defense of slavery and not an honorable heritage as most South Carolinians believe." They conclude their statement with these arguments:

> The controversy is no longer a mere housekeeping matter for South Carolina. The fact is that the nationalization of the issue has made our [Confederate battle] flag the symbol to millions of Americans of a last stand against Political Correctness and increasingly uniform and dictated views of our history. And, finally, racial reconciliation is best sought by the mutual understanding of black and white South Carolinians, not by the distortion or suppression of the Southern heritage.

II

These earnest Lost Cause Champions are respectable academicians, mostly at Southern institutions. They are particularly disturbed by the suggestion that the attempted secession and the consequent Southern sacrifices had been primarily in defense of slavery. Those massive sacrifices are described thus:

> [The War for Southern Independence of 1861–1865 was] a war in which an estimated one quarter of the white men of South Carolina lost their lives and in which we suffered invasion and devastation, aimed with malice aforethought at civilians, unprecedented in American history, devastation which brought suffering and death to black as well as to white South Carolinians.

Considerable emphasis is placed in this statement on the pre–Civil War commercial aggressiveness of Northerners. One can hear echoes of the decades-long tariff debates. "A reasonable interpretation of secession," it is suggested, "is that Southerners left the Union because they saw an inveterate hostility toward their society, culture, political heritage, and economic interests, which promised endless irritation and strife in a Union which their fathers had founded in a spirit of harmony."

It is appropriate that this battle flag controversy should have been provoked by events in South Carolina. After all, it *had* been there that the first of eleven Ordinances of Secession was enacted (in December 1860). And it was also there that there had been, at Fort Sumter, that firing on a federal post which helped move Virginia to join the secessionist movement, a critical step if any separation by Southerners was to have a serious hope of prevailing.

III

These Southern Champions do see themselves as offering "a last stand against [both] Political Correctness" and a deadening uniformity in views. The modernity they resist may be even more pervasive than they recognize. Thus they themselves can argue, "There are no immutable truths in secular history."

Considerable emphasis is placed by them on materialistic explanations for historical events. However old-fashioned they try to be in tone, they are very much moderns, if not even politically correct, in critical respects. This may be seen in their tendency toward relativism, especially as they discount the significance of the moral opposition to slavery that their opponents had made so much of.

That is, it does not seem to be recognized by these Champions of the Lost Cause that significant elements in the North (if not also in the South) had long considered slavery simply wrong, which affected what compromises they were willing to continue to make for the sake of national harmony. Particularly to be resisted by them were measures that allowed for an expansion and hence an indefinite perpetuation of slavery in the United States (an expectation that was evident in the Confederate Constitution of 1861). Not to recognize the moral seriousness of the Unionists' resistance to "slavery forever" is to fail to recognize that ideas have consequences.

IV

Of course, ideas may be seen in any thoughtful insistence upon states' rights. But, it can be suspected, some rather dubious passions were more readily appealed to and engaged here by the secessionists than any enduring principles critical to Western civilization. This is dramatized by the Southern inclination to ignore the "created equal" language in the Declaration of Independence when that instrument was drawn on by the secessionists in 1860–1861.

Instructive here is the Alabama secessionist ordinance which called (as we have seen) for a convention of fifteen states. Only "slaveholding States" were called on to act thus (including the eleven states that eventually came to declare themselves seceded). The people of that day, South as well as North, recognized again and again that slavery was somehow the underlying issue that threatened the continued unity of the country.

Secessionist movements were obviously triggered in 1860–1861 by the election to the presidency of the United States of the candidate of the Republican Party, something that was recognized again and again in secessionist manifestoes. Critical to their hostile assessments of the Republican Party was its steady insistence that there should be no new slave states established in any of the Territories of the United States. It was not the economic policy of the Republican Party that was so threatening to Southern interests, however much some elements in the Republican Party shamelessly exploited the economic opportunities provided by the war.

V

At the heart of the 2000 statement by our Champions of the Lost Cause is this proposition:

> Had Southerners been motivated solely by the desire to preserve slavery they would hardly have chosen secession since slavery was securely protected under the Constitution. Lincoln avowed repeatedly that he had no intention to interfere with slavery in the States and was willing to accept what could have become the Thirteenth Amendment—a permanent guarantee of slavery. It is also clear that Lincoln and most of his supporters did not believe in racial equality and that his preferred solution to the racial problem was to ship the African-Americans away, and short of that to leave them to "root hog or die."

What was truly Lincoln's "preferred solution to the racial problem" can be debated, a debate which should be respectful of Frederick Douglass's generous assessment of the president. But it cannot be seriously denied that the Free Soil policy of the Republican Party profoundly troubled Southerners who yearned to perpetuate chattel slavery indefinitely.

These Champions of the Lost Cause would not have been thanked by their secessionist ancestors for the defense that is now mounted on their behalf. For it is in effect said, in their 2000 statement, that the position that their ancestors had made so much of (as in Alexander H. Stephens's remarkable 1861 "Corner-stone Speech") was so clearly indefensible that it could not really have been held by them. How it was that decent Southerners could indeed be trapped as they obviously were in the 1850s by the suicidal determination not only to perpetuate and defend, but even eventually to extend, slavery does remain something of a mystery.

An instructive comment on these matters was provided by Ulysses S. Grant in his assessment of the now-iconic Robert E. Lee at Appomattox:

> When I went into the house [at Appomattox Court House] I found General Lee. We greeted each other, and after shaking hands took our seats. . . . What General Lee's feelings were I do not know. As he was a man of much dignity, with an impassible face, it was impossible to say whether he felt inwardly glad that the end had finally come, or felt sad over the result, and was too manly to show it. Whatever his feelings, they were entirely concealed from my observation; but my own feelings, which had been quite jubilant on the receipt of his letter [offering to surrender his army], were sad and depressed. I felt like anything rather than rejoicing at the downfall of a foe who had fought so long and valiantly, and had suffered so much for a cause, though that cause was, I believe, one of the worst for which a people ever fought, and one for which there was the least excuse. I do not question, however, the sincerity of the great mass of those who were opposed to us.

Is it not evident that not only were the slaves set on the road to genuine emancipation by the Civil War but so were their masters as well? Thus, is not the most severe criticism of the secessionists' 1860–1865 cause implicit in how their descendants have radically revised, as in their April 2000 statement, what Southern men and women had once sincerely believed to have called for appalling sacrifices?

VI

It was always hard to make the case for slavery, especially in light of the liberty-minded principles of the Anglo-American tradition (if not even of the Christianized Western tradition). The difficulty in making the case for slavery may be seen upon recalling once again the 1772 case of *Somerset* v. *Stewart*. That a great commercial judge could speak there as he did about slavery as "odious" anticipated the problems Southerners would have when moderate Free Soilers as well as radical abolitionists challenged chattel slavery in the United States.

We have noticed that the Free Soil principles of the Republican Party meant, in effect, that the slave states in the Union would find themselves more and more a minority and hence increasingly vulnerable, however much Northerners assured them that that original "bargain" would be honored which had permitted them to retain slavery. We have also noticed that pre–Civil War Southerners could well wonder what would happen if Congress should someday place limits upon the movement of slaves (if not also upon the movement of the products of slave labor) in what we now know as "interstate commerce." Already, Northern abolitionist sentiment, grounded for some in Christianity, threatened in various ways to undermine the absolute control by Southerners of their slaves, that property which they had gained "by honest toil."

Northerners were routinely condemned in 1860–1861 by secessionists not only for wanting to keep slavery out of the Territories of the United States, Territories regarded as owned by all the states in common. They were also condemned, sometimes perhaps even more, for not readily returning fugitive slaves to their masters in accordance with the original expectations of Southerners. We have noticed as well that it was becoming evident by the 1850s that the Africans who had been kidnapped into slavery were becoming more and more "American," a transformation which contributed to their own growing recognition that they as human beings were also entitled to "Life, Liberty, and the Pursuit of Happiness."

VII

The secessionists made much, in 1860–1861, of allegations of Yankee oppressiveness and insult, particularly in how slavery was talked about and dealt with by Northerners. But it should have been apparent to the dispassionate observer of that day that no oppressiveness and insult expressed by Northerners could begin to match as grievances what enslaved human beings had long been routinely subjected to in the United States. Certainly, we have suggested, our contemporary Champions of the Lost Cause tacitly concede what the abolitionists were saying during the decades before the Civil War about the obvious indefensibility of chattel slavery.

That abolitionists could sometimes be imprudent in how they tried to deal with slavery was evident to sober politicians in the North who were fundamentally anti-slavery. It very much depended on chance what measures would truly be useful from time to time. Prudence included an awareness of how much decent Southerners were indeed trapped by circumstances that they had inherited.

It was unfortunate that Southern statesmen were also trapped as much as they were by South Carolinian passions. It should have been explicitly recalled how critical South Carolina had been, in 1787, in preventing for twenty years the immediate repudiation by the United States of an international slave trade that had come to be generally condemned as barbarous. Our contemporary Champions of the Lost Cause could usefully assess the folly of John C. Calhoun, a far more influential South Carolinian than those historians who issued the March 31, 2000, anti-Confederate-flag-flying statement that has been so severely condemned by these Champions.

VIII

Much is made by our Champions of the Lost Cause, with some justice, of the way that the Union conducted its war against Southern secession. But (we must again wonder) did not even this harshness pale by comparison with that routinely relied upon by those who subjected kidnapped Africans to generations of slavery? Those descendants of Southerners who identify themselves as "justifiably proud of a great heritage" should be (and indeed are) reluctant to accept substantial, if not even vital, aspects of that heritage which can no longer be plausibly defended.

It is this understandable reluctance that led our Champions of the Lost Cause to speak as they did in the 2000 statement that we have been examining. All this is aside from what should be done about flying Confederate flags. It could even be argued that such displays can be used as salutary reminders of (among other things) the follies associated with slavery.

Indeed, one can again ask about Southern statesmen of the 1850s a question inspired for us by the First World War: "Did *anyone* 'in charge' know what he was doing?" This is not to deny that Northern statesmen also conducted themselves foolishly at times. But Northerners did have the long-term advantage of having the sounder case to work with.

IX

All this means that the Union cause requires far less distortion of the relevant facts for it to be made plausible today than does the Lost Cause. One consequence of the secessionists' reckless actions, therefore, was to put their pious descendants in an impossible situation. The obligations one has toward one's descendants are suggested by the question, "What did Hamlet's father really want?"

The Union cause continues to be expressed best by Abraham Lincoln. He examined, in his First Inaugural Address of March 4, 1861, that right of revolution that the secessionists were, in effect, invoking. His assessment, grounded in respect for the rule of law, was usefully put this way:

> All profess to be content in the Union, if all constitutional rights can be maintained. Is it true, then, that any right, plainly written in the Constitution, has been denied? I think not. Happily the human mind is so constituted, that no party can reach to the audacity of doing this. Think, if you can, of a single instance in which a plainly written provision of the Constitution has ever been denied. If, by the mere force of numbers, a majority should deprive a minority of any clearly written constitutional right, it might, in a moral point of view, justify revolution—certainly would, if such right were a vital one. But such is not our case. All the vital rights of minorities, and of individuals, are so plainly assured to them, by affirmations and negations, guaranties and prohibitions, in the Constitution, that controversies never arise concerning them. But no organic law can ever be framed with a provision specifically applicable to every question which may occur in practical administration. No foresight can anticipate, nor any document of reasonable length contain express provisions for all possible questions. Shall fugitives from labor be surrendered by national or by State authority? The Constitution does not expressly say. *May* Congress prohibit slavery in the territories? The Constitution does not expressly say. *Must* Congress protect slavery in the territories? The Constitution does not expressly say. From questions of this class spring all our constitutional controversies, and we divide upon them into majorities and minorities. If the minority will not acquiesce, the majority must, or the government must cease. There is no other alternative; for continuing the government, [there must be] acquiescence on one side or the other. If a minority, in such a case, will secede rather than acquiesce, they make a precedent which, in turn, will divide and ruin them; for a minority of their own will secede from them, whenever a majority refuses to be controlled by such minority. For instance, why may not any portion of a new confederacy, a year or two hence, arbitrarily secede again, precisely as portions of the present Union now claim to secede from it? All who cherish disunion sentiments, are now being educated to the exact temper of doing this. Is there such perfect identity of interests among the States to compose a new Union, as to produce harmony only, and prevent renewed secession? Plainly, the central idea of secession, is the essence of anarchy. A majority held in restraint by constitutional checks, and limitations, and always changing easily, with deliberate changes of popular opinions and sentiments, is the only true sovereign of a free people. Whoever rejects it, does, of necessity, fly to anarchy or to despotism. Unanimity is impossible; the rule of a minority, as a permanent arrangement,

is wholly inadmissible; so that, rejecting the majority principle, anarchy, or despotism in some form, is all that is left.

But it was at the end of the war that the president made an assessment of the causes of the conflict that our contemporary Champions of the Lost Cause may not yet be equipped to deal with properly. Consider how he spoke of those causes in his Second Inaugural Address of March 4, 1865:

> [At the outset of the Civil War,] one eighth of the whole population were colored slaves, not distributed generally over the Union, but localized in the Southern part of it. These slaves constituted a peculiar and powerful interest. All knew that this interest was, somehow, the cause of the war. To strengthen, perpetuate, and extend this interest was the object for which the insurgents would rend the Union, even by war; while the government claimed no right to do more than to restrict the territorial enlargement of it. Neither party expected for the war, the magnitude, or the duration, which it has already attained. Neither anticipated that the *cause* of the conflict might cease with, or even before, the conflict itself should cease. Each looked for an easier triumph, and a result less fundamental and astounding. Both read the same Bible, and pray to the same God; and each invokes His aid against the other. It may seem strange that any men should dare to ask a just God's assistance in wringing their bread from the sweat of other men's faces; but let us judge not that we be not judged. The prayers of both could not be answered; that of neither has been answered fully. The Almighty has His own purposes. "Woe unto the world because of offences! for it must needs be that offences come; but woe to that man by whom the offence cometh!" If we shall suppose that American Slavery is one of those offences which, in the providence of God, must needs come, but which, having continued through His appointed time, He now wills to remove, and that He gives to both North and South, this terrible war, as the woe due to those by whom the offence came, shall we discern therein any departure from those divine attributes which the believers in a Living God always ascribe to Him? Fondly do we hope—fervently do we pray—that this mighty scourge of war may speedily pass away. Yet, if God wills that it continue, until all the wealth piled by the bond-man's two hundred and fifty years of unrequited toil shall be sunk, and until every drop of blood drawn with the lash, shall be paid by another drawn with the sword, as was said three thousand years ago, so still it must be said "the judgments of the Lord, are true and righteous altogether."

It is salutary to notice once again that the triumphant Champions of the *Union* cause were urged, in effect, by a principled Free Soiler to recognize how their forebears, too, had contributed to and perhaps benefited substantially from "the bond-man's two hundred and fifty years of unrequited toil."

APPENDIX A

~

The Declaration of Independence (1776)

In Congress, July 4, 1776. A DECLARATION By the REPRESENTATIVES of the UNITED STATES OF AMERICA, In GENERAL CONGRESS assembled.

When in the Course of human Events, it becomes necessary for one People to dissolve the Political Bands which have connected them with another, and to assume among the Powers of the Earth, the separate and equal Station to which the Laws of Nature and of Nature's God entitle them, a decent Respect to the Opinions of Mankind requires that they should declare the causes which impel them to the Separation.

We hold these Truths to be self-evident, that all Men are created equal, that they are endowed by their Creator with certain unalienable Rights, that among these are Life, Liberty, and the Pursuit of Happiness—That to secure these Rights, Governments are instituted among Men, deriving their just Powers from the Consent of the Governed, that whenever any Form of Government becomes destructive of these Ends, it is the Right of the People to alter or to abolish it, and to institute new Government, laying its Foundation on such Principles, and organizing its Powers in such Form, as to them

Sources: See *The Declaration of Independence and the Constitution of the United States*, 96th Cong., 1st sess., House Document No. 96–143 (Washington, D.C.: Government Printing Office, 1979). See, also, George Anastaplo, *The Constitution of 1787: A Commentary* (Baltimore: Johns Hopkins University Press, 1989), 235, 239–44. See, as well, George Anastaplo, *Abraham Lincoln: A Constitutional Biography* [preferred title, *Thoughts on Abraham Lincoln: A Discourse on Prudence*] (Lanham, Md.: Rowman & Littlefield, 1999), 1–38.

shall seem most likely to effect their Safety and Happiness. Prudence, indeed, will dictate that Governments long established should not be changed for light and transient Causes; and accordingly all Experience hath shewn, that Mankind are more disposed to suffer, while Evils are sufferable, than to right themselves by abolishing the Forms to which they are accustomed. But when a long Train of Abuses and Usurpations, pursuing invariably the same Object, evinces a Design to reduce them under absolute Despotism, it is their Right, it is their Duty, to throw off such Government, and to provide new Guards for their future Security. Such has been the patient Sufferance of these Colonies; and such is now the Necessity which constrains them to alter their former Systems of Government. The History of the present King of Great-Britain is a History of repeated Injuries and Usurpations, all having in direct Object the Establishment of an absolute Tyranny over these States. To prove this, let Facts be submitted to a candid World.

He has refused his Assent to Laws, the most wholesome and necessary for the public Good.

He has forbidden his Governors to pass Laws of immediate and pressing Importance, unless suspended in their Operation till his Assent should be obtained; and when so suspended, he has utterly neglected to attend to them.

He has refused to pass other Laws for the Accommodation of large Districts of People, unless those People would relinquish the Right of Representation in the Legislature, a Right inestimable to them, and formidable to Tyrants only.

He has called together Legislative Bodies at Places unusual, uncomfortable, and distant from the Depository of their public Records, for the sole Purpose of fatiguing them into Compliance with his Measures.

He has dissolved Representative Houses repeatedly, for opposing with manly Firmness his Invasions on the Rights of the People.

He has refused for a long Time, after such Dissolutions, to cause others to be elected; whereby the Legislative Powers, incapable of Annihilation, have returned to the People at large for their exercise; the State remaining in the mean time exposed to all the Dangers of Invasion from without, and Convulsions within.

He has endeavoured to prevent the Population of these States; for that Purpose obstructing the Laws for Naturalization of Foreigners; refusing to pass others to encourage their Migrations hither, and raising the Conditions of new Appropriations of Lands.

He has obstructed the Administration of Justice, by refusing his Assent to Laws for establishing Judiciary Powers.

He has made Judges dependent on his Will alone, for the Tenure of their Offices, and the Amount and Payment of their Salaries.

He has erected a Multitude of new Offices, and sent hither Swarms of Officers to harass our People, and eat out their Substance.

He has kept among us, in Times of Peace, Standing Armies, without the consent of our Legislatures.

He has affected to render the Military independent of and superior to the Civil Power.

He has combined with others to subject us to a Jurisdiction foreign to our Constitution, and unacknowledged by our Laws; giving his Assent to their Acts of pretended Legislation:

For quartering large Bodies of Armed Troops among us:

For protecting them, by a mock Trial, from Punishment for any Murders which they should commit on the Inhabitants of these States:

For cutting off our Trade with all Parts of the World:

For imposing Taxes on us without our Consent:

For depriving us, in many Cases, of the Benefits of Trial by Jury:

For transporting us beyond Seas to be tried for pretended Offences:

For abolishing the free System of English Laws in a neighbouring Province, establishing therein an arbitrary Government, and enlarging its Boundaries, so as to render it at once an Example and fit Instrument for introducing the same absolute Rule into these Colonies:

For taking away our Charters, abolishing our most valuable Laws, and altering fundamentally the Forms of our Governments:

For suspending our own Legislatures, and declaring themselves invested with Power to legislate for us in all Cases whatsoever.

He has abdicated Government here, by declaring us out of his Protection and waging War against us.

He has plundered our Seas, ravaged our Coasts, burnt our Towns, and destroyed the Lives of our People.

He is, at this Time, transporting large Armies of foreign Mercenaries to compleat the Works of Death, Desolation, and Tyranny, already begun with circumstances of Cruelty and Perfidy, scarcely paralleled in the most barbarous Ages, and totally unworthy the Head of a civilized Nation.

He has constrained our fellow Citizens taken Captive on the high Seas to bear Arms against their Country, to become the Executioners of their Friends and Brethren, or to fall themselves by their Hands.

He has excited domestic Insurrections amongst us, and has endeavoured to bring on the Inhabitants of our Frontiers, the merciless Indian Savages, whose known Rule of Warfare, is an undistinguished Destruction, of all Ages, Sexes and Conditions.

In every stage of these Oppressions we have Petitioned for Redress in the most humble Terms: Our repeated Petitions have been answered only by repeated Injury. A Prince, whose Character is thus marked by every act which may define a Tyrant, is unfit to be the Ruler of a free People.

Nor have we been wanting in Attentions to our British Brethren. We have warned them from Time to Time of Attempts by their Legislature to extend an unwarrantable Jurisdiction over us. We have reminded them of the Circumstances of our Emigration and Settlement here. We have appealed to their native Justice and Magnanimity, and we have conjured them by the Ties of our common Kindred to disavow these Usurpations, which would inevitably interrupt our Connections and Correspondence. They too have been deaf to the Voice of Justice and of Consanguinity. We must, therefore, acquiesce in the Necessity, which denounces our Separation, and hold them, as we hold the rest of Mankind, Enemies in War, in Peace, Friends.

We, therefore, the Representatives of the UNITED STATES OF AMERICA, in General Congress, Assembled, appealing to the Supreme Judge of the World for the Rectitude of our Intentions, do, in the Name, and by Authority of the good People of these Colonies, solemnly Publish and Declare, That these United Colonies are, and of Right ought to be, Free and Independent States; that they are absolved from all Allegiance to the British Crown, and that all political Connection between them and the State of Great-Britain, is and ought to be totally dissolved; and that as Free and Independent States, they have full Power to levy War, conclude Peace, contract Alliances, establish Commerce, and to do all other Acts and Things which Independent States may of right do. And for the support of this Declaration, with a firm Reliance on the Protection of divine Providence, we mutually pledge to each other our Lives, our Fortunes, and our sacred Honor.

Signed by Order and in Behalf of the Congress . . .

[The signatures are provided in George Anastaplo, *Reflections on Constitutional Law* (Lexington: University Press of Kentucky, 2006) 190–92.]

APPENDIX B

The Northwest Ordinance (1787)

An Ordinance for the Government of the Territory of the United States, North-West of the River Ohio

[Section 1.] BE IT ORDAINED by the United States in Congress assembled, That the said territory, for the purposes of temporary government, be one district; subject, however, to be divided into two districts, as future circumstances may, in the opinion of Congress, make it expedient.

[Section 2.] Be it ordained by the authority aforesaid, That the estates both of resident and non-resident proprietors in the said territory, dying intestate, shall descend to, and be distributed among their children, and the descendants of a deceased child in equal parts; the descendants of a deceased child or grand-child, to take the share of their deceased parent in equal parts among them: And where there shall be no children or descendants, then in equal parts to the next of kin, in equal degree; and among collaterals, the children of a deceased brother or sister of the intestate, shall have in equal parts among them their deceased parents' share; and there shall in no case be a distinction between kindred of the whole and half blood; saving in all cases to the widow of the intestate, her third part of the real estate for life, and one third part of the personal estate; and this law relative to descents and dower,

Sources: See *The Northwest Ordinance 1787: A Bicentennial Handbook* (Indianapolis: Indiana Historical Society, 1987). See, also, George Anastaplo, *The Constitution of 1787: A Commentary* (Baltimore: Johns Hopkins University Press, 1989), 236, 258–65. See, as well, George Anastaplo, *Abraham Lincoln: A Constitutional Biography* [preferred title, *Thoughts on Abraham Lincoln: A Discourse on Prudence*] (Lanham, Md.: Rowman & Littlefield, 1999), 39–49, 69–79.

shall remain in full force until altered by the legislature of the district.—And until the governor and judges shall adopt laws as herein after mentioned, estates in the said territory may be devised or bequeathed by wills in writing, signed and sealed by him or her, in whom the estate may be, (being of full age) and attested by three witnesses;—and real estates may be conveyed by lease and release, or bargain and sale, signed, sealed, and delivered by the person being of full age, in whom the estate may be, and attested by two witnesses, provided such wills be duly proved, and such conveyances be acknowledged, or the execution thereof duly proved, and be recorded within one year after proper magistrates, courts, and registers shall be appointed for that purpose; and personal property may be transferred by delivery, saving, however, to the French and Canadian inhabitants, and other settlers of the Kaskaskies, Saint Vincent's, and the neighbouring villages, who have heretofore professed themselves citizens of Virginia, their laws and customs now in force among them, relative to the descent and conveyance of property.

[Section 3.] Be it ordained by the authority aforesaid, That there shall be appointed from time to time, by Congress, a governor, whose commission shall continue in force for the term of three years, unless sooner revoked by Congress; he shall reside in the district, and have a freehold estate therein, in one thousand acres of land, while in the exercise of his office.

[Section 4.] There shall be appointed from time to time, by Congress, a secretary, whose commission shall continue in force for four years, unless sooner revoked, he shall reside in the district, and have a freehold estate therein, in five hundred acres of land, while in the exercise of his office; it shall be his duty to keep and preserve the acts and laws passed by the legislature, and the public records of the district, and the proceedings of the governor in his executive department; and transmit authentic copies of such acts and proceedings, every six months, to the secretary of Congress: There shall also be appointed a court to consist of three judges, any two of whom to form a court, who shall have a common law jurisdiction, and reside in the district, and have each therein a freehold estate in five hundred acres of land, while in the exercise of their offices; and their commissions shall continue in force during good behaviour.

[Section 5.] The governor and judges, or a majority of them, shall adopt and publish in the district, such laws of the original states, criminal and civil, as may be necessary, and best suited to the circumstances of the district, and report them to Congress, from time to time, which laws shall be in force in the district until the organization of the general assembly therein, unless disapproved of by Congress; but afterwards the legislature shall have authority to alter them as they shall think fit.

[Section 6.] The governor for the time being, shall be commander in chief of the militia, appoint and commission all officers in the same, below the rank of general officers; all general officers shall be appointed and commissioned by Congress.

[Section 7.] Previous to the organization of the general assembly, the governor shall appoint such magistrates and other civil officers, in each county or township, as he shall find necessary for the preservation of the peace and good order in the same: After the general assembly shall be organized, the powers and duties of magistrates and other civil officers shall be regulated and defined by the said assembly; but all magistrates and other civil officers, not herein otherwise directed, shall, during the continuance of this temporary government, be appointed by the governor.

[Section 8.] For the prevention of crimes and injuries, the laws to be adopted or made shall have force in all parts of the district, and for the execution of process, criminal and civil, the governor shall make proper divisions thereof—and he shall proceed from time to time, as circumstances may require, to lay out the parts of the district in which the Indian titles shall have been extinguished, into counties and townships, subject, however, to such alterations as may thereafter be made by the legislature.

[Section 9.] So soon as there shall be five thousand free male inhabitants, of full age, in the district, upon giving proof thereof to the governor, they shall receive authority, with time and place, to elect representatives from their counties or townships, to represent them in the general assembly; provided that for every five hundred free male inhabitants there shall be one representative, and so on progressively with the number of free male inhabitants, shall the right of representation increase, until the number of representatives shall amount to twenty-five, after which the number and proportion of representatives shall be regulated by the legislature; provided that no person be eligible or qualified to act as a representative, unless he shall have been a citizen of one of the United States three years and be a resident in the district, or unless he shall have resided in the district three years, and in either case shall likewise hold in his own right, in fee simple, two hundred acres of land within the same:—Provided also, that a freehold in fifty acres of land in the district, having been a citizen of one of the states, and being resident in the district; or the like freehold and two years residence in the district shall be necessary to qualify a man as an elector of a representative.

[Section 10.] The representatives thus elected, shall serve for the term of two years, and in case of the death of a representative, or removal from office, the governor shall issue a writ to the county or township for which he was a member, to elect another in his stead, to serve for the residue of the term.

[Section 11.] The general assembly, or legislature, shall consist of the governor, legislative council, and a house of representatives. The legislative council shall consist of five members, to continue in office five years, unless sooner removed by Congress, any three of whom to be a quorum, and the members of the council shall be nominated and appointed in the following manner, to wit: As soon as representatives shall be elected, the governor shall appoint a time and place for them to meet together, and, when met, they shall nominate ten persons, resident in the district, and each possessed of a freehold in five hundred acres of land, and return their names to Congress; five of whom Congress shall appoint and commission to serve as aforesaid; and whenever a vacancy shall happen in the council, by death or removal from office, the house of representatives shall nominate two persons, qualified as aforesaid, for each vacancy, and return their names to Congress; one of whom Congress shall appoint and commission for the residue of the term; and every five years, four months at least before the expiration of the time of service of the members of council, the said house shall nominate ten persons, qualified as aforesaid, and return their names to Congress, five of whom Congress shall appoint and commission to serve as members of the council five years, unless sooner removed. And the governor, legislative council, and house of representatives, shall have authority to make laws in all cases for the good government of the district, not repugnant to the principles and articles in this ordinance established and declared. And all bills having passed by a majority in the house, and by a majority in the council, shall be referred to the governor for his assent; but no bill or legislative act whatever, shall be of any force without his assent. The governor shall have power to convene, prorogue and dissolve the general assembly, when in his opinion it shall be expedient.

[Section 12.] The governor, judges, legislative council, secretary, and such other officers as Congress shall appoint in the district, shall take an oath or affirmation of fidelity, and of office, the governor before the president of Congress, and all other officers before the governor. As soon as a legislature shall be formed in the district, the council and house, assembled in one room, shall have authority by joint ballot to elect a delegate to Congress, who shall have a seat in Congress, with a right of debating, but not of voting, during this temporary government.

[Section 13.] And for extending the fundamental principles of civil and religious liberty, which form the basis whereon these republics, their laws and constitutions are erected; to fix and establish those principles as the basis of all laws, constitutions and governments, which for ever hereafter shall be formed in the said territory;—to provide also for the establishment of states, and permanent government therein, and for their admission to a share in the federal councils on an equal footing with the original states, at as early periods as may be consistent with the general interest:

[Section 14.] It is hereby ordained and declared by the authority aforesaid, That the following articles shall be considered as articles of compact between the original states and the people and states in the said territory, and forever remain unalterable, unless by common consent, to wit:

Article the First. No person, demeaning himself in a peaceable and orderly manner, shall ever be molested on account of his mode of worship or religious sentiments in the said territory.

Article the Second. The inhabitants of the said territory shall always be entitled to the benefits of the writ of habeas corpus, and of the trial by jury; of a proportionate representation of the people in the legislature, and of judicial proceedings according to the course of the common law; all persons shall be bailable unless for capital offenses, where the proof shall be evident, or the presumption great; all fines shall be moderate, and no cruel or unusual punishments shall be inflicted; no man shall be deprived of his liberty or property but by the judgment of his peers, or the law of the land; and should the public exigencies make it necessary for the common preservation to take any person's property, or to demand his particular services, full compensation shall be made for the same;—and in the just preservation of rights and property it is understood and declared, that no law ought ever to be made, or have force in the said territory, that shall in any manner whatever interfere with, or affect private contracts or engagements, bona fide and without fraud previously formed.

Article the Third. Religion, morality and knowledge, being necessary to good government and the happiness of mankind, schools and the means of education shall forever be encouraged. The utmost good faith shall always be observed towards the Indians; their lands and property shall never be taken from them without their consent; and in their property, rights and liberty, they never shall be invaded or disturbed, unless in just and lawful wars authorized by Congress; but laws founded in justice and humanity shall from time to time be made, for preventing wrongs being done to them; and for preserving peace and friendship with them.

Article the Fourth. The said territory, and the states which may be formed therein, shall forever remain a part of this confederacy of the United States of America, subject to the articles of confederation, and to such alterations therein as shall be constitutionally made; and to all the acts and ordinances of the United States in Congress assembled, conformable thereto. The inhabitants and settlers in the said territory, shall be subject to pay a part of the federal debts contracted or to be contracted, and a proportional part of the expences of government, to be apportioned on them by Congress, according to the same common rule and measure by which apportionments thereof shall be made on the other states; and the taxes for paying their proportion, shall be laid and levied by the authority and direction of the legislatures of the district or districts or new states, as in the original states, within the time agreed upon by the United States in Congress assembled. The legislatures of those districts, or new states, shall never interfere with the primary disposal of the soil by the United States in Congress assembled, nor with any regulations Congress may find necessary for securing the title in such soil to the bona fide purchasers. No tax shall be imposed on lands the property of the United States; and in no case shall non-resident proprietors be taxed higher than residents. The navigable waters leading into the Mississippi and St. Lawrence, and the carrying places between the same shall be common highways, and forever free, as well as to the inhabitants of the said territory, as to the citizens of the United States, and those of any other states that may be admitted into the confederacy, without any tax, impost or duty therefor.

Article the Fifth. There shall be formed in the said territory, not less than three nor more than five states; and the boundaries of the states, as soon as Virginia shall alter her act of cession and consent to the same, shall become fixed and established as follows, to wit: The western state in the said territory, shall be bounded by the Mississippi, the Ohio and Wabash rivers; a direct line drawn from the Wabash and Post Vincent's due north to the territorial line between the United States and Canada, and by the said territorial line to the lake of the Woods and Mississippi. The middle state shall be bounded by the said direct line, the Wabash from Post Vincent's to the Ohio; by the Ohio, by a direct line drawn due north from the mouth of the Great Miami to the said territorial line, and by the said territorial line. The eastern state shall be bounded by the last mentioned direct line, the Ohio, Pennsylvania, and the said territorial line; Provided however, and it is further understood and declared, that the boundaries of these three states, shall be subject so far to be altered, that if Congress shall hereafter find it expedient, they shall have authority to form one or two states in that part of the said territory which lies north of an east and west line drawn through the southerly bend or extreme of lake Michigan: and whenever any of the said states shall have sixty thousand free inhabitants therein, such state shall be admitted by its delegates into the Congress of the United States, on an equal footing with the original states in all respects whatever; and shall be at liberty to form a permanent constitution and state government: Provided the constitution and government so to be formed, shall be republican, and in conformity to the principles contained in these articles, and so far as it can be consistent with the general interest of the confederacy, such admission shall be allowed at an earlier period, and when there may be a less number of free inhabitants in the state than sixty thousand.

Article the Sixth. There shall be neither slavery nor involuntary servitude in the said territory, otherwise than in punishment of crimes whereof the party shall have been duly convicted: Provided always, that any person escaping into the same, from whom labor or service is lawfully claimed in any one of the original states, such fugitive may be lawfully reclaimed and conveyed to the person claiming his or her labor or service as aforesaid.

Be it ordained by the authority aforesaid, That the resolutions of the 23d of April, 1784, relative to the subject of this ordinance, be, and the same are hereby repealed and declared null and void.

DONE by the UNITED STATES in CONGRESS assembled, the 13th day of July, in the year of our Lord 1787, and of their sovereignty and independence the 12th.*

*The following Act of the First Congress, approved August 7, 1789, reenacted the Northwest Ordinance as modified to conform to the United States Constitution of 1787:

An Act to provide for the government of the Territory northwest of the river Ohio.

Whereas, in order that the ordinance of the United States in Congress assembled, for the government of the Territory northwest of the river Ohio may continue to have full effect, it is requisite that certain provisions should be made so as to adapt the same to the present Constitution of the United States:

Be it enacted, etc., That in all cases in which, by the said ordinance, any information is to be given, or communication made by the Governor of the said Territory to the United States in Congress assembled, or to any of their officers, it shall be the duty of the said Governor to give such information, and to make such communication to the President of the United States; and the President shall nominate, and by and with the advice and consent of the Senate shall appoint all officers which by the said ordinance were to have been appointed by the United States in Congress assembled, and all officers so appointed shall be commissioned by him; and in all cases where the United States in Congress assembled might, by the said ordinance, revoke any commission, or remove from any office, the President is hereby declared to have the same powers of revocation and removal.

Sec. 2. *And be it further enacted*. That in case of the death, removal, resignation, or necessary absence of the Governor of the said Territory, the Secretary thereof shall be, and he is hereby authorized and required to execute all the powers and perform all the duties of the Governor, during the vacancy occasioned by the removal, resignation, or necessary absence of the said Governor.

APPENDIX C

~

The United States Constitution (1787)

The Constitution of the United States

We the People of the United States, in Order to form a more perfect Union, establish Justice, insure domestic Tranquility, provide for the common defence, promote the general Welfare, and secure the Blessings of Liberty to ourselves and our Posterity, do ordain and establish this Constitution for the United States of America.

Article. I.

Section. 1. All legislative Powers herein granted shall be vested in a Congress of the United States, which shall consist of a Senate and a House of Representatives.

Section. 2. The House of Representatives shall be composed of Members chosen every second Year by the People of the several States, and the Electors in each State shall have the Qualifications requisite for Electors of the most numerous Branch of the State Legislature.

No person shall be a Representative who shall not have attained to the Age of twenty five Years, and been seven Years a Citizen of the United

Sources: See *Document Illustrative of the Formation of the Union of the American States*, 69th Cong., 1st sess., House Document No. 398 (Washington, D.C.: Government Printing Office, 1927). See, also, George Anastaplo, *The Constitution of 1787: A Commentary* (Baltimore: Johns Hopkins University Press, 1989), 236, 266–79. See, on Constitutionalism, George Anastaplo, *The Constitutionalist: Notes on the First Amendment* (Dallas: Southern Methodist University Press, 1971; Lanham, Md.: Lexington Books, 2005).

States, and who shall not, when elected, be an Inhabitant of that State in which he shall be chosen.

Representatives and direct Taxes shall be apportioned among the several States which may be included within this Union, according to their respective Numbers, which shall be determined by adding to the whole Number of free Persons, including those bound to Service for a Term of Years, and excluding Indians not taxed, three fifths of all other Persons. The actual Enumeration shall be made within three Years after the first Meeting of the Congress of the United States, and within every subsequent Term of ten Years, in such Manner as they shall by Law direct. The Number of Representatives shall not exceed one for every thirty Thousand, but each State shall have at Least one Representative; and until such enumeration shall be made, the State of New Hampshire shall be entitled to chuse three, Massachusetts eight, Rhode-Island and Providence Plantations one, Connecticut five, New-York six, New Jersey four, Pennsylvania eight, Delaware one, Maryland six, Virginia ten, North Carolina five, South Carolina five, and Georgia three.

When vacancies happen in the Representation from any State, the Executive Authority thereof shall issue Writs of Election to fill such Vacancies.

The House of Representatives shall chuse their Speaker and other Officers; and shall have the sole Power of Impeachment.

Section. 3. The Senate of the United States shall be composed of two Senators from each State, chosen by the Legislature thereof, for six Years; and each Senator shall have one Vote.

Immediately after they shall be assembled in Consequence of the first Election, they shall be divided as equally as may be into three Classes. The Seats of the Senators of the first Class shall be vacated at the Expiration of the second Year, of the second Class at the Expiration of the fourth Year, and of the third Class at the Expiration of the sixth Year, so that one third may be chosen every second Year; and if Vacancies happen by Resignation, or otherwise, during the Recess of the Legislature of any State, the Executive thereof may make temporary Appointments until the next Meeting of the Legislature, which shall then fill such Vacancies.

No Person shall be a Senator who shall not have attained to the Age of thirty Years, and been nine Years a Citizen of the United States, and who shall not, when elected, be an Inhabitant of that State for which he shall be chosen.

The Vice President of the United States shall be President of the Senate, but shall have no Vote, unless they be equally divided.

The Senate shall chuse their other Officers, and also a President pro tempore, in the Absence of the Vice President, or when he shall exercise the Office of President of the United States.

The Senate shall have the sole Power to try all Impeachments. When sitting for that Purpose, they shall be on Oath or Affirmation. When the President of the United States is tried, the Chief Justice shall preside: And no Person shall be convicted without the Concurrence of two thirds of the Members present.

Judgment in Cases of Impeachment shall not extend further than to removal from Office, and disqualification to hold and enjoy any Office of honor, Trust or Profit under the United States: but the Party convicted shall nevertheless be liable and subject to Indictment, Trial, Judgment and Punishment, according to Law.

Section. 4. The Times, Places and Manner of holding Elections for Senators and Representatives, shall be prescribed in each State by the Legislature thereof; but the Congress may at any time by Law make or alter such Regulations, except as to the Places of chusing Senators.

The Congress shall assemble at least once in every Year, and such Meeting shall be on the first Monday in December, unless they shall by Law appoint a different Day.

Section. 5. Each House shall be the Judge of the Elections, Returns and Qualifications of its own Members, and a Majority of each shall constitute a Quorum to do Business; but a smaller Number may adjourn from day to day, and may be authorized to compel the Attendance of absent Members, in such Manner, and under such Penalties as each House may provide.

Each House may determine the Rules of its Proceedings, punish its Members for disorderly Behaviour, and, with the Concurrence of two thirds, expel a Member.

Each House shall keep a Journal of its Proceedings, and from time to time publish the same, excepting such Parts as may in their Judgment require Secrecy; and the Yeas and Nays of the Members of either House on any question shall, at the Desire of one fifth of those Present, be entered on the Journal.

Neither House, during the Session of Congress, shall, without the Consent of the other, adjourn for more than three days, nor to any other Place than that in which the two Houses shall be sitting.

Section. 6. The Senators and Representatives shall receive a Compensation for their Services, to be ascertained by Law, and paid out of the Treasury of the United States. They shall in all Cases, except Treason, Felony and Breach of the Peace, be privileged from Arrest during their Attendance at the Session of their respective Houses, and in going to and returning from the same; and for any Speech or Debate in either House, they shall not be questioned in any other Place.

No Senator or Representative shall, during the Time for which he was elected, be appointed to any civil Office under the Authority of the United

States, which shall have been created, or the Emoluments whereof shall have been encreased during such time; and no Person holding any Office under the United States, shall be a Member of either House during his Continuance in Office.

Section. 7. All Bills for raising Revenue shall originate in the House of Representatives; but the Senate may propose or concur with Amendments as on other Bills.

Every Bill which shall have passed the House of Representatives and the Senate, shall, before it become a Law, be presented to the President of the United States; If he approve he shall sign it, but if not he shall return it, with his Objections to that House in which it shall have originated, who shall enter the Objections at large on their Journal, and proceed to reconsider it. If after such Reconsideration two thirds of that House shall agree to pass the Bill, it shall be sent, together with the Objections, to the other House, by which it shall likewise be reconsidered, and if approved by two thirds of that House, it shall become a Law. But in all such Cases the Votes of both Houses shall be determined by Yeas and Nays, and the Names of the Persons voting for and against the Bill shall be entered on the Journal of each House respectively. If any Bill shall not be returned by the President within ten Days (Sundays excepted) after it shall have been presented to him, the Same shall be a Law, in like Manner as if he had signed it, unless the Congress by their Adjournment prevent its Return, in which Case it shall not be a Law.

Every Order, Resolution, or Vote to which the Concurrence of the Senate and House of Representatives may be necessary (except on a question of Adjournment) shall be presented to the President of the United States; and before the Same shall take Effect, shall be approved by him, or being disapproved by him, shall be repassed by two thirds of the Senate and House of Representatives, according to the Rules and Limitations prescribed in the Case of a Bill.

Section. 8. The Congress shall have Power

To lay and collect Taxes, Duties, Imposts and Excises, to pay the Debts and provide for the common Defence and general Welfare of the United States; but all Duties, Imposts and Excises shall be uniform throughout the United States;

To borrow Money on the credit of the United States;

To regulate Commerce with foreign Nations, and among the several States, and with the Indian Tribes;

To establish an uniform Rule of Naturalization, and uniform Laws on the subject of Bankruptcies throughout the United States;

To coin Money, regulate the Value thereof, and of foreign Coin, and fix the Standard of Weights and Measures;

To provide for the Punishment of counterfeiting the Securities and current Coin of the United States;

To establish Post Offices and post Roads;

To promote the Progress of Science and useful Arts, by securing for limited Times to Authors and Inventors the exclusive Right to their respective Writings and Discoveries;

To constitute Tribunals inferior to the supreme Court;

To define and punish Piracies and Felonies committed on the high Seas, and Offences against the Law of Nations;

To declare War, grant Letters of Marque and Reprisal, and make Rules concerning Captures on Land and Water;

To raise and support Armies, but no Appropriation of Money to that Use shall be for a longer Term than two Years;

To provide and maintain a Navy;

To make Rules for the Government and Regulation of the land and naval Forces;

To provide for calling forth the Militia to execute the Laws of the Union, suppress Insurrections and repel Invasions;

To provide for organizing, arming, and disciplining the Militia, and for governing such Part of them as may be employed in the Service of the United States, reserving to the States respectively, the Appointment of the Officers, and the Authority of training the Militia according to the discipline prescribed by Congress;

To exercise exclusive Legislation in all Cases whatsoever, over such District (not exceeding ten Miles square) as may, by Cession of particular States, and the Acceptance of Congress, become the Seat of the Government of the United States, and to exercise like Authority over all Places purchased by the Consent of the Legislature of the State in which the Same shall be, for the Erection of Forts, Magazines, Arsenals, dock-Yards, and other needful Buildings; —And

To make all Laws which shall be necessary and proper for carrying into Execution the foregoing Powers, and all other Powers vested by this Constitution in the Government of the United States, or in any Department or Officer thereof.

Section. 9. The Migration or Importation of such Persons as any of the States now existing shall think proper to admit, shall not be prohibited by the Congress prior to the Year one thousand eight hundred and eight, but a

Tax or duty may be imposed on such Importation, not exceeding ten dollars for each Person.

The Privilege of the Writ of Habeas Corpus shall not be suspended, unless when in Cases of Rebellion or Invasion the public Safety may require it.

No Bill of Attainder or ex post facto Law shall be passed.

No Capitation, or other direct, Tax shall be laid, unless in Proportion to the Census or Enumeration herein before directed to be taken.

No Tax or Duty shall be laid on Articles exported from any State.

No Preference shall be given by any Regulation of Commerce or Revenue to the Ports of one State over those of another: nor shall Vessels bound to, or from, one State, be obliged to enter, clear, or pay Duties in another.

No Money shall be drawn from the Treasury, but in Consequence of Appropriations made by Law; and a regular Statement and Account of the Receipts and Expenditures of all public Money shall be published from time to time.

No Title of Nobility shall be granted by the United States: And no Person holding any Office of Profit or Trust under them, shall, without the Consent of the Congress, accept of any present, Emolument, Office, or Title, of any kind whatever, from any King, Prince, or foreign State.

Section. 10. No State shall enter into any Treaty, Alliance, or Confederation; grant Letters of Marque and Reprisal; coin Money; emit Bills of Credit; make any Thing but gold and silver Coin a Tender in Payment of Debts; pass any Bill of Attainder, ex post facto Law, or Law impairing the Obligation of Contracts, or grant any Title of Nobility.

No State shall, without the Consent of the Congress, lay any Imposts or Duties on Imports or Exports, except what may be absolutely necessary for executing it's inspection Laws: and the net Produce of all Duties and Imposts, laid by any State on Imports or Exports, shall be for the Use of the Treasury of the United States; and all such Laws shall be subject to the Revision and Controul of the Congress.

No State shall, without the Consent of Congress, lay any Duty of Tonnage, keep Troops, or Ships of War in time of Peace, enter into any Agreement or Compact with another State, or with a foreign Power, or engage in War, unless actually invaded, or in such imminent Danger as will not admit of delay.

Article. II.

Section. 1. The executive Power shall be vested in a President of the United States of America. He shall hold his Office during the Term of four Years, and, together with the Vice President, chosen for the same Term, be elected, as follows

Each State shall appoint, in such Manner as the Legislature thereof may direct, a Number of Electors, equal to the whole Number of Senators and Representatives to which the State may be entitled in the Congress: but no Senator or Representative, or Person holding an Office of Trust or Profit under the United States, shall be appointed an Elector.

The Electors shall meet in their respective States, and vote by Ballot for two Persons, of whom one at least shall not be an Inhabitant of the same State with themselves. And they shall make a List of all the Persons voted for, and of the Number of Votes for each; which List they shall sign and certify, and transmit sealed to the Seat of the Government of the United States, directed to the President of the Senate. The President of the Senate shall, in the Presence of the Senate and House of Representatives, open all the Certificates, and the Votes shall then be counted. The Person having the greatest Number of Votes shall be the President, if such Number be a Majority of the whole Number of Electors appointed; and if there be more than one who have such Majority, and have an equal Number of Votes, then the House of Representatives shall immediately chuse by Ballot one of them for President; and if no Person have a Majority, then from the five highest on the List the said House shall in like Manner chuse the President. But in chusing the President, the Votes shall be taken by States, the Representation from each State having one Vote; A quorum for this Purpose shall consist of a Member or Members from two thirds of the States, and a Majority of all the States shall be necessary to a Choice. In every Case, after the Choice of the President, the Person having the greatest Number of Votes of the Electors shall be the Vice President. But if there should remain two or more who have equal Votes, the Senate shall chuse from them by Ballot the Vice President.

The Congress may determine the Time of chusing the Electors, and the Day on which they shall give their Votes; which Day shall be the same throughout the United States.

No Person except a natural born Citizen, or a Citizen of the United States, at the time of the Adoption of this Constitution, shall be eligible to the Office of President; neither shall any person be eligible to that Office who shall not have attained to the Age of thirty five Years, and been fourteen Years a Resident within the United States.

In Case of the Removal of the President from Office, or of his Death, Resignation, or Inability to discharge the Powers and Duties of the said Office, the Same shall devolve on the Vice President, and the Congress may by Law provide for the Case of Removal, Death, Resignation or Inability, both of the President and Vice President, declaring what Officer shall then act as President, and such Officer shall act accordingly, until the Disability be removed, or a President shall be elected.

The President shall, at stated Times, receive for his Services, a Compensation, which shall neither be encreased nor diminished during the Period for which he shall have been elected, and he shall not receive within that Period any other Emolument from the United States, or any of them.

Before he enter on the Execution of his Office, he shall take the following Oath or Affirmation:— "I do solemnly swear (or affirm) that I will faithfully execute the Office of President of the United States, and will to the best of my Ability, preserve, protect and defend the Constitution of the United States."

Section. 2. The President shall be Commander in Chief of the Army and Navy of the United States, and of the Militia of the several States, when called into the actual Service of the United States; he may require the Opinion, in writing, of the principal Officer in each of the executive Departments, upon any Subject relating to the Duties of their respective Offices, and he shall have Power to grant Reprieves and Pardons for Offences against the United States, except in Cases of Impeachment.

He shall have Power, by and with the Advice and Consent of the Senate, to make Treaties, provided two thirds of the Senators present concur; and he shall nominate, and by and with the Advice and Consent of the Senate, shall appoint Ambassadors, other public Ministers and Consuls, Judges of the supreme Court, and all other Officers of the United States, whose Appointments are not herein otherwise provided for, and which shall be established by Law: but the Congress may by Law vest the Appointment of such inferior Officers, as they think proper, in the President alone, in the Courts of Law, or in the Heads of Departments.

The President shall have Power to fill up all Vacancies that may happen during the Recess of the Senate, by granting Commissions which shall expire at the End of their next Session.

Section. 3. He shall from time to time give to the Congress Information of the State of the Union, and recommend to their Consideration such Measures as he shall judge necessary and expedient; he may, on extraordinary Occasions, convene both Houses, or either of them, and in Case of Disagreement between them, with Respect to the Time of Adjournment, he may adjourn them to such Time as he shall think proper; he shall receive Ambassadors and other public Ministers; he shall take Care that the Laws be faithfully executed, and shall Commission all the Officers of the United States.

Section. 4. The President, Vice President and all civil Officers of the United States, shall be removed from Office on Impeachment for, and Conviction of, Treason, Bribery, or other high Crimes and Misdemeanors.

Article. III.

Section. 1. The judicial Power of the United States, shall be vested in one supreme Court, and in such inferior Courts as the Congress may from time to time ordain and establish. The Judges, both of the supreme and inferior Courts, shall hold their Offices during good Behaviour, and shall, at stated Times, receive for their Services, a Compensation, which shall not be diminished during their Continuance in Office.

Section. 2. The judicial Power shall extend to all Cases, in Law and Equity, arising under this Constitution, the Laws of the United States, and Treaties made, or which shall be made, under their Authority;—to all Cases affecting Ambassadors, other public Ministers and Consuls;—to all Cases of admiralty and maritime Jurisdiction;—to Controversies to which the United States shall be a Party;—to Controversies between two or more States;—between a State and Citizens of another State;—between Citizens of different States,—between Citizens of the same State claiming Lands under Grants of different States, and between a State, or the Citizens thereof, and foreign States, Citizens or Subjects.

In all Cases affecting Ambassadors, other public Ministers and Consuls, and those in which a State shall be a Party, the supreme Court shall have original Jurisdiction. In all the other Cases before mentioned, the supreme Court shall have appellate Jurisdiction, both as to Law and Fact, with such Exceptions, and under such Regulations as the Congress shall make.

The Trial of all Crimes, except in Cases of Impeachment, shall be by Jury; and such Trial shall be held in the State where the said Crimes shall have been committed; but when not committed within any State, the Trial shall be at such Place or Places as the Congress may by Law have directed.

Section. 3. Treason against the United States, shall consist only in levying War against them, or in adhering to their Enemies, giving them Aid and Comfort. No Person shall be convicted of Treason unless on the Testimony of two Witnesses to the same overt Act, or on Confession in open Court.

The Congress shall have Power to declare the Punishment of Treason, but no Attainder of Treason shall work Corruption of Blood, or Forfeiture except during the Life of the Person attainted.

Article. IV.

Section. 1. Full Faith and Credit shall be given in each State to the public Acts, Records, and judicial Proceedings of every other State. And the Congress may by general Laws prescribe the Manner in which such Acts, Records and Proceedings shall be proved, and the Effect thereof.

Section. 2. The Citizens of each State shall be entitled to all Privileges and Immunities of Citizens in the several States.

A Person charged in any State with Treason, Felony, or other Crime, who shall flee from Justice, and be found in another State, shall on Demand of the executive Authority of the State from which he fled, be delivered up, to be removed to the State having Jurisdiction of the Crime.

No Person held to Service or Labour in one State, under the Laws thereof, escaping into another, shall, in Consequence of any Law or Regulation therein, be discharged from such Service or Labour, but shall be delivered up on Claim of the Party to whom such Service or Labour may be due.

Section. 3. New States may be admitted by the Congress into this Union; but no new State shall be formed or erected within the Jurisdiction of any other State; nor any State be formed by the Junction of two or more States, or Parts of States, without the Consent of the Legislatures of the States concerned as well as of the Congress.

The Congress shall have Power to dispose of and make all needful Rules and Regulations respecting the Territory or other Property belonging to the United States; and nothing in this Constitution shall be so construed as to Prejudice any Claims of the United States, or of any particular State.

Section. 4. The United States shall guarantee to every State in this Union a Republican Form of Government, and shall protect each of them against Invasion; and on Application of the Legislature, or of the Executive (when the Legislature cannot be convened) against domestic Violence.

Article. V.

The Congress, whenever two thirds of both Houses shall deem it necessary, shall propose Amendments to this Constitution, or, on the Application of the Legislatures of two thirds of the several States, shall call a Convention for proposing Amendments, which, in either Case, shall be valid to all Intents and Purposes, as Part of this Constitution, when ratified by the Legislatures of three fourths of the several States, or by Conventions in three fourths thereof, as the one or the other Mode of Ratification may be proposed by the Congress; Provided that no Amendment which may be made prior to the Year One thousand eight hundred and eight shall in any Manner affect the first and fourth Clauses in the Ninth Section of the first Article; and that no State, without its Consent, shall be deprived of it's equal Suffrage in the Senate.

Article. VI.

All Debts contracted and Engagements entered into, before the Adoption of this Constitution, shall be as valid against the United States under this Constitution, as under the Confederation.

This Constitution, and the Laws of the United States which shall be made in Pursuance thereof; and all Treaties made, or which shall be made, under the Authority of the United States, shall be the supreme Law of the Land; and the Judges in every State shall be bound thereby, any Thing in the Constitution or Laws of any State to the Contrary notwithstanding.

The Senators and Representatives before mentioned, and the Members of the several State Legislatures, and all executive and judicial Officers, both of the United States and of the several States, shall be bound by Oath or Affirmation, to support this Constitution; but no religious Test shall ever be required as a Qualification to any Office or public Trust under the United States.

Article. VII.

The Ratification of the Conventions of nine States, shall be sufficient for the Establishment of this Constitution between the States so ratifying the Same.

DONE in Convention by the Unanimous Consent of the States present the Seventeenth Day of September in the Year of our Lord one thousand seven hundred and Eighty seven and of the Independence of the United States of America the Twelfth. In Witness whereof We have hereunto subscribed our Names, . . .

[The signatures of these "witnesses" are provided in George Anastaplo, *Reflections on Constitutional Law* (Lexington: University Press of Kentucky, 2006), 221–23.]

APPENDIX D

The Amendments to the United States Constitution (1791–1992)

Articles in Addition to, and Amendment of, the Constitution of the United States, Proposed by Congress and Ratified by the Several States, Pursuant to the Fifth Article of the Original Constitution

Amendment I [1791]

Congress shall make no law respecting an establishment of religion, or prohibiting the free exercise thereof; or abridging the freedom of speech, or of the press; or the right of the people peaceably to assemble, and to petition the Government for a redress of grievances.

Amendment II [1791]

A well regulated Militia, being necessary to the security of a free State, the right of the people to keep and bear Arms, shall not be infringed.

Amendment III [1791]

No Soldier shall, in time of peace be quartered in any house, without the consent of the Owner, nor in time of war, but in a manner to be prescribed by law.

Sources: See *The Declaration of Independence and the Constitution of the United States*, 96th Cong., 1st sess., House Document No. 96–143 (Washington, D.C.: Government Printing Office, 1979). See, also, George Anastaplo, *The Constitution of 1787: A Commentary* (Baltimore: Johns Hopkins University Press, 1989), 237, 288–97; George Anastaplo, *The Amendments to the Constitution: A Commentary* (Baltimore: Johns Hopkins University Press, 1995), 243, 375–84. The dates of ratification of the Amendments are provided in brackets. "Sec." is written as "Section" in all Amendments.

Amendment IV [1791]

The right of the people to be secure in their persons, houses, papers, and effects, against unreasonable searches and seizures, shall not be violated, and no Warrants shall issue, but upon probable cause, supported by Oath or affirmation, and particularly describing the place to be searched, and the persons or things to be seized.

Amendment V [1791]

No person shall be held to answer for a capital, or otherwise infamous crime, unless on a presentment or indictment of a Grand Jury, except in cases arising in the land or naval forces, or in the Militia, when in actual service in time of War or public danger; nor shall any person be subject for the same offence to be twice put in jeopardy of life or limb; nor shall be compelled in any criminal case to be a witness against himself, nor be deprived of life, liberty, or property, without due process of law; nor shall private property be taken for public use, without just compensation.

Amendment VI [1791]

In all criminal prosecutions, the accused shall enjoy the right to a speedy and public trial, by an impartial jury of the State and district wherein the crime shall have been committed, which district shall have been previously ascertained by law, and to be informed of the nature and cause of the accusation; to be confronted with the witnesses against him; to have compulsory process for obtaining witnesses in his favor, and to have the Assistance of Counsel for his defence.

Amendment VII [1791]

In Suits at common law, where the value in controversy shall exceed twenty dollars, the right of trial by jury shall be preserved, and no fact tried by a jury, shall be otherwise re-examined in any Court of the United States, than according to the rules of the common law.

Amendment VIII [1791]

Excessive bail shall not be required, nor excessive fines imposed, nor cruel and unusual punishments inflicted.

Amendment IX [1791]

The enumeration in the Constitution, of certain rights, shall not be construed to deny or disparage others retained by the people.

Amendment X [1791]

The powers not delegated to the United States by the Constitution, nor prohibited by it to the States, are reserved to the States respectively, or to the people.

Amendment XI [1798]

The Judicial power of the United States shall not be construed to extend to any suit in law or equity, commenced or prosecuted against one of the United States by Citizens of another State, or by Citizens or Subjects of any Foreign State.

Amendment XII [1804]

The Electors shall meet in their respective states, and vote by ballot for President and Vice-President, one of whom, at least, shall not be an inhabitant of the same state with themselves; they shall name in their ballots the person voted for as President, and in distinct ballots the person voted for as Vice-President, and they shall make distinct lists of all persons voted for as President, and of all persons voted for as Vice-President, and of the number of votes for each, which lists they shall sign and certify, and transmit sealed to the seat of the government of the United States, directed to the President of the Senate;—The President of the Senate shall, in the presence of the Senate and House of Representatives, open all the certificates and the votes shall then be counted;—The person having the greatest number of votes for President, shall be the President, if such number be a majority of the whole number of Electors appointed; and if no person have such majority, then from the persons having the highest numbers not exceeding three on the list of those voted for as President, the House of Representatives shall choose immediately, by ballot, the President. But in choosing the President, the votes shall be taken by states, the representation from each state having one vote; a quorum for this purpose shall consist of a member or members from two-thirds of the states, and a majority of all the states shall be necessary to a choice. And if the House of Representatives shall not choose a President whenever the right of choice shall devolve upon them, before the fourth day of March next following, then the Vice-President shall act as President, as in the case of the death or other constitutional disability of the President.—The person having the greatest number of votes as Vice-President, shall be the Vice-President, if such number be a majority of the whole number of Electors appointed, and if no person have a majority, then from the two highest numbers on the list, the Senate shall choose the Vice-President; a quorum for the purpose shall consist of two-thirds of the whole number of Senators, and a majority of the whole number shall be necessary to a choice. But no person constitutionally ineligible to the office of President shall be eligible to that of Vice-President of the United States.

Amendment XIII [1865]

Section 1. Neither slavery nor involuntary servitude, except as a punishment for crime whereof the party shall have been duly convicted, shall exist within the United States, or any place subject to their jurisdiction.

Section 2. Congress shall have power to enforce this article by appropriate legislation.

Amendment XIV [1868]

Section 1. All persons born or naturalized in the United States, and subject to the jurisdiction thereof, are citizens of the United States and of the State wherein they reside. No State shall make or enforce any law which shall abridge the privileges or immunities of citizens of the United States; nor shall any State deprive any person of life, liberty, or property, without due process of law; nor deny to any person within its jurisdiction the equal protection of the laws.

Section 2. Representatives shall be apportioned among the several States according to their respective numbers, counting the whole number of persons in each State, excluding Indians not taxed. But when the right to vote at any election for the choice of electors for President and Vice President of the United States, Representatives in Congress, the Executive and Judicial officers of a State, or the members of the Legislature thereof, is denied to any of the male inhabitants of such State, being twenty-one years of age, and citizens of the United States, or in any way abridged, except for participation in rebellion, or other crime, the basis of representation therein shall be reduced in the proportion which the number of such male citizens shall bear to the whole number of male citizens twenty-one years of age in such State.

Section 3. No person shall be a Senator or Representative in Congress, or elector of President and Vice President, or hold any office, civil or military, under the United States, or under any State, who, having previously taken an oath, as a member of Congress, or as an officer of the United States, or as a member of any State legislature, or as an executive or judicial officer of any State, to support the Constitution of the United States, shall have engaged in insurrection or rebellion against the same, or given aid or comfort to the enemies thereof. But Congress may by a vote of two-thirds of each House, remove such disability.

Section 4. The validity of the public debt of the United States, authorized by law, including debts incurred for payment of pensions and bounties for services in suppressing insurrection or rebellion, shall not be questioned. But neither the United States nor any State shall assume or pay any debt or obligation incurred in aid of insurrection or rebellion against the United States, or any claim for the loss or emancipation of any slave; but all such debts, obligations and claims shall be held illegal and void.

Section 5. The Congress shall have power to enforce, by appropriate legislation, the provisions of this article.

Amendment XV [1870]

Section 1. The right of citizens of the United States to vote shall not be denied or abridged by the United States or by any State on account of race, color, or previous condition of servitude.

Section 2. The Congress shall have power to enforce this article by appropriate legislation.

Amendment XVI [1913]

The Congress shall have power to lay and collect taxes on incomes, from whatever source derived, without apportionment among the several States, and without regard to any census or enumeration.

Amendment XVII [1913]

The Senate of the United States shall be composed of two Senators from each State, elected by the people thereof, for six years; and each Senator shall have one vote. The electors in each State shall have the qualifications requisite for electors of the most numerous branch of the State legislatures.

When vacancies happen in the representation of any State in the Senate, the executive authority of such State shall issue writs of election to fill such vacancies: *Provided*, That the legislature of any State may empower the executive thereof to make temporary appointments until the people fill the vacancies by election as the legislature may direct.

This amendment shall not be so construed as to affect the election or term of any Senator chosen before it becomes valid as part of the Constitution.

Amendment XVIII [1919]

Section 1. After one year from the ratification of this article the manufacture, sale, or transportation of intoxicating liquors within, the importation thereof into, or the exportation thereof from the United States and all territory subject to the jurisdiction thereof for beverage purposes is hereby prohibited.

Section 2. The Congress and the several States shall have concurrent power to enforce this article by appropriate legislation.

Section 3. This article shall be inoperative unless it shall have been ratified as an amendment to the Constitution by the legislatures of the several States, as provided in the Constitution, within seven years from the date of the submission hereof to the States by the Congress.

Amendment XIX [1920]

The right of citizens of the United States to vote shall not be denied or abridged by the United States or by any State on account of sex.

Congress shall have power to enforce this article by appropriate legislation.

Amendment XX [1933]

Section 1. The terms of the President and Vice President shall end at noon on the 20th day of January, and the terms of Senators and Representatives at noon on the 3d day of January, of the years in which such terms would have ended if this article had not been ratified; and the terms of their successors shall then begin.

Section 2. The Congress shall assemble at least once in every year, and such meeting shall begin at noon on the 3d day of January, unless they shall by law appoint a different day.

Section 3. If, at the time fixed for the beginning of the term of the President, the President elect shall have died, the Vice President elect shall become President. If a President shall not have been chosen before the time fixed for the beginning of his term, or if the President elect shall have failed to qualify, then the Vice President elect shall act as President until a President shall have qualified; and the Congress may by law provide for the case wherein neither a President elect nor a Vice President elect shall have qualified, declaring who shall then act as President, or the manner in which one who is to act shall be selected, and such person shall act accordingly until a President or Vice President shall have qualified.

Section 4. The Congress may by law provide for the case of the death of any of the persons from whom the House of Representatives may choose a President whenever the right of choice shall have devolved upon them, and for the case of the death of any of the persons from whom the Senate may choose a Vice President whenever the right of choice shall have devolved upon them.

Section 5. Sections 1 and 2 shall take effect on the 15th day of October following the ratification of this article.

Section 6. This article shall be inoperative unless it shall have been ratified as an amendment to the Constitution by the legislatures of three-fourths of the several States within seven years from the date of its submission.

Amendment XXI [1933]

Section 1. The eighteenth article of amendment to the Constitution of the United States is hereby repealed.

Section 2. The transportation or importation into any State, Territory, or possession of the United States for delivery or use therein of intoxicating liquors, in violation of the laws thereof, is hereby prohibited.

Section 3. This article shall be inoperative unless it shall have been ratified as an amendment to the Constitution by conventions in the several States, as provided in the Constitution, within seven years from the date of the submission hereof to the States by the Congress.

Amendment XXII [1951]

Section 1. No person shall be elected to the office of the President more than twice, and no person who has held the office of President, or acted as President, for more than two years of a term to which some other person was elected President shall be elected to the office of the President more than once. But this Article shall not apply to any person holding the office of President when this Article was proposed by the Congress, and shall not prevent any person who may be holding the office of President, or acting as President, during the term within which this Article becomes operative from holding the office of President or acting as President during the remainder of such term.

Section 2. This article shall be inoperative unless it shall have been ratified as an amendment to the Constitution by the legislatures of three-fourths of the several States within seven years from the date of its submission to the States by the Congress.

Amendment XXIII [1961]

Section 1. The District constituting the seat of Government of the United States shall appoint in such manner as the Congress may direct:

A number of electors of President and Vice President equal to the whole number of Senators and Representatives in Congress to which the District would be entitled if it were a State, but in no event more than the least populous State; they shall be in addition to those appointed by the States, but they shall be considered, for the purposes of the election of President and Vice President, to be electors appointed by a State; and they shall meet in the District and perform such duties as provided by the twelfth article of amendment.

Section 2. The Congress shall have power to enforce this article by appropriate legislation.

Amendment XXIV [1964]

Section 1. The right of citizens of the United States to vote in any primary or other election for President or Vice President, for electors for President or Vice President, or for Senator or Representative in Congress, shall not be denied or abridged by the United States or any State by reason of failure to pay any poll tax or other tax.

Section 2. The Congress shall have power to enforce this article by appropriate legislation.

Amendment XXV [1967]

Section 1. In case of the removal of the President from office or of his death or resignation, the Vice President shall become President.

Section 2. Whenever there is a vacancy in the office of the Vice President, the President shall nominate a Vice President who shall take office upon confirmation by a majority vote of both Houses of Congress.

Section 3. Whenever the President transmits to the President pro tempore of the Senate and the Speaker of the House of Representatives his written declaration that he is unable to discharge the powers and duties of his office, and until he transmits to them a written declaration to the contrary, such powers and duties shall be discharged by the Vice President as Acting President.

Section 4. Whenever the Vice President and a majority of either the principal officers of the executive departments or of such other body as Congress may by law provide, transmit to the President pro tempore of the Senate and the Speaker of the House of Representatives their written declaration that the President is unable to discharge the powers and duties of his office, the Vice President shall immediately assume the powers and duties of the office as Acting President.

Thereafter, when the President transmits to the President pro tempore of the Senate and the Speaker of the House of Representatives his written declaration that no inability exists, he shall resume the powers and duties of his office unless the Vice President and a majority of either the principal officers of the executive department or of such other body as Congress may by law provide, transmit within four days to the President pro tempore of the Senate and the Speaker of the House of Representatives their written declaration that the President is unable to discharge the powers and duties of his office. Thereupon Congress shall decide the issue, assembling within forty-eight hours for that purpose if not in session. If the Congress, within twenty-one days after receipt of the latter written declaration, or, if Congress is not in session, within twenty-one days after Congress is required to assemble, determines by two-thirds vote of both Houses that the President is unable to discharge the powers and duties of his office, the Vice President shall continue to discharge the same as Acting President; otherwise, the President shall resume the powers and duties of his office.

Amendment XXVI [1971]

Section 1. The right of citizens of the United States, who are eighteen years of age or older, to vote shall not be denied or abridged by the United States or by any State on account of age.

Section 2. The Congress shall have power to enforce this article by appropriate legislation.

Amendment XXVII [1992]

No law varying the compensation for the services of the Senators and Representatives shall take effect until an election of Representatives shall have intervened. [This amendment was originally submitted by Congress to the States in 1789 for ratification.]

APPENDIX E

The Confederate Constitution (1861)

The Constitution of the Confederate States of America

[*The texts of the first twelve amendments to the United States Constitution of 1787 are substantially incorporated in Articles I, II, III, and VI of the Confederate Constitution, which itself works from the 1787 Constitution. The numbering and most of the words added in 1861 to the Constitution of 1787 and to its first twelve amendments incorporated therein are emphasized below except for the numbers routinely added within each section. The 1861 changes in the spelling, capitalization, punctuation, and italicization are* not *noted by emphasis here. These changes are not uniform in all editions available to us of the Confederate Constitution of 1861.*]

We, the people of the *Confederate* States, *each State acting in its sovereign and independent character*, in order to form *a permanent federal government*, establish justice, insure domestic tranquillity, and secure the blessings of liberty to ourselves and our posterity—*invoking the favor and guidance of Almighty God*—do ordain and establish this Constitution for the *Confederate* States of America.

Sources: See Senate Document No. 234, 58th Cong., 2nd sess. (Washington, D.C.: Government Printing Office, 1904), 909–23; Roger L. Ransom, *The Confederate States of America* (New York: W. W. Norton and Co., 2005), 265–86. See, also, George Anastaplo, *The Amendments to the Constitution: A Commentary* (Baltimore: Johns Hopkins University Press, 1995), 243, 344–61. See, as well, George Anastaplo, *Abraham Lincoln: A Constitutional Biography* [preferred title, *Thoughts on Abraham Lincoln: A Discourse on Prudence*] (Lanham, Md.: Rowman & Littlefield, 1999).

Article I.

Section 1.

All legislative powers herein *delegated* shall be vested in a Congress of the *Confederate* States, which shall consist of a Senate and a House of Representatives.

Section 2.

1. The House of Representatives shall be composed of members chosen every second year by the people of the several States; and the electors in each State shall *be citizens of the Confederate States, and* have the qualifications requisite for electors of the most numerous branch of the State Legislature; *but no person of foreign birth, not a citizen of the Confederate States, shall be allowed to vote for any officer, civil or political, State or Federal.*

2. No person shall be a Representative who shall not have attained the age of twenty-five years, and *be* a citizen of the *Confederate* States, and who shall not when elected, be an inhabitant of that State in which he shall be chosen.

3. Representatives and direct taxes shall be apportioned among the several States, which may be included within this *Confederacy*, according to their respective numbers, which shall be determined, by adding to the whole number of free persons, including those bound to service for a term of years, and excluding Indians not taxed, three-fifths of all *slaves*. The actual enumeration shall be made within three years after the first meeting of the Congress of the *Confederate* States, and within every subsequent term of ten years, in such manner as they shall by law direct. The number of Representatives shall not exceed one for every *fifty* thousand, but each State shall have at least one Representative; and until such enumeration shall be made, *the State of South Carolina* shall be entitled to choose *six; the State of Georgia ten; the State of Alabama nine; the State of Florida two; the State of Mississippi seven; the State of Louisiana six; and the State of Texas six.*

4. When vacancies happen in the representation from any State the executive authority thereof shall issue writs of election to fill such vacancies.

5. The House of Representatives shall choose their Speaker and other officers; and shall have the sole power of impeachment; *except that any judicial or other Federal officer, resident and acting solely within the limits of any State, may be impeached by a vote of two-thirds of both branches of the Legislature thereof.*

Section 3.

1. The Senate of the *Confederate* States shall be composed of two Senators from each State, chosen for six years by the Legislature thereof, *at the regular*

session next immediately preceding the commencement of the term of service; and each Senator shall have one vote.

2. Immediately after they shall be assembled, in consequence of the first election, they shall be divided as equally as may be into three classes. The seats of the Senators of the first class shall be vacated at the expiration of the second year; of the second class at the expiration of the fourth year; and of the third class at the expiration of the sixth year; so that one-third may be chosen every second year; and if vacancies happen by resignation, or otherwise, during the recess of the Legislature of any State, the Executive thereof may make temporary appointments until the next meeting of the Legislature, which shall then fill such vacancies.

3. No person shall be a Senator who shall not have attained the age of thirty years, and *be* a citizen of the *Confederate* States; and who shall not, when elected, be an inhabitant of the State for which he shall be chosen.

4. The Vice President of the *Confederate* States shall be President of the Senate, but shall have no vote unless they be equally divided.

5. The Senate shall choose their other officers; and also a president pro tempore in the absence of the Vice President, or when he shall exercise the office of President of the *Confederate* States.

6. The Senate shall have the sole power to try all impeachments. When sitting for that purpose, they shall be on oath or affirmation. When the President of the *Confederate* States is tried, the Chief Justice shall preside; and no person shall be convicted without the concurrence of two-thirds of the members present.

7. Judgment in cases of impeachment shall not extend further than to removal from office, and disqualification to hold any office of honor, trust, or profit under the *Confederate* States; but the party convicted shall, nevertheless, be liable and subject to indictment, trial, judgment and punishment according to law.

Section 4.

1. The times, places, and manner of holding elections for Senators and Representatives, shall be prescribed in each State by the Legislature thereof, *subject to the provisions of this Constitution*; but the Congress may, at any time, by law, make or alter such regulations, except as to the *times and* places of choosing Senators.

2. The Congress shall assemble at least once in every year; and such meeting shall be on the first Monday in December, unless they shall, by law, appoint a different day.

Section 5.

1. Each House shall be the judge of the elections, returns, and qualifications of its own members, and a majority of each shall constitute a quorum to do business; but a smaller number may adjourn from day to day, and may be authorized to compel the attendance of absent members, in such manner and under such penalties as each House may provide.

2. Each House may determine the rules of its proceedings, punish its members for disorderly behavior, and, with the concurrence of two-thirds *of the whole number*, expel a member.

3. Each House shall keep a journal of its proceedings, and from time to time publish the same, excepting such parts as may in their judgment require secrecy; and the yeas and nays of the members of either House, on any question, shall, at the desire of one-fifth of those present, be entered on the journal.

4. Neither House, during the session of Congress, shall without the consent of the other, adjourn for more than three days, nor to any other place than that in which the two Houses shall be sitting.

Section 6.

1. The Senators and Representatives shall receive a compensation for their services, to be ascertained by law, and paid out of the Treasury of the *Confederate* States. They shall, in all cases, except treason, felony, and breach of the peace, be privileged from arrest during their attendance at the session of their respective Houses, and in going to and returning from the same; and for any speech or debate in either House, they shall not be questioned in any other place.

2. No Senator or Representative shall, during the time for which he was elected, be appointed to any civil office under the authority of the *Confederate* States, which shall have been created, or the emoluments whereof shall have been increased during such time; and no person holding any office under the *Confederate* States shall be a member of either House during his continuance in office. *But Congress may, by law, grant to the principal officer in each of the Executive Departments a seat upon the floor of either House, with the privilege of discussing any measures appertaining to his department.*

Section 7.

1. All bills for raising revenue shall originate in the House of Representatives; but the Senate may propose or concur with amendments, as on other bills.

2. Every bill which shall have passed *both Houses*, shall, before it becomes a law, be presented to the President of the *Confederate* States; if he approve, he shall sign it; but if not, he shall return it, with his objections, to that House in which it shall have originated, who shall enter the objections at large on their journal, and proceed to reconsider it. If, after such reconsideration, two-thirds of that House shall agree to pass the bill, it shall be sent, together with the objections, to the other House, by which it shall likewise be reconsidered, and if approved by two-thirds of that House, it shall become a law. But in all such cases, the votes of both Houses shall be determined by yeas and nays, and the names of the persons voting for and against the bill shall be entered on the journal of each House respectively. If any bill shall not be returned by the President within ten days (Sundays excepted) after it shall have been presented to him, the same shall be a law, in like manner as if he had signed it, unless the Congress, by their adjournment, prevent its return; in which case it shall not be a law. *The President may approve any appropriation and disapprove any other appropriation in the same bill. In such case he shall, in signing the bill, designate the appropriations disapproved; and shall return a copy of such appropriations, with his objections, to the House in which the bill shall have originated; and the same proceedings shall then be had as in case of other bills disapproved by the President.*

3. Every order, resolution, or vote, to which the concurrence of both Houses may be necessary (except on a question of adjournment) shall be presented to the President of the *Confederate* States; and before the same shall take effect, shall be approved by him; or being disapproved by him, shall be repassed by two-thirds of *both Houses*, according to the rules and limitations prescribed in case of a bill.

Section 8.

The Congress shall have power—

1. To lay and collect taxes, duties, imposts, and excises *for revenue, necessary* to pay the debts, provide for the common defence, *and carry on the Government of the Confederate States; but no bounties shall be granted from the Treasury; nor shall any duties or taxes on importations from foreign nations be laid to promote or foster any branch of industry*; and all duties, imposts, and excises shall be uniform throughout the *Confederate* States;

2. To borrow money on the credit of the *Confederate* States;

3. To regulate commerce with foreign nations, and among the several States, and with the Indian tribes; *but neither this, nor any other clause contained in the Constitution, shall ever be construed to delegate the power to*

Congress to appropriate money for any internal improvement intended to facilitate commerce; except for the purpose of furnishing lights, beacons, and buoys, and other aids to navigation upon the coasts, and the improvement of harbors and the removing of obstructions in river navigation; in all which cases such duties shall be laid on the navigation facilitated thereby as may be necessary to pay the costs and expenses thereof;

4. To establish uniform *laws* of naturalization, and uniform laws on the subject of bankruptcies, throughout the *Confederate* States; *but no law of Congress shall discharge any debt contracted before the passage of the same*;

5. To coin money, regulate the value thereof, and of foreign coin, and fix the standard of weights and measures;

6. To provide for the punishment of counterfeiting the securities and current coin of the *Confederate* States;

7. To establish post offices and post *routes; but the expenses of the Post Office Department, after the first day of March, in the year of our Lord eighteen hundred and sixty-three, shall be paid out of its own revenues*;

8. To promote the progress of science and useful arts, by securing for limited times to authors and inventors the exclusive right to their respective writings and discoveries;

9. To constitute tribunals inferior to the Supreme Court;

10. To define and punish piracies and felonies committed on the high seas, and offenses against the law of nations;

11. To declare war, grant letters of marque and reprisal, and make rules concerning captures on land and water;

12. To raise and support armies; but no appropriation of money to that use shall be for a longer term than two years;

13. To provide and maintain a navy;

14. To make rules for the government and regulation of the land and naval forces;

15. To provide for calling forth the militia to execute the laws of the *Confederate* States, suppress insurrections, and repel invasions;

16. To provide for organizing, arming, and disciplining the militia, and for governing such part of them as may be employed in the service of the *Confederate* States; reserving to the States, respectively, the appointment of the officers, and the authority of training the militia according to the discipline prescribed by Congress;

17. To exercise exclusive legislation, in all cases whatsoever, over such district (not exceeding ten miles square) as may, by cession of *one or more* States and the acceptance of Congress, become the seat of the Government of the *Confederate* States; and to exercise like authority over all places pur-

chased by the consent of the Legislature of the State in which the same shall be, for the erection of forts, magazines, arsenals, dockyards, and other needful buildings; and

18. To make all laws which shall be necessary and proper for carrying into execution the foregoing powers, and all other powers vested by this Constitution in the Government of the *Confederate* States, or in any department or officer thereof.

Section 9.

1. The importation of *negroes of the African race from any foreign country other than the slaveholding States or Territories of the United States of America, is hereby forbidden; and Congress is required to pass such laws as shall effectually prevent the same.*

2. *Congress shall also have power to prohibit the introduction of slaves from any State not a member of, or Territory not belonging to, this Confederacy.*

3. The privilege of the writ of *habeas corpus* shall not be suspended, unless when in cases of rebellion or invasion the public safety may require it.

4. No bill of attainder, *ex post facto* law, *or law denying or impairing the right of property in negro slaves* shall be passed.

5. No capitation or other direct tax shall be laid, unless in proportion to the census or enumeration hereinbefore directed to be taken.

6. No tax or duty shall be laid on Articles exported from any State, *except by a vote of two-thirds of both Houses.*

7. No preference shall be given by any regulation of commerce or revenue to the ports of one State over those of another.

8. No money shall be drawn from the Treasury, but in consequence of appropriations made by law; and a regular statement and account of the receipts and expenditures of all public money shall be published from time to time.

9. *Congress shall appropriate no money from the Treasury except by a vote of two-thirds of both Houses, taken by yeas and nays, unless it be asked and estimated for by some one of the heads of departments and submitted to Congress by the President; or for the purpose of paying its own expenses and contingencies; or for the payment of claims against the Confederate States, the justice of which shall have been judicially declared by a tribunal for the investigation of claims against the Government, which it is hereby made the duty of Congress to establish.*

10. *All bills appropriating money shall specify in Federal currency, the exact amount of each appropriation and the purposes for which it is made; and Congress shall grant no extra compensation to any public contractor, officer, agent, or servant, after such contract shall have been made or such service rendered.*

11. No title of nobility shall be granted by the *Confederate* States; and no person holding any office of profit or trust under them shall, without the consent of the Congress, accept of any present, emolument, office or title of any kind whatever, from any king, prince, or foreign state.

12. Congress shall make no law respecting an establishment of religion, or prohibiting the free exercise thereof; or abridging the freedom of speech, or of the press; or the right of the people peaceably to assemble and petition the Government for a redress of grievances.

13. A well-regulated militia being necessary to the security of a free State, the right of the people to keep and bear arms shall not be infringed.

14. No soldier shall, in time of peace, be quartered in any house, without the consent of the owner; nor in time of war, but in a manner to be prescribed by law.

15. The right of the people to be secure in their persons, houses, papers, and effects, against unreasonable searches and seizures, shall not be violated; and no warrants shall issue but upon probable cause, supported by oath or affirmation, and particularly describing the place to be searched and the persons or things to be seized.

16. No person shall be held to answer for a capital or otherwise infamous crime, unless on a presentment or indictment of a grand jury, except in cases arising in the land or naval forces, or in the militia, when in actual service in time of war or public danger; nor shall any person be subject for the same offense to be twice put in jeopardy of life or limb; nor be compelled, in any criminal case, to be a witness against himself; nor be deprived of life, liberty, or property, without due process of law; nor shall private property be taken for public use, without just compensation.

17. In all criminal prosecutions the accused shall enjoy the right to a speedy and public trial, by an impartial jury of the State and district wherein the crime shall have been committed, which district shall have been previously ascertained by law, and to be informed of the nature and cause of the accusation; to be confronted with the witnesses against him; to have compulsory process for obtaining witnesses in his favor; and to have the assistance of counsel for his defense.

18. In suits at common law, where the value in controversy shall exceed twenty dollars, the right of trial by jury shall be preserved; and no fact *so* tried by a jury shall be otherwise reexamined in any court of the *Confederacy*, than according to the rules of common law.

19. Excessive bail shall not be required, nor excessive fines imposed, nor cruel and unusual punishments inflicted.

20. *Every law, or resolution having the force of law, shall relate to but one subject, and that shall be expressed in the title.*

Section 10.

1. No State shall enter into any treaty, alliance, or confederation; grant letters of marque and reprisal; coin money; make anything but gold and silver coin a tender in payment of debts; pass any bill of attainder, or ex post facto law, or law impairing the obligation of contracts; or grant any title of nobility.

2. No State shall, without the consent of the Congress, lay any imposts or duties on imports or exports, except what may be absolutely necessary for executing its inspection laws; and the net produce of all duties and imposts, laid by any State on imports or exports, shall be for the use of the Treasury of the *Confederate* States; and all such laws shall be subject to the revision and control of Congress.

3. No State shall, without the consent of Congress, lay any duty on tonnage, *except on sea-going vessels, for the improvement of its rivers and harbors navigated by the said vessels; but such duties shall not conflict with any treaties of the Confederate States with foreign nations; and any surplus revenue, thus derived, shall, after making such improvement, be paid into the common treasury. Nor shall any State* keep troops or ships-of-war in time of peace, enter into any agreement or compact with another State, or with a foreign power, or engage in war, unless actually invaded, or in such imminent danger as will not admit of delay. *But when any river divides or flows through two or more States they may enter into compacts with each other to improve the navigation* thereof.

Article II.

Section 1.

1. The executive power shall be vested in a President of the *Confederate* States of America. *He and the Vice President* shall hold *their* offices *for* the term of *six* years; *but the President shall not be re-eligible. The President and Vice President shall* be elected as follows:

2. Each State shall appoint, in such manner as the legislature thereof may direct, a number of electors equal to the whole number of Senators and Representatives to which the State may be entitled in the Congress; but no Senator or Representative or person holding an office of trust or profit under the *Confederate* States shall be appointed an elector.

3. The electors shall meet in their respective States and vote by ballot for President and Vice President, one of whom, at least, shall not be an inhabitant of the same State with themselves; they shall name in their ballots the person

voted for as President, and in distinct ballots the person voted for as Vice President, and they shall make distinct lists of all persons voted for as President, and of all persons voted for as Vice President, and of the number of votes for each, which lists they shall sign and certify, and transmit, sealed, to the seat of the government of the *Confederate* States, directed to the President of the Senate; the President of the Senate shall, in the presence of the Senate and House of Representatives, open all the certificates, and the votes shall then be counted; the person having the greatest number of votes for President shall be the President, if such number be a majority of the whole number of electors appointed; and if no person have such majority, then, from the persons having the highest numbers, not exceeding three, on the list of those voted for as President, the House of Representatives shall choose immediately, by ballot, the President. But in choosing the President the votes shall be taken by States—the representation from each State having one vote; a quorum for this purpose shall consist of a member or members from two-thirds of the States, and a majority of all the States shall be necessary to a choice. And if the House of Representatives shall not choose a President, whenever the right of choice shall devolve upon them, before the fourth day of March next following, then the Vice President shall act as President, as in case of the death, or other constitutional disability of the President.

4. The person having the greatest number of votes as Vice President shall be the Vice President, if such number be a majority of the whole number of electors appointed; and if no person have a majority, then, from the two highest numbers on the list, the Senate shall choose the Vice President; a quorum for the purpose shall consist of two-thirds of the whole number of Senators, and a majority of the whole number shall be necessary to a choice.

5. But no person constitutionally ineligible to the office of President shall be eligible to that of Vice President of the *Confederate* States.

6. The Congress may determine the time of choosing the electors, and the day on which they shall give their votes; which day shall be the same throughout the *Confederate* States.

7. No person except a natural born citizen *of the Confederate* States, or a citizen *thereof* at the time of the adoption of this Constitution, *or a citizen thereof born in the United States prior to the 20th of December, 1860*, shall be eligible to the office of President; neither shall any person be eligible to that office who shall not have attained the age of thirty-five years, and been fourteen years a resident within *the limits of the Confederate States, as they may exist at the time of his election.*

8. In case of the removal of the President from office, or of his death, resignation, or inability to discharge the powers and duties of said office, the

same shall devolve on the Vice President; and the Congress may, by law, provide for the case of removal, death, resignation, or inability, both of the President and Vice President, declaring what officer shall then act as President; and such officer shall act accordingly, until the disability be removed or a President shall be elected.

9. The President shall, at stated times, receive for his services a compensation, which shall neither be increased nor diminished during the period for which he shall have been elected; and he shall not receive within that period any other emolument from the *Confederate* States, or any of them.

10. Before he enters on the execution of his office, he shall take the following oath or affirmation: "I do solemnly swear (or affirm) that I will faithfully execute the office of President of the *Confederate* States, and will, to the best of my ability, preserve, protect, and defend the Constitution *thereof*."

Section 2.

1. The President shall be Commander-in-Chief of the Army and Navy of the *Confederate* States, and of the militia of the several States, when called into the actual service of the *Confederate* States; he may require the opinion, in writing, of the principal officer in each of the executive departments, upon any subject relating to the duties of their respective offices; and he shall have power to grant reprieves and pardons for offenses against the *Confederate* States, except in cases of impeachment.

2. He shall have power, by and with the advice and consent of the Senate, to make treaties; provided two-thirds of the Senators present concur; and he shall nominate, and by and with the advice and consent of the Senate, shall appoint ambassadors, other public ministers and consuls, judges of the Supreme Court, and all other officers of the *Confederate* States whose appointments are not herein otherwise provided for, and which shall be established by law; but the Congress may, by law, vest the appointment of such inferior officers, as they think proper, in the President alone, in the courts of law, or in the heads of departments.

3. *The principal officer in each of the Executive Departments, and all persons connected with the diplomatic service, may be removed from office at the pleasure of the President. All other civil officers of the Executive Departments may be removed at any time by the President, or other appointing power, when their services are unnecessary, or for dishonesty, incapacity. inefficiency, misconduct, or neglect of duty; and when so removed, the removal shall be reported to the Senate, together with the reasons therefor.*

4. The President shall have power to fill all vacancies that may happen during the recess of the Senate, by granting commissions which shall expire

at the end of their next session; *but no person rejected by the Senate shall be re-appointed to the same office during their ensuing recess*.

Section 3.

1. *The President* shall, from time to time, give to the Congress information of the state of the *Confederacy*, and recommend to their consideration such measures as he shall judge necessary and expedient; he may, on extraordinary occasions, convene both Houses, or either of them; and in case of disagreement between them, with respect to the time of adjournment, he may adjourn them to such time as he shall think proper; he shall receive ambassadors and other public ministers; he shall take care that the laws be faithfully executed, and shall commission all the officers of the *Confederate* States.

Section 4.

1. The President, Vice President, and all civil officers of the *Confederate* States, shall be removed from office on impeachment for, and conviction of, treason, bribery, or other high crimes and misdemeanors.

Article III.

Section 1.

1. The judicial power of the *Confederate* States shall be vested in one Supreme Court, and in such inferior courts as the Congress may, from time to time, ordain and establish. The judges, both of the Supreme and inferior courts, shall hold their offices during good behavior, and shall, at stated times, receive for their services a compensation which shall not be diminished during their continuance in office.

Section 2.

1. The judicial power shall extend to all cases arising under this Constitution, the laws of the *Confederate* States; and treaties made, or which shall be made, under their authority; to all cases affecting ambassadors, other public ministers and consuls; to all cases of admiralty and maritime jurisdiction; to controversies to which the *Confederate* States shall be a party; to controversies between two or more States; between a State and citizens of another State, *where the State is plaintiff*; between citizens claiming lands under grants of different States; and between a State or the citizens thereof, and foreign states, citizens, or subjects; but no State shall be sued by a citizen or subject of any foreign state.

2. In all cases affecting ambassadors, other public ministers and consuls, and those in which a State shall be a party, the Supreme Court shall have original jurisdiction. In all the other cases before mentioned, the Supreme Court shall have appellate jurisdiction both as to law and fact, with such exceptions and under such regulations as the Congress shall make.

3. The trial of all crimes, except in cases of impeachment, shall be by jury, and such trial shall be held in the State where the said crimes shall have been committed; but when not committed within any State, the trial shall be at such place or places as the Congress may by law have directed.

Section 3.

1. Treason against the *Confederate* States shall consist only in levying war against them, or in adhering to their enemies, giving them aid and comfort. No person shall be convicted of treason unless on the testimony of two witnesses to the same overt act, or on confession in open court.

2. The Congress shall have power to declare the punishment of treason; but no attainder of treason shall work corruption of blood, or forfeiture, except during the life of the person attainted.

Article IV.

Section I.

1. Full faith and credit shall be given in each State to the public acts, records, and judicial proceedings of every other State. And the Congress may, by general laws, prescribe the manner in which such acts, records, and proceedings shall be proved, and the effect thereof.

Section 2.

1. The citizens of each State shall be entitled to all the privileges and immunities of citizens in the several States; *and shall have the right of transit and sojourn in any State of this Confederacy, with their slaves and other property; and the right of property in said slaves shall not be thereby impaired.*

2. A person charged in any State with treason, felony, or other crime *against the laws of such State*, who shall flee from justice, and be found in another State, shall, on demand of the Executive authority of the State from which he fled, be delivered up, to be removed to the State having jurisdiction of the crime.

3. No *slave or other* person held to service or labor in *any* State *or Territory of the Confederate States*, under the laws thereof, escaping *or lawfully carried*

into another, shall, in consequence of any law or regulation therein, be discharged from such service or labor; but shall be delivered up on claim of the party to whom *such slave belongs; or to whom* such service or labor may be due.

Section 3.

1. *Other* States may be admitted *into this Confederacy by a vote of two-thirds of the whole House of Representatives and two-thirds of the Senate, the Senate voting by States;* but no new State shall be formed or erected within the jurisdiction of any other State, nor any State be formed by the junction of two or more States, or parts of States, without the consent of the legislatures of the States concerned, as well as of the Congress.

2. The Congress shall have power to dispose of and make all needful rules and regulations *concerning the* property of *the Confederate States, including the lands thereof.*

3. *The Confederate States may acquire new territory; and Congress shall have power to legislate and provide governments for the inhabitants of all territory belonging to the Confederate States, lying without the limits of the several States; and may permit them, at such times, and in such manner as it may by law provide, to form States to be admitted into the Confederacy. In all such territory, the institution of negro slavery, as it now exists in the Confederate States, shall be recognized and protected by Congress and by the territorial government; and the inhabitants of the several Confederate States and Territories shall have the right to take to such territory any slaves lawfully held by them in any of the States or Territories of the Confederate States.*

4. The *Confederate* States shall guarantee to every State *that now is, or hereafter may become, a member of this Confederacy*, a republican form of government; and shall protect each of them against invasion; and on application of the Legislature (or of the Executive when the Legislature *is not in session*), against domestic violence.

Article V.

Section I.

1. *Upon the demand of any three States, legally assembled in their several conventions, the Congress shall summon a convention of all the States, to take into consideration such amendments to the Constitution as the said States shall concur in suggesting at the time when the said demand is made; and should any of the proposed amendments to the Constitution be agreed on by the said convention—voting by States—and the same be* ratified by the Legislatures of *two-thirds* of the several States, or by conventions in *two-thirds* thereof—as the one or the

other mode of ratification may be proposed by the *general convention*—they *shall thenceforward form* a part of this Constitution. *But* no State *shall*, without its consent, be deprived of its equal *representation* in the Senate.

Article VI.

1. *The Government established by this Constitution is the successor of the Provisional Government of the Confederate States of America, and all the laws passed by the latter shall continue in force until the same shall be repealed or modified; and all the officers appointed by the same shall remain in office until their successors are appointed and qualified, or the offices abolished.*

2. All debts contracted and engagements entered into before the adoption of this Constitution shall be as valid against the *Confederate* States under this Constitution, as under the *Provisional Government*.

3. This Constitution, and the laws of the *Confederate* States, made in pursuance thereof, and all treaties made, or which shall be made, under the authority of the *Confederate* States, shall be the supreme law of the land; and the judges in every State shall be bound thereby, anything in the Constitution or laws of any State to the contrary notwithstanding.

4. The Senators and Representatives before mentioned, and the members of the several State Legislatures, and all executive and judicial officers, both of the *Confederate* States and of the several States, shall be bound by oath or affirmation to support this Constitution; but no religious test shall ever be required as a qualification to any office or public trust under the *Confederate* States.

5. The enumeration, in the Constitution, of certain rights shall not be construed to deny or disparage others retained by the people *of the several States*.

6. The powers not delegated to the *Confederate* States by the Constitution, nor prohibited by it to the States, are reserved to the States, respectively, or to the people *thereof*.

Article VII.

1. The ratification of the conventions of *five* States shall be sufficient for the establishment of this Constitution between the States so ratifying the same.

2. *When five States shall have ratified this Constitution, in the manner before specified, the Congress under the Provisional Constitution shall prescribe the time for holding the election of President and Vice President; and for the meeting of the Electoral College; and for counting the votes, and inaugurating the President. They shall, also, prescribe the time for holding the first election of members of Congress*

under this Constitution, and the time for assembling the same. Until the assembling of such Congress, the Congress under the Provisional Constitution shall continue to exercise the legislative powers granted them; not extending beyond the time limited by the Constitution of the Provisional Government.

Adopted unanimously by the Congress of the Confederate States of South Carolina, Georgia, Florida, Alabama, Mississippi, Louisiana, and Texas, sitting in Convention at the capitol, in the city of Montgomery, Alabama, on the Eleventh day of March, in the Year Eighteen Hundred and Sixty-one . . .

[The numbering and most of the words added by the Confederate States Convention in 1861 to the Constitution of 1787 and to its first twelve amendments incorporated therein are underlined in the version of the Confederate Constitution provided in George Anastaplo, *Reflections on Constitutional Law* (Lexington: University Press of Kentucky, 2006, 239–55). The 1861 changes in spelling, capitalization, punctuation and italicization are not indicated by underlining there, or otherwise noticed either there or here.]

APPENDIX F

On the Relations of Slaves to Masters Who Considered Them "Nothings"

This conversation of May 25, 2000, is one of thirteen conversations in a six-hundred-page transcript of recorded conversations between George Anastaplo and Simcha Brudno, *Simply Unbelievable: Conversations with a Holocaust Survivor*. The first such conversation (March 23, 2000) is included in *Reflections on Life, Death, and the Constitution* (2009). The second such conversation (March 30, 2000) is included in *The Christian Heritage: Problems and Prospects* (2010). The third such conversation (May 4, 2000) is included in *Abraham Lincoln, Lawyers, and the Civil War: Bicentennial Explorations* (Volume 35 of the *Oklahoma City University Law Review* [2010]). It has been translated into Spanish by Manuel Vela Rodriguez, with the title *Simplemente Increible: Conversaciones con un supervivente del Holocausto*. A fourth conversation is included in Volume 35 of the *Southern Illinois University Law Journal* (2011). The tapes of these thirteen conversations were transcribed by Adam Reinherz, who was then a student at Loyola University Chicago School of Law. The current availability of these conversations in print has very much depended on both his diligence and his knowledge of Jewish things. All of these conversations were recorded in Regenstein Library at the University of Chicago.

Simcha Brudno, a recognized mathematician, lived in Siauliai, Lithuania, until he was deported to Dachau, Germany, in 1944. After the war he lived in Israel before settling in the United States. For more information on Simcha Brudno, see Joel Noel, Obituary, *Chicago Tribune*, June 13, 2006. See, also, George Anastaplo, *The Bible: Respectful Readings* (Lexington Books, 2008).

There are provided, at pages 299–300 of this Appendix, scholarly recollections of the dreadful experiences of Jews in Lithuania at the hands of both the Lithuanians and the Germans during the Second World War. The Lithuania occupied by the Nazis since 1941, from which a Dachau-bound contingent of Jews was shipped in 1944, is glanced at in the Afterword added to this Year 2000 Conversation in Chicago.

Anastaplo: You say there were other places that were more interesting than Dachau?
Brudno: Stutthof, no doubt.
A: How long were you at Stutthof?
B: Only one month. In Dachau I was nine.
A: When did you get to Dachau? We have recorded this before but I want to collect the information here.
B: I think we left Stutthof the 20th of August, 1944, and I think we were five days on the road. So I think the 25th of August, 1944, was when we got to Dachau. It was a very interesting trip.
A: How did you go, by train?
B: Yes, of course, by train.
A: Why do you say "of course"?
B: Because train transportation is the most efficient transportation over a long distance. I quote a German newspaper.
A: So that's what they used for people?
B: For people and soldiers.
A: Where did you catch the train?
B: Tiegenhoff. That is near Stutthof.
A: Now from Stutthof, how did you get to the train station?
B: We marched to a small-gauge train.
A: You took a narrow-gauge from Stutthof to—
B: —to Tiegenhoff.
A: And Tiegenhoff is spelled how?
B: T-I-E-G-E-N-H-O-F-F, I think.
A: How many of you left on that occasion?
B: I think four hundred.
A: And who were those people?
B: Wait, wait, I'm lying to you. Many more than four hundred, but how many I don't know.
A: Who were they?
B: Jews, Jews, Jews, and Jews.
A: Jews and Jews, but were they people you knew?
B: Yes.

A: These were people that had come from Lithuania?
B: Yes.
A: Were these Lithuanian Jews?
B: Yes.
A: They had kept you together so far?
B: Yes.
A: Those that came out of Lithuania?
B: Out of the Baltic, yes.
A: Out of the Baltic, they kept you together?
B: Yes.
A: You had gone to Stutthof, where they held you for a month?
B: Yes.
A: And from there they sent you to a train station, where you got on a train?
B: Yes.
A: To go to Dachau?
B: To go where, we don't know.
A: You didn't know where you were going when you left?
B: No, we didn't know where we were going. When I talked with the guards, they said we were going to Austria.
A: Did they believe that, do you think?
B: Yes, why not?
A: I don't know.
B: Our destination was not far from the Austrian border. That is true.
A: Dachau was not far?
B: Dachau and our special branch of Dachau. We didn't go straight to Dachau.
A: When you went from Stutthof to the train station, you went under guard?
B: Yes.
A: The guards were with you on the train?
B: Yes.
A: And were you in passenger cars, or were you in freight cars, or were you in—
B: Freight cars, freight cars.
A: No passenger cars?
B: No, no.
A: No chairs, no seats?
B: Ach, no. We were fifty people to a carriage.
A: Yes.
B: So we were sitting, you know, one into another, one into another. The guards gave us advice, how to sit, how to save space.
A: So they knew how to pack you?

B: Oh yes, oh yes.
A: And you did?
B: What choice did we have? That was the most efficient way to sit.
A: It was the most efficient?
B: Yes.
A: Where were the guards sitting?
B: In the middle.
A: By themselves?
B: Yes.
A: How many guards in a car?
B: Two.
A: Just like before, coming out of Lithuania?
B: Yes, two.
A: Armed how?
B: With rifles.
A: And so there were fifty to two in each car?
B: Positive.
A: And there were what, four cars at least? No, eight cars at least?
B: No, no, many more, there were many more.
A: Well, four hundred would be eight cars?
B: Four hundred, at least. At least four hundred.
A: So there were at least eight cars, and two guards for each car?
B: Yes.
A: So you could easily have taken over—
B: It was never a problem of running away; it's where to go that was the problem.
A: Nor was it a problem of overcoming the guards?
B: They were only two and from time to time they have to sleep.
A: That's right.
B: Regardless of any law which says that one must always be awake, both of them could sleep very healthily.
A: They were fairly sure they were safe when they slept?
B: They considered us "nothings." That bothers me to this day.
A: I see. What would have happened if the—
B: I don't know. I don't know anything about "what if."
A: Well, let me again ask you: you must have thought of the possibility of doing something to the guards?
B: That was never the problem. I'll tell you again. Where do I go from there?
A: I mean that if the guards themselves had been attacked systematically, they would have had to have many more guards. Is that right or not?

B: It would have cost them much more. It was too easy for the Germans. From the first day of our conversations I told you this. It was too easy.

A: Partly because of the way the victims were cooperating?

B: Brainwashed, I would say, just brainwashed.

A: The picture you draw of the way people were sitting—

B: We had no choice but to sit that way. We were so tightly packed. We had to sit this way. This was the most efficient way.

A: —if you were going to be able to be moved efficiently. But what if you had decided you were not going to cooperate in any way, what would have happened?

B: What do you mean "not cooperate"? It was definitely for our benefit to sit this way.

A: How long a trip was it?

B: I told you, about five days.

A: Five days and nights?

B: Yes.

A: And this was constant movement.

B: No. Of course, you stop here, you stop there.

A: How long, would you say, was the trip itself? How many miles was it, or kilometers?

B: I don't know. You'll have to look at a map. I was the lucky one who was standing at the window. I told you why.

A: Yes.

B: Because all these learned and older people than me, they trusted my geographic sense.

A: Yes.

B: We made a rotation of being at the window, I told you—

A: Yes.

B: Because we are fair. But I was the only one who was allowed at the window all the time, because by going to the window, I know where we are. And we went through Bromberg, which is Poland. And we went still further. You can look it up on the map.

A: Yes.

B: The guards themselves would always ask where we are. They also didn't know. And I was very impressed when we came to Jena. Jena was a place that I knew from the Napoleonic Wars.

A: You mean from the battle?

B: Yes. And I thought, Here I am in Jena, here I am in territory that is now being attacked by the British and Americans. Before in Lithuania, there had been no British planes, no American planes, nothing.

A: But now you're in—
B: Now I am in the range of the British, so I already felt better.
A: Now, what country were you in then?
B: Germany. It was all the time Germany. I thought if we go to Austria we will cross Czechoslovakia. The reality is no, we went around Czechoslovakia.
A: Okay.
B: Wait, wait. Then we stopped in a place named, I think, Kaufering. It turned out that Kaufering already had enough people.
A: Enough people for—
B: —for work, what they needed. So we have been sorted out to go further.
A: So far as you know, Dachau was not your original destination? If they had needed you elsewhere, they would have taken you off the train? Is that it?
B: Kaufering belonged to Dachau. This was a branch of Dachau. These were all branches of Dachau.
A: How far apart are they from Dachau?
B: I don't know.
A: You say "branches." What does that mean?
B: It means there is a main camp that's named Dachau.
A: Yes.
B: And there are branches, Dachau Number One, Dachau Number Two, and so forth.
A: How far from Dachau would they be?
B: Not far. Probably in the vicinity.
A: Well, by that you mean a mile, two miles, or do you mean one hundred miles?
B: More or less like fifty miles.
A: And they're all considered branches of Dachau?
B: Yes.
A: You found out they didn't want you at the first branch you reached.
B: Not that I "found out." They sorted us out. I was in the last columns, and we were turned back.
A: Some of them were left there?
B: However many workers they needed, they took. This is why I say there were more than four hundred, because in the end we were four hundred.
A: So, by the time you had gotten to your destination, you had already gotten rid of a number of passengers?
B: They fared much worse.
A: Who, the ones that had been dropped off earlier?
B: At Kaufering, yes. They died at a much greater rate.
A: Because of what?

B: I keep telling you, because we had a very good SS guy in our camp. And we also had our own guy who had been our representative in the ghetto [back in Lithuania]. He also took over and he tried to treat us as nice as possible. He himself was Jewish. He helped us survive.
A: The leader from your own ghetto?
B: Yes.
A: As well as the SS man that you earlier described?
B: These two things helped. I tell my Jewish friends: "Burgin, always Burgin, he made us all survive. But the truth is, without the German guy, no Burgin would have been of help."
A: Burgin is spelled how?
B: B-U-R-G-I-N.
A: And the German again is—
B: B-I-E-R.
A: These were all men.
B: Of course, the women had already been separated in Stutthof.
A: So you don't see the women?
B: No.
A: They are left behind or something else?
B: We know nothing.
A: You don't know anything about them nor do you know what you are going to be doing?
B: No, of course we don't know.
A: You don't know, and the guards don't know, really?
B: The guards don't know. The truth is they always used to be guards, and they had already transported ten thousand before us.
A: And is there a commanding officer on the trip?
B: The Germans, of course, have someone.
A: Did you see him?
B: Yes, but I have no impression of him.
A: But there *was* somebody in command?
B: Of course.
A: But you never had the occasion to hear him talking, or explaining things?
B: Not that I remember.
A: No one in the beginning said anything to all of you as to what's going to happen to you now?
B: They didn't have to tell us anything. You go to work and that's it. They treated us as nonexistent.
A: So they didn't have to explain anything?
B: Nothing.

A: They didn't have to ask for your cooperation?
B: Definitely not.
A: They fed you, of course?
B: Yes.
A: Boxed lunches, or how was it done on the train? You spoke of a boxed lunch on an earlier trip?
B: Boxed lunch?
A: I'm calling it a boxed lunch, a package of food for each person, right?
B: Each person gets food.
A: In a package of some kind?
B: Not in a package.
A: Well, how was it given to you?
B: If it was meat, then it was in a can. And if it was margarine, then it was, you know, in paper.
A: Was it given to you every day or was it given—
B: Every day, every day, every day. And they cut the margarine to exactly how many pieces, per person.
A: And it would be given to you when, each day, on the train trip?
B: I don't know.
A: Well, each morning, for the day? Or at night, for the next day? Or was it more than one time a day?
B: One time a day.
A: You don't remember whether it was morning or afternoon?
B: At this moment I don't remember.
A: Where was the food coming from?
B: From Allah, from God. This was the same food that was distributed for the civil population.
A: But how were they getting the food, do you know how?
B: Who?
A: The guards. The guards were distributing it, weren't they?
B: Yes.
A: Where were they getting it? Were they picking it up on the road? Or was it all put on the train in the beginning?
B: I think it was all put on in the beginning.
A: You believe that they were supplied with the food necessary for the trip?
B: Yes.
A: And then they gave it out day by day, during the trip?
B: Yes.
A: Of course, you slept the best you could?
B: Yes.

A: And did all the people that started the trip survive it, so far as you know?

B: From the beginning of the trip till the end of the trip, all of them survived.

A: Nothing happened to anybody on that trip, so far—

B: No, nothing happened to anybody on that trip.

A: You had ventilation?

B: What are you saying? What are you—

A: I mean you weren't suffocated, that's what I am trying to find out.

B: No, no, no.

A: You were fifty to a railroad car?

B: Yes.

A: You had your food brought in?

B: Yes.

A: Now, what were you doing for bathroom facilities?

B: Once a day, I think, the train would stop and we would go out. We went out in one place where it looked like a tremendous amount of people had gone through there.

A: Did they have latrines? Did they have buildings?

B: One of the places had latrines and everything.

A: A building?

B: Buildings, buildings, and everything was written in Russian so I knew that many Ukrainians went through there.

A: Now when they let you out to the bathrooms or for anything else, would they count you back in? Would there be a counting of people on and off the cars?

B: I don't think they counted. They treated us like docile sheep, that's all. They didn't give a damn. They didn't think even for one moment that—

A: And nobody did anything unexpected, so far as—

B: Nobody did, nobody did.

A: Nobody that you know?

B: Nobody even thought about it.

A: It could have been done easily?

B: Where to? I need to underline that for you.

A: I understand.

B: Of course, it could be done.

A: It could have been done easily? Somebody could have stayed behind when the train left and the guards wouldn't have known it? That's what I am wondering. What we are talking about now is that you people were not counted off or back on the train wherever you stopped.

B: Not counted, nothing.

A: And again, so far as you know, no one ever stayed behind on that trip?

B: Nobody stayed behind.
A: Would you have known it if they had?
B: Of course, because they counted us at the end, just as in the beginning.
A: And no one turned up missing?
B: No one turned up missing, ever.
A: Did each of you have identity cards?
B: Oh, God have pity on you! So now I will tell you. Everything has been taken away from us.
A: I'm wondering, was there any identity—
B: Oh, identity, very good. The trip is finished and we are already in a new place. The trip itself is always more interesting. Anyway, we come to the place.
A: The place where—
B: —where we will stay, Dachau Number Ten. When we came there, we were put in a row. There were already people in the camp to register us. Each one of us has been given a number.
A: When, there, on that occasion?
B: There, on that occasion.
A: You had nothing like that before?
B: Nothing.
A: From the Germans?
B: In Stutthof we also had numbers. But there, nothing was written on us. Here we got our number.
A: On your jackets?
B: Yes. 92,126.
A: That was your number?
B: That's me.
A: Ninety-two thousand—
B: —a hundred and twenty-six—
A: —a hundred and twenty-six.
B: That's it.
A: That's the number you had all the time you were at Dachau?
B: Yes. And they didn't—I want to underline this—they didn't play any games by tattooing our hands. You understand?
A: They did not?
B: No. They didn't play any games. By then Germany needed workers: no more sadism, no more anything, they needed work. So they didn't have time to put on tattoos and waste time on that.
A: That *was* done earlier?
B: Earlier there were tattoos, all those people got tattoos.

A: So there was no tattooing when you got there?
B: No tattooing, finished. 92,126 (right here is a number [pointing]), that's it, no more names, no more family names.
A: Was it at that point that the SS leader took over?
B: I don't know.
A: Well, was he there? When did you first see him?
B: I don't remember.
A: Was it in Dachau or outside of Dachau?
B: We didn't even go into Dachau, I'm telling you—straight to the branch.
A: So you didn't go to the main camp?
B: We didn't go to the main camp.
A: How far away was the main camp?
B: I don't know. We once walked it in two nights. I don't know how far it could be. On the map you could—
A: You never went to the main camp?
B: In the end we went to the main camp.
A: But your nine months, almost all, were at Number Ten?
B: Yes.
A: And how many of you were there?
B: I told you, four hundred from our hometown, no doubt. Four hundred people.
A: That's all that were there in that branch, just the ones from your hometown?
B: Then they brought over two hundred from ghetto Lodz. Lodz, have you heard about it? Lodz, a city in Poland.
A: These were Polish Jews?
B: These were Polish Jews.
A: The others had been Lithuanian Jews?
B: We are four hundred Lithuanian Jews.
A: And what language are you speaking among yourselves?
B: Yiddish.
A: All of you?
B: Yes.
A: You could understand the Poles when they spoke Yiddish?
B: Yes.
A: They could understand you?
B: Yes.
A: How about the guards, what did they speak?
B: German.
A: And you were expected to understand that, too?

B: Exactly.
A: And you could?
B: Of course.
A: Not just you?
B: Everyone.
A: Everybody could?
B: Yes.
A: So two hundred from Poland are added to the four hundred from Lithuania. That's six hundred altogether?
B: Yes.
A: Is that all of this camp?
B: Yes.
A: Dachau Number Ten?
B: Yes.
A: Now, how large was Number Ten?
B: I really don't know but it's twelve blocks, that much I can tell you. There were—
A: Do you mean twelve barracks?
B: No, no, no, huts. Don't call them barracks because that means there are walls. I explained to you, there were only roofs.
A: I missed that. They have only roofs, you say? They were that way, even in the winter?
B: Yes, I'll make it. [Drawing] Here is the thing for the smoke to go out, like a chimney. This is an entrance. You have to go down in order to enter. We sleep on the floor. There are no walls, only the roof.
A: The roof is a wall?
B: The roof is everything.
A: Yes, the roof is everything.
B: On the other side, there's a window.
A: With glass?
B: Glass.
A: And how many of you would be in that?
B: Fifty.
A: In the hut?
B: Six hundred people divided by twelve is fifty.
A: In other words, the same number of people as in the carriages?
B: Basically, yes.
A: Would it be the same people? Or were you redistributed?
B: We were redistributed.
A: It wasn't that the people in one carriage went into one hut?

B: No, there was no one-to-one correspondence.
A: Was this fairly warm in the winter?
B: We had an oven.
A: What did you burn in it?
B: Wood.
A: Where did the wood come from?
B: We stole wood whenever we could.
A: You stole wood from wherever you could?
B: Yes.
A: But the Germans must have expected you to burn something in there to keep you warm. Did they supply you anything to burn?
B: No.
A: They did supply you food. Let's start with that.
B: They supplied the kitchen with wood.
A: But they didn't supply the huts with wood?
B: Nope.
A: What *did* they expect you to do?
B: Steal. Wait a minute, don't look so unbelieving.
A: No, I'm not.
B: When we came, my hut had not been finished. There was no window, so it was very cold.
A: Right.
B: So this Bier, this commandant, God bless him, said that he'll overlook it if we steal glass somewhere and put it in. He'll overlook it. What else can you ask him? So that's what happened.
A: So where did you get it?
B: There was a big place for building supplies.
A: Supplies for—
B: Supplies for whatever work we did.
A: And so you stole some wood from there to burn?
B: Yes, definitely, yes.
A: As well as glass to make windows with?
B: Yes.
A: You were expected then to finish building your own huts?
B: In due course the glass came and everything.
A: Who built these huts?
B: When we came there the huts were already built.
A: By whom?
B: By other Jews. I think Hungarian Jews.
A: I see. They were all gone by now?

B: Gone.
A: Where were they?
B: I don't know. They may have been in other camps of Dachau.
A: But why hadn't they kept them, if they needed workers?
B: Don't ask me. I give you, as I told you, only the facts.
A: So you don't know what had happened to your predecessors?
B: They were in other camps. They were transported there to build a camp and then they were taken to other camps.
A: Okay. So you move in here?
B: Yes.
A: Four hundred of you are allocated among these twelve barracks.
B: I think twelve, maybe there was a thirteenth, but I don't remember.
A: Twelve would be room for six hundred, I guess.
B: Yes.
A: So you have a dozen barracks, I'm sorry, not barracks, huts?
B: Yes.
A: What did *you* all call them? What did you call these buildings?
B: Blocks.
A: Blocks?
B: Yes.
A: That's a good German word?
B: Yes.
A: What block were you in?
B: I was in block number eleven.
A: Over how large an area?
B: I don't know. You squeeze me for what I cannot answer. I don't remember.
A: Well, is it—
B: A very small area.
A: For the entire camp?
B: For the entire camp. We were so tight, like sardines.
A: The buildings, you mean, next to each other?
B: The buildings were also next to each other. [Drawing]
A: Were they in two rows, then? Is that what you are showing?
B: There were two rows, and of course there was the eleventh block, where I was.
A: It was separated from the others?
B: It was not in the row.
A: Now, did you have to stay in the block you were assigned?
B: The whole camp was free. You could walk in the camp as much as you liked.

A: And you could sleep where you wanted to?
B: If you have any other place.
A: You could?
B: By all means.
A: You could if you wanted to?
B: Yes, if you wanted to sleep on the outside.
A: In the summertime, could you sleep outside if you wanted to?
B: Of course, if you wanted.
A: The camp itself was surrounded by—
B: Barbed wire.
A: And guards?
B: Yes. They said that the barbed wire was electric.
A: Was it electric?
B: I don't know.
A: They said it was?
B: They said. I don't know.
A: And you didn't want to—
B: I never went to find out. My personal opinion was that it was not electric. But this is only my personal opinion.
A: There were guards, of course?
B: Guards there were, yes. Here is the place were the latrine was and the washing place. [Drawing]
A: All in one place?
B: Yes—washing on one side, latrine on the other side. And here is the main entrance, and here are guards, a guard tower, with of course barbed wire all around.
A: Yes.
B: Here is another two blocks.
A: And this one over here is yours?
B: That's mine, of course. Why I always get something special I don't know, but I always get something special.
A: Special in the sense that it's a different orientation?
B: Yes. I'll tell you why this was special for me.
A: Why?
B: On this side is the barbed wire. So I see only the barbed wire and the fields around it, *fields*. So what I did, and I'm sure that nobody else did, I went and I laid down on it. I took my blanket, laid down on it, and sunned myself. I'm sure I was the only one who did this.
A: Laid down on what?
B: On the roof.

A: On the roof of your building?

B: Yes. And I sunned myself. Nobody else did it in the whole camp, I'm sure. But nobody saw me from the camp; only the guards saw me.

A: And the guards didn't bother you?

B: Why would the guards give a damn?

A: They didn't care.

B: They didn't care. It was only once that I had problems with a guard. I had bleeding wounds, and it was very cold. I was sleeping near the stove, in the middle of the night. At that time there was an alarm which meant American bombers were flying over us. So you are not allowed to make any fire because they see its sparks. So a guard shouted, "Fire, fire." He is on the other side, so he has to go around to go to the tower in order to get to us. I realized that he is serious, so I ran to the washing house to get two pails of water, and put out the fire. So when he came, everybody was asleep. He could do nothing. But I had to think very quick, you know, because he would catch me with the fire.

A: That was a serious offense.

B: A very serious offense.

A: You could hear the bombers going over sometimes?

B: Yes, we could hear them. One day we saw, how do you call them, the salvation planes?

A: You mean American observation planes?

B: Yes. They have a name, for God's sake.

A: I don't remember what you're talking about, but I know—

B: What is a plane that's not going to bomb but is going to take pictures, what's the name?

A: Reconnaissance.

B: Reconnaissance? Okay. They would fly and they would make a lot of steam behind them, so we called them "the painters" because they painted the sky full of lines.

A: Oh yes, the vapor trails. And those were by day?

B: Then there were alarms, so we don't have to work. We were not to move, so they would not notice us.

A: I see.

B: All this is covered with earth, with green. The roofs are covered, so from the air you cannot notice them. This was camouflage.

A: Now, where did you take your meals?

B: They are brought to each one in the block.

A: Some food would be brought there to each one? And it would be distributed?

B: Yes.
A: Was there somebody in charge of each block?
B: Yes, of course.
A: Who was it in your block?
B: I think Leibel, I don't remember. A nice guy.
A: From?
B: From my hometown. We decided that he is the one, and that's it.
A: Did you choose your own man?
B: Yes.
A: He was the one who negotiated with the Germans?
B: He didn't negotiate. What was there to negotiate about?
A: I don't know. If the Germans wanted something done, would they go talk to somebody?
B: He is only to stay in the block. He takes care that the block should be clean. He takes care, you know, of the distribution of the food, that it should be fair. We were very fair in the distribution of the food. That's very important. We would get a huge pail of soup, you know, and then with a spoon everybody would get his. It doesn't fit precisely, this many people, and so there would always be leftovers. We made amongst ourselves a line for leftovers, each one was in line. Today, let's say the first five people, and the next day, the next five people, on a rotational basis. Very fair.
A: You worked that out?
B: Yes.
A: And that was throughout the nine months? That's the way you did it?
B: Yes, very fair.
A: I see.
B: I tried to be very clever, so I asked if I can clean the pail afterwards. Of course, at first nobody objected. And I would clean and I would be happy. And they realized that it is substance. So it also was done on a rotational basis.
A: The privilege of cleaning would be passed around?
B: Yes.
A: I see. Now, what age group are you talking about here?
B: All those capable of work.
A: So what ages were they?
B: Some as young as fourteen. There were five old people.
A: By old you mean what?
B: By old, definitely in the sixties.
A: And they would do a day's work, too?

B: They had to do a day's work, too. If they did not, they are the ones who did the dying.

A: By dying you mean what?

B: By dying I mean dying.

A: Do you mean that they were dying because of the work, or dying because of the food, or dying because they were killed?

B: No, no, not killed.

A: You mean that they just couldn't stay with the pace, is that it?

B: They just couldn't, just couldn't.

A: And they would collapse or—

B: They died, collapse or no collapse, each one died.

A: Were there any medical services?

B: Yes, there was a place for the sick. This sick block had lofts, it was not like our blocks. Let me go back. It happened that each camp had its bad things. Stutthof didn't give us some things—I don't remember what. Dachau didn't give us socks. In Stutthof I think we got socks. So there always was the idea that there should be a shortage. Whatever they gave us was always with a little sadism, such as no socks. Then, what else? Hats. Of course, each one got one hat.

A: Was it all the same for everybody?

B: There were all kinds of hats. They were from other people, from Russian prisoners of war, from Jews who have been killed, everything. What they had when we came, that is what's given to us.

A: There was a sort of an international warehouse of things?

B: Recycling.

A: Recycling, okay. Now you have your work parties.

B: Wait, wait, wait. I have to—

A: Go ahead.

B: I have to start telling. So, what came the first day? We had to work in the camp, where we had to make the drainage go outside of the camp.

A: Yes.

B: We worked on the drainage here and there the first days. Then we started going out to work. I was with my best friend. Itgolov was his name.

A: From your hometown?

B: From my hometown. From my own courtyard there, and we decided to be together. I promised his mother that I would go with him wherever he goes. And let me tell you, I did not keep my promise. I feel guilty about it to this day. So anyway, I worked with him, and we were sorted out to go to work in the woods.

A: Yes.

B: That was a very privileged kind of work. So we are going out every day. The forester was a guy whose father was in the First World War in Lithuania. So he treated us very fair. Matter of fact, he would give us every day a loaf of bread. He was afraid of the German guard, so he would cut the loaf of bread into exactly how many people we are. He would tell us beneath which tree it is. And each one would go and take his slice. Completely fair, that was very important, completely fair. So we have a slice of bread more than the other people. We were treated fair and we were cutting trees. This forester would go and mark trees, usually by cutting something on a tree, and this tree had to be cut down. Now, at first everything had been done with a saw, and an axe. Later on, electricals appear. The electrical saw was used after the tree was already laying down, to cut into pieces. But to cut down the tree we still did with the saw. So my friend and—

A: You cut trees manually?

B: Manually, yes.

A: So you and your friend—

B: We were cutting the tree. We then had two non-Jews working with us, one an Italian and one a Czech.

A: Also prisoners?

B: No, they were free. Labor forces had been taken all over Europe, you know, to work in Germany.

A: And they were doing the same work that you were?

B: Exactly the same work.

A: But they are not living—

B: They are not in a camp and they are getting paid. But as far as work is concerned, they do exactly what we do. We would cut down ten trees a day, not big trees, not small trees. The trees were used to make ties for a railroad.

A: You knew that's what these things were for?

B: Yes.

A: Roughly how long did you work there?

B: I'll give you everything, wait. So, we are working there, we are cutting trees, and of course I try to be clever. I try to see it like a war. In Germany, it's not a natural forest, it's a made-forest. Therefore the trees are in rows and columns like soldiers. So my impression was that I am cutting down a soldier every time. And when you cut the tree it's noticeable because there is a gap in the row.

A: Yes.

B: So later on I decided I can cut any tree I want. And the sign that it has to be cut, I'll make later, when the tree is already lying down. The forester was very much in love with me and my coworker because we worked hard. So he trusts us completely that we will cut down whatever tree is necessary. Why did he trust us still more? One day a tree fell on the road. Now the road has to be cleared, right, so there'll be traffic? But it was between twelve and one, it was the time when you eat. So he asked for volunteers. I and my friend went and we volunteered and we did it. We went up, in his estimate. Then something wrong happened to me. Wherever I cut myself it wouldn't heal.

A: On your hand?

B: Everywhere. And it got worse and worse. So I went to the doctor; I didn't want to go to work.

A: And this would be a German doctor?

B: No, a Jewish doctor. He is right now still alive in New York. He is ninety-six.

A: Was he also from your hometown?

B: Yes, Isokovitch. He is now in bad shape. They cut off half of his leg. I talk with him on the phone. I go to the doctor, so that I should not go to work, but go to the hospital. Others go to the hospital, and I am still sent to work. But it turns out I had here a huge sack of pus.

A: On your leg?

B: On my leg, and I didn't know to complain about it. So once I show it to the doctor, I go to the hospital. Before I went to the hospital I want to tell you other things. For example, working in the trees was a good thing. It's a real romantic thing. One day I really enjoyed it. There was a huge rain. Our guard was a German from Palestine.

A: From Palestine?

B: Yes. The Palestinian Germans had been sent back to Germany. I don't know how it was exactly; there was an arrangement. And he hated the Jews very much because of Palestine. He was especially sadistic. The previous guard, if it was raining, would let us go into a hut. This guy didn't let us, and it was raining, and we got soaked tremendously, and then the rain stopped and the sun came out. And we are all wet and everything. So we undress and hang our clothes on the trees to dry. So we all undressed and we worked naked.

A: You worked that way?

B: Yes. It was a laughing matter to me. I mean it was so strange, one tree got caught in another tree, and my friend had to go up in order to untangle it. And he looked like an ape working on the tree, and it was really, really a joke.

A: How long did you work in the—

B: Wait, wait, wait. This is one time I liked, toward the end of the summer, 1944. Then another time, it was already later in the winter. There was snow. We were going seven kilometers from our camp, we were going to the trees. There was a tremendous snow. Are you going to fall asleep?

A: No, go ahead.

B: So, it was a snow. Because there was a snow, the tractor that has to come and fetch us couldn't come.

A: So you were not expected to walk that?

B: Wait a minute, so we have been taken, every day, there and back.

A: By a cart?

B: By a cart pulled by a tractor. But now, it is a snow, and the tractor couldn't come to fetch us. So the decision is that we walk, we'll walk the seven kilometers. And here is something interesting. I was surprised by what the Jewish people talked about amongst themselves. There was an argument between two Jewish people as to why the revolution in 1905 did not succeed. Honest to God! I thought, For God's sake, don't you know where you are? They didn't. That was the argument, why didn't in 1905—

A: How many people would be arguing that? Just a couple of them or—

B: A couple of them.

A: As you're walking along?

B: As we're walking along. This is the great argument. Then we came to some clearing. It's a little place. The German guard is also walking with us. He is fed up with all these things. He says, "You promise not to run away?" Of course, we promise not to run away. So he went into one of these places to have a cup of tea. The moment he left us, of course we spread around to go *shnoré*, to beg.

A: To beg?

B: To beg. I go in one place and there is a woman. She is boiling unpeeled potatoes. I say to her, "Here you have unpeeled potatoes, I am hungry." She gave me unpeeled potatoes. Then there was another woman—

A: Boiled potatoes?

B: Boiled, yes, but with their peels. Then another woman—there were no men, no men—then there was another woman and she says, "Poor people, who knows, maybe my husband and my son are now in a Russian prison and maybe they are also treated this way." So I told her, "But at least they are not being burned." She says, "Oh, how can you say such words? People are not burned." I'm sure she didn't know that Jews were being burned. I am dead sure. And she had two pails of milk.

A: Now you hadn't had milk for some time?

B: What do you mean "for some time"? Since I came to the camp.

A: And this is the same woman who didn't believe that the Jews were being burned?

B: That anyone was being burned. "How can you say such a thing? How can you say such a thing?"

[A portion of this conversation here is inaudible on the tape.]

A: They would take some people from the hospital?

B: From the hospital. Weak people have been sorted out. Usually twenty-five people.

A: Did you know what was going to happen to them?

B: No.

A: Did you suspect anything?

B: I suspected the worst, of course, that they are taken to die. But at least these were not taken to die.

A: How do you know that?

B: Because after I survived I met people that had been in these groups. So this is why I feel bad about my best friend. I had been sorted out to go. I had a way to wiggle out, which I'll tell. He didn't have a way to wiggle out and he was sent away. I should have gone with him.

A: Sorted out to go where?

B: To another camp.

A: What happened there?

B: I know only people that survived. Some guy that went with his father, some guy who went because his son was sick, and they survived. It means that even there, there were conditions that people could survive. Most of them died, that goes without saying.

A: Not killed?

B: Not killed.

A: Died because of conditions?

B: Died because they died. But not killed, not straightforwardly killed. This is what I found out later. I was suspicious that everyone was taken there to be killed, but that's me being pessimistic.

A: Now in Dachau itself nobody was being straightforwardly killed?

B: I don't know.

A: That you know about?

B: I can't talk about Dachau itself—

A: What about in Number Ten?

B: Nobody was taken to be killed, nobody.

A: People would be taken away and you don't know what happened to them when they left?

B: Yes.

A: But so far as you know, nobody in the camp was killed.

B: In the camp, nobody.

A: It was a work camp?

B: A work camp. Some people died.

A: Yes, and how far away was the most you'd go to work?

B: Seven kilometers.

A: In the forest?

B: Yes. Nothing was done in the camp. Outside there was a place that much was going on. We worked on fabricated walls, three fabricated walls.

A: They were to be used someplace else?

B: We didn't know. They never managed to finish it, but that was the plan. So this is what our daily work was. Anyway, I worked a lot in the forest. But you can see I am really beginning to forget little details.

A: What had you heard about Dachau before you got there?

B: I heard about Dachau when I was still in Lithuania in 1944.

A: What had you heard about it?

B: That it's a horrible camp and people work very hard. And the guards go into the women's quarters whenever they feel like it. And, of course, there was no comparison to what I really saw there later. We knew Dachau was horrible. It was one of the first camps that the National Socialists had made.

A: But you didn't go to that part of it, the first part, the one the Nazis originally made? You didn't go to the main camp yourself until—

B: —later. I was in the main camp.

A: How long were you in the main camp?

B: Three days. I'll tell you about the three days, basically, only two nights.

A: The Dachau you knew for nine months was far better than what you had expected? Is that right?

B: I don't know. It depends where you were. The living conditions were much worse than in Dachau proper, much worse. In Dachau proper they had locks where people slept. Dachau proper was the camp that you now see in the movies.

A: How large was the main camp, do you think?

B: I have no idea.

A: Well, thousands of people?

B: There were thousands of people.

A: Many thousands?

B: Oh yes, no doubt.
A: Compared to that, yours was very small?
B: Very small.
A: Now in your camp, Number Ten, did you have a sense, did you feel safe there?
B: In what sense safe?
A: Physically.
B: My motto was, If we work, that's it. Work is the price for staying alive, that's all.
A: I see. By the way, how many days of the week did you work? Was it every day of the week?
B: One Sunday in two weeks they asked me to work.
A: Every other Sunday was free of work?
B: We have a two-weeks week.
A: And the day off would be a Sunday, not the Jewish Sabbath?
B: Of course, Sunday. What kind of question is that?
A: I don't know. I'm just wondering, I'm just trying to find out.
B: If you're religious—
A: —you would be free to do what?
B: Whatever you want.
A: And what would you do?
B: Whatever anyone wants, for God's sake. Usually cleaning our lice.
A: There was lice?
B: Oh ho, oh ho. Lice is a thing that is too horrible to—
A: Were they constantly a problem?
B: A constant problem.
A: Year round, even in the winter?
B: Yes. I can tell you about the lice.
A: You got up at what time?
B: I told you, I think four or five. I don't remember. And then coffee is given in the morning.
A: Would they wake you up or would you?
B: The light would turn on.
A: The light would turn on in the hut?
B: Yes.
A: In the block?
B: Yes.
A: And you know how long you have to get dressed, to get ready to go out, right?

B: The coffee is coming in, the coffee is distributed. If you're ready not to drink the coffee, you can sleep another half an hour.

A: Okay, and then what time did you expect to leave?

B: I drank the coffee. I managed to go through the camp without drinking unboiled water. I would drink the coffee instead of water.

A: The whole time you were there?

B: This thing of not drinking unboiled water has stayed with me till this day.

A: So the water I bring you from the water fountain is suspect?

B: Suspect, definitely.

A: What time were you expected to leave to go to work?

B: We had to be at work at seven in the morning.

A: And you would all go together to the various—

B: Every column goes to each work. Everyone to where he was assigned.

A: With a guard?

B: With a guard.

A: Everything was with a guard, is that it?

B: Everything was with a guard.

A: All the movements out through that main gate?

B: Yes.

A: With a guard?

B: Yes.

A: And the same guard would be with you all day?

B: I don't know what he did all day.

A: Would he be with you all day?

B: No.

A: Well, what would he do, just leave you?

B: He would bring us to work and that's it.

A: And then he would come to get you at the end of the day, is that it?

B: I don't think it was arranged that way. At first we were put into lines and rows and counted every morning, every morning, and then every evening when we come from work. Later, because this Bier was a very nice guy, each column leader, a Jew (not a guard) would report how many people there were. Nobody was missed, never, and we went back to the barracks.

A: Now, during the nine months you were there, nobody ran away?

B: Nobody ran away.

A: At all?

B: At all. Please, I explain to you again, in order to run away you have to have a destination where to run away. If you know that you will be turned in the first day, you don't run away.

A: And you did have the sense that if you somehow cooperated—

B: That was the only thing to do in order to survive.

A: And you expected to survive?

B: I didn't.

A: You did not expect that?

B: No, because I thought they cannot leave witnesses to these horrible things. I thought even if the Germans win the war, how can they show themselves to their own allies with this atrocity? How can they?

A: Now what atrocity? You didn't see any atrocities, did you?

B: What I saw was enough. What I saw was enough, I don't need any more.

A: Well, you saw people that were being imprisoned and forced to work, right? You didn't see anything else, did you?

B: People were taken away to be killed in Lithuania, that is enough, I don't need more.

A: In Lithuania, all right.

B: And in Germany, when we were in Stutthof.

A: How much control did you feel you had over your life?

B: Zero. Zero.

A: I don't believe that.

B: So, don't believe.

A: No, I don't believe it. You yourself don't believe it. You had some control, didn't you, about—

B: I'll tell you "control." It was very cold, it's wintertime, we have only this little nothing to wear. So I would take the blanket, put my hands around me, and just wear a blanket instead of clothes. But for wearing a blanket you would get five on your behind as a punishment. It was illegal.

A: Seriously?

B: Yes.

A: Why?

B: You're abusing the government's property. What are you talking? Oh, you sometimes—really I have to give it to you straight. In another place that the people didn't have socks, they took the blanket, cut it into five parts, and made socks for themselves. All five of them were hanged for destroying government property. Maybe that will—

A: How do you know that?

B: There were too many witnesses. What do you mean, How do I know?

A: Oh, there were witnesses to that?

B: Of course. They were hanged officially. Not in my camp.

A: Not in your camp?

B: No, not in my camp.

A: So, people were whipped in your camp?
B: Oh yes, the whipping was official and legalized—
A: Who would do the whipping?
B: Usually some *cappo*.
A: Some *cappo*, meaning?
B: *Cappo* is one of the, you know, administration.
A: Germans or Jews?
B: They were Jews.
A: Jews?
B: A Jew or maybe a Pole. Yes, some *cappos* had been brought over from the main camp.
A: From the main camp?
B: Yes, and one was a Frenchman, one was a Polack. Sometimes they would do it. The hard thing was that this was legal. There were all kinds of crimes. Again in the evening they would say number so and so. We had only numbers. You ask how much choice I had. This was how much choice I had: yes, to wear the blanket or not to wear it. My calculation was: If I don't wear it, I'll die from cold; if I wear it, maybe I'll be caught, maybe not. Nobody turned me in so I was never caught.
A: So you were never caught?
B: Never caught.
A: So you were never whipped, then?
B: I was never whipped.
A: But you saw others whipped?
B: Yes. The whipping ceremony was very ugly.
A: It was in public?
B: Public.
A: Out in the open?
B: Yes.
A: Outside?
B: Yes.
A: And the entire camp would be assembled or how many would there be?
B: The whole thing, everyone.
A: With the commanding officer?
B: With everyone, yes, yes, with Bier and all the others. It was a great ceremony, with a light shining on it. It was ugly; I hate the ugly.
A: Yes. I see.
B: The only point that I will give here is about this Bier. I told you about one guy who had to get ten. He stole some cabbage.
A: Cabbage?

B: Cabbage, he stole one head of cabbage. He had to get, I don't remember, twenty, I think, perhaps a hundred. But he was a deaf mute. I told you this story.

A: Yes, I remember.

B: He was a deaf mute, so he started making noises that would break the heart of any human being. And Bier said, "Stop!" It was too much even for him. But usually people would get twenty. And either they shouted or did not shout.

A: And that would be in the evening?

B: Yes, after they had done the work. That was a ceremony.

A: Would there be something like that every evening?

B: No, no, only if there were people who had done something.

A: How often would you estimate?

B: I don't remember.

A: Now, all this time, the Germans had a sense that they're losing the war?

B: No, the opposite. They will win the war. They never had a sense of losing the war.

A: They're still hopeful?

B: What do you mean hopeful? I have to be personal. You don't let me be personal. You want me to be—

A: No, no, I want you to tell me about your experience.

B: Yes. So here is one, for example, my relation with the foreman, the German guy under whom I worked. Of course, you know me, I always have personal relations. I talk to him, he talks to me, I talk to him, he talks to me. He's an Austrian. He had a medal for taking Sevastopol. Now, Sevastopol is being taken back by the Russians. But he got a medal for conquering it. He had been one of the soldiers. I talked and talked to him. One day it was raining and ugly and terrible, and of course I didn't want to work. He had always a stick with which he would hit everybody. He comes over and hits me with the stick. I told him, "You should be ashamed of yourself." So he apologizes and he says he behaved this way because he was two years in Russia, and this is how they treated the Russians. They just beat them. I said, "How are we Russians? And how dare you compare us to them?" And he apologized, and he never used the stick again. So that's about him.

A: Now, you spoke of the *cappos* earlier?

B: There are good *cappos* and bad *cappos*. The *cappos* got another portion of soup, more than anybody else.

A: To what extent did they run the camp?

B: I don't know. I really don't remember. Usually people have a very bad feeling about *cappos*. But our *cappos* were chosen by ourselves. Only two *cappos* came over from the main camp. And one of them was a little bastard.

A: Now what could one do on one's own in the camp? Was there anything that you could do in your spare time, in your leisure or every other Sunday, besides cleaning lice?

B: You have to repair your things. I don't remember how often, but you could shave.

A: Was there any kind of—

B: No. No.

A: No what?

B: You want activities.

A: Yes, any activities—

B: No.

A: —at all—

B: No.

A: —that you all could do together?

B: No.

A: No sports?

B: What are you talking about?

A: I don't know.

B: No.

A: You could have done it among yourselves? Prisoners could have done something, if they had wanted? Would they have stopped you from doing it if you had wanted to?

B: Who would stop you from doing anything? Nobody gave a damn.

A: Did you have any games?

B: What games?

A: Chess. Were there any chess games? Don't look at me as if I'm asking you about something—

B: No. Where can you get the pieces?

A: Pieces of paper.

B: We did have pieces of paper for playing checkers.

A: Okay, now we're on our way. You did do that?

B: Checkers.

A: You did play checkers?

B: Yes.

A: Did *you* play?

B: Yes.

A: Were you good at it?

B: Yes.

A: How often did you play?

B: There is no law.

A: What do you mean there is—

B: There is no law, whenever there was time, and when there was somebody who wanted to play.

A: That would be the game you played, if you played anything?

B: That's the game I remember we did play.

A: No cards?

B: No cards. How can you have cards?

A: What do you mean?

B: Nobody had anything.

A: No, no, that isn't true. Even though you didn't have checkers, you played checkers?

B: Yes, because you don't need any special thing. Stones can be good for playing checkers.

A: So the only game you played was checkers?

B: As much as I remember, that's the only game.

A: No boxing?

B: What are you talking? People were—

A: No running?

B: No, no.

A: Anybody exercising?

B: Anyone who wanted could exercise.

A: No, but would there be any people trying to keep themselves in a certain kind of shape?

B: You washed yourself every day. What was there to "keeping in shape"? You were working under the fresh air. What is this "keeping in shape"?

A: I don't know. I'm just trying to see what there was. Was there any kind of storytelling?

B: No, no, definitely not.

A: No plays?

B: No, what are you talking about?

A: No singing.

B: No. But wait, wait, I'm lying, I'm lying.

A: Okay.

B: There was a time we made something for singing on the block, and people were going and singing. And one guy got a fiddle and he was a good fiddler.

A: Yes.

B: And I was a performer. This is how I saved my life. Okay, I'll be very personal. I was young then. All of a sudden, poetry overtook me, and I wanted to write poetry. I wrote some poetry—of course, everything is by heart—and the people liked it. And one block decided they will give me another portion of soup. And another block invited me and gave me another portion of soup. So I was reading my poetry and he was fiddling. That was the show. And then there were some people who decided they will sing. They were singing very nice. Some people felt inferior to us. They were much hungrier, because they had already been two years more under German occupation. They fell into German hands in '39, we only in '41. And not long ago I was in New York and I met one of these soldier guys, and I was shocked when he told me that in the concentration camp they got more food than in the ghetto. In our case, it was the opposite.

[The remainder of this May 25, 2000 Anastaplo-Brudno conversation is missing because the tape again becomes inaudible here. A recent Internet account suggests what the Lithuania was like from which Simcha Brudno and his Jewish neighbors in Siauliai (and many others) were shipped to Dachau, Germany (and elsewhere) in 1944 ("Lithuania and the Holocaust," http://www.virtualjerusalem.com/news.php?option=com_content&view=article&id=2019:lithuania-and-the-holocaust&catid=3:world&Itemid=2019, Posted December 24, 2010):

> This past week, the Prime Minister of Lithuania . . . was a guest of the Israeli government, on a state visit to Israel. For many Jews, just the mention of the name 'Lithuania' is painful; after all, the Lithuanians were among the most enthusiastic supporters of Nazis outside Germany, with Lithuanians from various backgrounds volunteering to help round up and kill Jews even before the Nazis arrived in the country in 1941. . . . The assistance rendered by the Lithuanians, historians say, was one of the reasons the German killing machine that operated in the country between 1941 and 1945 was the among the most efficient in the entire Nazi empire—with 95% of Lithuanian Jews murdered by the time it was all over. . . . Rabbi [Yisrael] Rosenson, director of Michlelet Efrata, . . . says he understands why many Jews think of Lithuania as an unreformed land of Nazi sympathizers. "While the Holocaust was of course a horror everywhere, it was unique in Lithuania. Before the war, there were almost no public manifestations of anti-Semitism, yet even before the Nazis took over the country, many jumped on board with the Nazi agenda and began persecuting Jews, often outdoing the Germans."

> After the war, Lithuania fell into the hands of the Communists, being absorbed directly into the Soviet Union—further cause for anti-Semitism, as many Lithuanians identified Communism as a "Jewish plot."

Another Internet posting, an article by Andrew L. Jaffe ("Lithuanians, Jews, Nazis, the Holocaust, and Collective Guilt," April 14, 2003) includes these observations: "According to the *Jewish Telegraph Agency*, there is an ongoing debate as to how many 'righteous Lithuanians' there were. After thirteen years of extensive research, the State Jewish Museum last week released *Saving the Jews in Lithuania from 1941–44*. The book by Viktorija Sakaite lists the names of 2,570 non-Jewish Lithuanians who risked their lives to protect Jews during the Nazi occupation of this Baltic nation." The Lithuanian Jewish experience is summed up thus in a report, "Under Nazi Occupation," *The Yivo Encyclopedia of Jews in Eastern Europe*, Gershom David Hundert, ed. (New Haven: Yale University Press, 2008), vol. 1, p. 1075: "Even in 1943, amid signs that the tide of war was turning against the Germans, some Lithuanians continued to display hostility to Jews, and there were many incidents in which Lithuanians betrayed them to the Gestapo. With some exceptions, Lithuanian clergy failed to caution the mostly Catholic population against hostile treatment of Jews." See, also, Martin Gilbert, *The Righteous: The Unsung Heroes of the Holocaust* (New York: Doubleday, 2002), pp. xi–xiii, 1–2, 65–86. A Jewish woman I happen to know, who is the survivor of a prominent Vilna family, recalls both that there were indeed some Lithuanians who risked their lives to help Jews and that the Germans had no difficulty recruiting many Lithuanians eager to engage in massive killing of Jews under Nazi direction. In short, bloodthirsty Nazis were once able to find enough Lithuanians to kill Jews for them by the tens of thousands just as generations of respectable slave owners in this country were once able to find enough Americans (including many Northerners) both to kidnap boatloads of innocent people from Africa and to hunt down desperate runaway slaves throughout the United States. See, for another recent account of matters dealt with in this Appendix, Ellen Cassedy, *We Are Here: Memories of the Lithuanian Holocaust* (University of Nebraska Press, 2012).]

APPENDIX G

Roster of Cases and Other Materials Drawn On

Cases

Barron v. Mayor and City of Baltimore, 32 U.S. 243 (1833).
Brown v. Board of Education, 347 U.S. 483 (1954).
Bush v. Gore, 531 U.S. 98 (2000).
Civil Rights Cases, 109 U.S. 3 (1883).
Dred Scott v. Sandford, 60 U.S. 393 (1857).
Marbury v. Madison, 1 Cranch (5 U.S.) 137 (1803).
Prigg v. Pennsylvania, 41 U.S. 539 (1842).
Somerset v. Stewart, 90 Eng. Rep. 499 (1772) (reprinted in George Anastaplo, ed., *Liberty, Equality, and Modern Constitutionalism*).
Swift v. Tyson, 41 U.S. 1 (1842).
The Antelope, 10 Wheat. (23 U.S.) 66 (1825).

Other Materials

Act to prohibit the importation of slaves into any port of place within the jurisdiction of the United States, from and after the first day of January, in the year of our Lord one thousand eight hundred and eight (United States Congress, 2 Stat. 426, March 2, 1807).

Anastaplo, George. "A Second Pearl Harbor? Let's Be Serious" (a talk given on September 12, 2001), in Anastaplo, "September Eleventh, The ABCs of a Citizen's Responses: Explorations," 29 *Oklahoma City University Law Review* 165, 175 (2004); supplemented by collections of periodic assessments in Anastaplo,

"September Eleventh, a Citizen's Responses (Continued)," 4 *Loyola University Chicago International Law Review* 135 (2006) and in Anastaplo, "September Eleventh, A Citizen's Responses (Continued Further)," 35 *Oklahoma City University Law Review* 625 (2010).

———. *Abraham Lincoln: A Constitutional Biography* (preferred title: *Thoughts on Abraham Lincoln: A Discourse on Prudence*). Lanham, Maryland: Rowman and Littlefield, 1999 (including an exegesis of the Emancipation Proclamation that has been generously endorsed by Harry V. Jaffa, the most vigorous champion of Abraham Lincoln in our time).

———. "An Instructive Encounter with Professor Sidney Hook of New York City," in *Selected Writings by and about George Anastaplo*, www.anastaplo.wordpress.com (an enterprise established by Joel Rich and maintained by John Metz). (Compare an exchange with B. F. Skinner in Anastaplo, "Constitutionalism and the Good: Explorations," 70 *Tennessee Law Review* 757, 796–99 [2003].)

———. "Ancient African (Including Egyptian) Thought." In Anastaplo, *But Not Philosophy: Seven Introductions to Non-Western Thought*. Lanham, Maryland: Lexington Books, 2002, p. 31.

———. Bibliography. *Leo Strauss and His Legacy: A Bibliography*, ed. John A Murley. Lanham, Maryland: Lexington Books, 2005, pp. 29, 733–855, 871.

———. "Did Anyone 'In Charge' Know What He Was Doing? The Thirty Years War of the Twentieth Century." In Anastaplo, *Campus Hate-Speech Codes, Natural Right, and Twentieth Century Atrocities*. Lewiston, New York: Edwin Mellen Press, 1999, p. 49–70.

———. *Further Thoughts on Abraham Lincoln: A Discourse on Chance and the Good* (submitted for publication).

———. *Human Being and Citizen: Essays on Virtue, Freedom, and the Common Good*. Chicago: Swallow Press/Athens: Ohio University Press, 1975.

———. "John Woolman on Slavery and on Wealth." In Anastaplo, "Legal Education, Economics, and Law School Governance: Explorations," 46 *South Dakota Law Review* 102, 253 (2001).

———. *Liberty, Equality, and Modern Constitutionalism: A Source Book* (in two volumes). Newburyport, Massachusetts: Focus Publishing / R. Pullins Company, 1999.

———. "On Truly Knowing What One Is Trying to Do: The Mystery of Evil." In Anastaplo, *The Christian Heritage: Problems and Prospects*. Lanham, Maryland: Lexington Books, 2010, p. 357.

———. *Reflections on Constitutional Law*. Lexington, Kentucky: University Press of Kentucky, 2006.

———. *Reflections on Freedom of Speech and the First Amendment*. Lexington, Kentucky: University Press of Kentucky, 2007.

———. *Reflections on Life, Death, and the Constitution*. Lexington, Kentucky: University Press of Kentucky, 2009.

———. *Reflections on Religion, the Divine, and Constitutionalism* (forthcoming)

———. "Slavery and the Constitution: Explorations." 19 *Texas Tech Law Review* 677 (1989).

———. *The Amendments to the Constitution: A Commentary*. Baltimore: Johns Hopkins University Press, 1995.
———. *The American Moralist: On Law, Ethics, and Government*. Athens, Ohio: Ohio University Press, 1992.
———. *The Bible: Respectful Readings*. Lanham, Maryland: Lexington Books, 2008.
———. *The Constitution of 1787: A Commentary*. Baltimore: Johns Hopkins University Press, 1989.
———. *The Constitutionalist: Notes on the First Amendment*. Dallas, Texas: Southern Methodist University Press, 1971; Lanham, Maryland: Lexington Books, 2005.
———. "Was the Constitution Pro-Slavery." *University of Chicago Magazine*, November–December, 2010, p. 6.
———. "What Did Hamlet's Father Really Want? On the Use and Abuse of Memory." In Anastaplo, "Law and Literature and Shakespeare: Explorations," 26 *Oklahoma City University Law Review* 1, 220 (2001).
Articles of Confederation and Perpetual Union (1776–1789). Reprinted in Anastaplo, *Reflections on Constitutional Law*.
Bartlett, John, ed. *Familiar Quotations*. Boston: Little, Brown and Company, 1941.
Blackstone, William. *Commentaries on the Laws of England*. Chicago: University of Chicago Press, 1979.
Boatner, Mark Mayo, ed. *The Civil War Dictionary*. New York: Vintage Civil War Library, 1991, 1998.
Braithwaite, William T. "The Common Law and the Judicial Power: An Introduction to Swift-Erie and the Problem of Transcendental versus Positive Law." In John A. Murley, Robert L. Stone, and William T. Braithwaite, eds., *Law and Philosophy*. Athens, Ohio: Ohio University Press, 1992, p. 774.
Calhoun, John. *Basic Documents*, John M. Anderson, ed. State College, Pennsylvania: Bald Eagle Press, 1952.
Cassedy, Ellen. *We Are Here: Memories of the Lithuanian Holocaust*. University of Nebraska Press, 2012.
Caton, Bruce. *U. S. Grant and the American Military Tradition*. Boston: Little, Brown and Company, 1954.
Chronology of World Slavery, Junius P. Rodriguez, ed. Santa Barbara, California: ABC-CLIO, 1979.
The Civil War Dictionary, Mark Mayo Boatner, ed. New York: David McKay Company, 1959.
Civil War Songs. In George Anastaplo, ed., *Liberty, Equality, and Modern Constitutionalism: A Source Book*. Newburyport, Massachusetts: Focus Publishing/R. Pullins Company, 1999.
Coates, Ta-Nehisi, "Why Do So Few Blacks Study the Civil War?" *Atlantic Monthly*, "The Civil War Issue," 2012 (http://www.theatlantic.com/magazine/archive/2012/02/why-do-so-few-blacks-study-the-civil-war/8831/).
Cobb, James C. "How Did Robert E. Lee Become an American Icon?" *Humanities*, July/August 2011, p. 28.

Constitution of the Confederate States of America (1861–1865). (Appendix E of this volume.)

Constitution of the United States of America and Amendments. (Appendixes C and D of this volume.)

Cox, Richard H. "Hugo Grotius (1583–1645)." Leo Strauss and Joseph Cropsey, eds., *History of Political Philosophy*. Chicago: University of Chicago Press, 1987 (3rd ed.), p. 386.

Death Penalty Information Center. "Facts about the Death Penalty." Washington, D.C., June 30, 2011.

Dictionary of American Biography. New York, New York: Charles Scribner's Sons, 1935.

Documents Illustrative of the Formation of the Union of the American States. Washington, D.C.: Government Printing Office, 1927.

Douglas, Stephen A. "In the Montgomery Address." *The Journal of Southern History*, vol. V. November 1939, p. 327.

Douglass, Frederick. *Life and Times*, 1881 (available in the Library of America collection).

Emerson, Ralph Waldo. *The Complete Essays and Other Writings*. New York, New York: Modern Library, 1950.

Encyclopedia Britannica, 15th edition. Chicago, Illinois.

Encyclopedia of the American Constitution. New York, New York: Macmillan, 1986.

The Federalist Papers, 1787–1788.

"The Flag Controversy and the Causes of the Civil War: A Statement by Historians." *Callalo* 24 (2001), 196–98.

Fornieri, Joseph R., *The Language of Liberty: The Political Speeches and Writings of Abraham Lincoln*. Washington, D.C.: Regnery Publishing Company, 2003 (revised edition).

Fugitive Slave Acts, United States Congress, 1 Stat. 302 (1793), 9 Stat. 463 (1850) (Repealed in 1864).

Grant, Ulysses S. *Personal Memoirs*. New York: C. L. Webster, 1885.

Grotius, Hugo. *The Law of War and Peace* (reprinted, in part, in Anastaplo, *Liberty, Equality, and Modern Constitutionalism*).

Jefferson, Thomas. "Original Rough Draft" of the Declaration of Independence. In David Armitage, *The Declaration of Independence: A Global History*. Cambridge, Massachusetts: Harvard University Press, 2007, pp. 161–62.

Lincoln, Abraham. *The Collected Works*, Roy P. Basler, ed. New Brunswick, New Jersey: Rutgers University Press, 1953.

Magna Carta, 1215. Reprinted in Anastaplo, *Reflections on Constitutional Law*.

McCord, Louisa S. (1810–1879). Critique of *Uncle Tom's Cabin*. *Southern Quarterly*, January 1853.

Miller, William Lee. *Arguing About Slavery: The Great Battles in the United States Congress*. New York, New York: A. A. Knopf, 1996.

Moody, Marjory M. "The Evolution of Emerson as an Abolitionist." *American Literature*, 17 (March 1945), 1.

More, Hannah (1745–1833). *The Works*. Philadelphia, Pennsylvania: Edward Earle /J. Maxwell, 1818, vol. I.

Murley, John A., ed. *Leo Strauss and His Legacy: A Bibliography*. Lanham, Maryland: Lexington Books, 2005.

Noel, Joel. Simcha Brudno Obituary. *Chicago Tribune*, June 13, 2006.

Northwest Ordinance of 1787. (Appendix B of this volume including an Act of Congress, August 7, 1789.)

Plato. *Meno*, translated by George Anastaplo and Laurence Berns. Newburyport, Mass.: Focus Publishing / R. Pullins Company, 2004.

Ransom, Roger L. *The Confederate States of America*. New York, New York: W. W. Norton & Co., 2005.

Shakespeare, William. *The Complete Works of William Shakespeare*, David Bevington, ed. New York, New York: Longman, 1997.

Smith, Ted J., III. *Steps Toward Restoration: The Consequences of Richard Weaver's Ideas*. Wilmington, Delaware: ISI Books, 1998.

Statement of College and University Professors in Support of the Confederate Battle Flag Atop the South Carolina Statehouse. April 2000. http://www.lewrockwell.com/orig/profs.html.

Stephens, Alexander H. *A Constitutional View of the Late War Between the States; Its Causes, Character, Conduct and Results*. Philadelphia, Pennsylvania: National Publishing Company, 1870 (excerpted in George Anastaplo, ed., *Liberty, Equality, and Modern Constitutionalism*, Focus Publishing Company, 1999.)

Stowe, Harriet Beecher. *Uncle Tom's Cabin: Life Among the Lowly*. 1852.

Victor, Orville I., *The History, Civil, Political, and Military of the Southern Rebellion*. New York, New York: J. D. Torrey, 1868 (the South Carolina Declaration of Secession is reprinted in George Anastaplo, ed., *Liberty, Equality, and Modern Constitutionalism*).

Weaver, Richard M. *Ideas Have Consequences*. Chicago, Illinois: University of Chicago Press, 1948.

———. *The Southern Tradition at Bay: A History of Postbellum Thought*, George Cove and M. E. Bradford, eds. New Rochelle, New York: Arlington House, 1968.

Wesley, John. Letter to William Wilberforce (1791). (Reprinted in George Anastaplo, ed., *Liberty, Equality, and Modern Constitutionalism*.)

———. *Thoughts Upon Slavery*. (Reprinted in George Anastaplo, ed., *Liberty, Equality, and Modern Constitutionalism*).

Wiecek, William M. "*Somerset*: Lord Mansfield and the Legitimacy of Slavery in the Anglo-American Word." 42 *University of Chicago Law Review* 86 (1974).

Wight, Martin. *Four Seminal Thinkers in International Theory: Machiavelli, Grotius, Kant, and Mazzini*. Oxford: Oxford University Press, 2005.

Wilson, Edmund. *Patriotic Gore: Studies in the Literature of the American Civil War*. New York, New York: Oxford University Press, 1962.

Index

About the Author

George Anastaplo was born in St. Louis, Missouri, in 1925, and grew up in southern Illinois. After serving three years as an aviation cadet and flying officer during and just after the Second World War, he earned A.B., J.D., and Ph.D. degrees from the University of Chicago. He is currently Lecturer in the Liberal Arts at the University of Chicago (in the Basic Program of Liberal Education for Adults), Professor of Law at Loyola University of Chicago, and Professor Emeritus of Political Science and of Philosophy at Dominican University.

His publications include a score of books and two dozen book-length collections in law reviews. His scholarship was reviewed in seven articles in the 1997 volume of the *Political Science Reviewer*. A two-volume Festschrift, *Law and Philosophy*, was issued in his honor in 1992 by the Ohio University Press. Between 1980 and 1992 he was nominated annually for a Nobel Peace Prize by a Chicago-based committee that had as its initial spokesman Malcolm P. Sharp (1897–1980), Professor Emeritus of the University of Chicago Law School. (See, for the Malcolm Sharp letter, www.anastaplo.wordpress.com)

Professor Anastaplo's career is assessed in a chapter in *Leo Strauss, the Straussians, and the American Regime* (Rowman & Littlefield, 1999). It is assessed as well in the cover story of the November 26, 2000, issue of the *Chicago Tribune Magazine* and in the 2012 volume of the University of Chicago Alumni Magazine. A bibliography of his work is included in the Anastaplo Festschrift, *Law and Philosophy* (v. II, pp. 1073–1145). See, also, "George Anastaplo: An Autobiographical Bibliography (1947–2001)," 20

Northern Illinois University Law Review 581–710 (2000); "George Anastaplo: Tables of Contents for His Books and Published Collections (1950–2001)," 39 *Brandeis Law Journal* 219–87 (2000–2001). See, as well, the massive bibliography in political philosophy compiled by John A. Murley, *Leo Strauss: A Bibliographical Legacy* (Lexington Books, 2005), pp. 733–855, 871. Various materials by and about him (including bibliographies) have been collected by Joel Rich and John Metz at www.anastaplo.wordpress.com. Professor Anastaplo acknowledges the considerable assistance in the development of his materials, by Loyola School of Law personnel, including Corinne Chomiczewski, James Faught, Elaine Gist, Charity Humphries, LaTrina Porter, Adam Reinherz, and Wendy Wermerskirchen.

www.ingramcontent.com/pod-product-compliance
Ingram Content Group UK Ltd.
Pitfield, Milton Keynes, MK11 3LW, UK
UKHW020127290926
15471UKWH00003B/329

9 780739 184318